Three Rivers and a Tree

Neelum Saran Gour is a professor of English literature at Allahabad University and a well-known writer. She has authored eight works of fiction and edited a pictorial volume on the history and culture of the city of Allahabad. Her critical writings and short fiction have been included in various anthologies. She has been a humour columnist for the Allahabad page of the *Hindustan Times* and a book reviewer for *The Indian Review of Books* and *The Times Literary Supplement*, UK. To know more about her, visit www.neelumsarangour.com

Three Rivers and a Tree

~ *The Story of Allahabad University* ~

NEELUM SARAN GOUR

RUPA

Published by
Rupa Publications India Pvt. Ltd 2015
7/16, Ansari Road, Daryaganj
New Delhi 110002

Sales Centres:

Allahabad Bengaluru Chennai
Hyderabad Jaipur Kathmandu
Kolkata Mumbai

Copyright © Neelum Saran Gour 2015

Page 359 is an extension of the copyrights page.

The views and opinions expressed in this book are the author's own and the facts are as reported by her which have been verified to the extent possible, and the publishers are not in any way liable for the same.

All rights reserved.
No part of this publication may be reproduced, transmitted, or stored in a retrieval system, in any form or by any means, electronic, mechanical, photocopying, recording or otherwise, without the prior permission of the publisher.

ISBN: 978-81-291-3492-9

First impression 2015

10 9 8 7 6 5 4 3 2 1

The moral right of the author has been asserted.

This book is sold subject to the condition that it shall not, by way of trade or otherwise, be lent, resold, hired out, or otherwise circulated, without the publisher's prior consent, in any form of binding or cover other than that in which it is published.

To the memory of my parents, Sitawar Saran and Vera, whose years at the Allahabad University were the high point of their lives.

THE QUADRANGLE, MUIR COLLEGE, ALLAHABAD UNIVERSITY, INDIA
W. EMERSON, ARCHITECT

CONTENTS

The Muir Overture	1
Act Two	36
High Noon	53
Tidal Wave	118
Picture Gallery	147
Autumn Afterglow	225
Waning Day	298
Real Time	322
Acknowledgements	357
Copyright Acknowledgements	359
Endnotes	360

The Allahabad University logo

1
THE MUIR OVERTURE

This is a storyteller's history of the Allahabad University, not a historian's, and for me it begins on a day in mid-October. The first breath of incoming winter is in the air and the surprising gossamer light of the morning has just been submerged in the afternoon simmer of an Allahabad autumn.

There is a sign on the gate: *Beware of the dog.* I unlatch the gate, look around for the dog and, not meeting it, step cautiously across the few paving stones. An old woman is sitting on her haunches, scrubbing a length of cloth with a bar of soap, beside what looks like a large cemented water-storage tank with a tap on one side. She is stocky and vigorous, and definitely not pleased to be interrupted. I have to explain myself several times before she gets the hang of what I'm driving at.

'They're all out,' she says. Her voice is abrasive and she is obviously Bengali, an old family servant, gruff in her confirmed authority. I seem to have stepped into a different time zone. 'And there's no point asking *her* anything. She can't hear. Stone-deaf.'

Then I see the old mistress moving down a shadowy corridor. She is tiny, shrunken, and her face has lapsed beyond any hope of recall from some former shape. She comes forward slowly, beneath the wide arch, supporting herself with a metal walker. But my eyes have seized upon the broad soaring archway of lime-washed stone. The thick, fluted girth of the tall pillar is streaked with ingrown murk and patchy monsoon mildew in its discoloured grooves, and caked all around its cloudy rim.

'Is this Darbhanga Castle?' I ask the mistress.

She must be skilled in lip-reading for she answers immediately: 'Yes. Yes it is.'

'Yes, it is,' repeats the old servant in the manner of a staunch retainer practising protocol sycophancy, or of a habitual interpreter for worlds that can no longer communicate without help.

'Is this all that's left?' I want to know.

'Go around the back,' says the mistress. 'See it for yourself. It's enormous.' Her voice has a faded ring of proprietorial pride.

Enormous it is, the bits and pieces that remain, swamped by mongrel constructions crowding close together. Alongside is a large dusty field where the bamboo frames of a soon-to-be Durga Puja pandal are being put up. My excitement is palpable and has clearly communicated itself to the two women.

'So this is Lowther Castle!' I exclaim. 'This is where it all began.'

This time my lip movements are not entirely decoded nor, perhaps, accessible to interpretation by that ready reckoner of unintelligible utterance.

All I can put across is: 'May I take photographs?'

'Come on Sunday when the men are home,' is the tentative answer, and I move away along the dusty field where the pandal frames are being assembled, in a state bordering on giddy exhilaration.

This is how a legend has the power to stir through a pillar, the crumbled remains of a house, and a history.

Lowther (now Darbhanga) Castle

That dusty field—what remains of the extensive grounds—was an orchard famous for the sweetness of its plums, raided and fondly remembered by the first batch of boys that came to study at Muir Central College. A former student, G.N. Chakravarti, mentions a 'well-kept garden and delightful orchard' which was 'a second home' to students 'who often resorted to secluded spots in its compound to find the quiet denied to them in their own homes.' In quaintly Victorian cadence, he warns: 'Let not those who have the privilege of getting University education in pillared halls and domed classrooms waste their pity on their predecessors who received their instructions in humbler surroundings, for despite various disadvantages inseparable from an improvised college building, there was an atmosphere of homeliness which is perhaps absent from stately edifices.'[1]

The rest of the grounds have been swallowed up by what is now known as the Darbhanga Colony.

Lowther Castle changed to Darbhanga Castle under dramatic circumstances, around 1888. After it was vacated by Muir Central College, it was temporarily rented by a local missionary school, St Mary's Convent, for an unspecified period of time. Later, the Maharaja of Darbhanga gallantly stepped in when a sticky situation arose and bought Lowther Castle from its owner in Lucknow—in a secret operation reportedly conducted by night—for the venue of a contentious historic event.

The lieutenant governor, Sir Auckland Colvin, had publicly declared his strong disapproval of the Congress, and the spokes-paper of British opinion, *The Pioneer*, had been steadily heaping scorn on Alan Octavian Hume, Sir Henry Cotton and other British 'inciters' of resistance politics. The fourth session of the Indian National Congress had been denied permission by the local representatives of the British Government for every possible venue including Khusru Bagh, the Magh Mela grounds and the premises of cantonment homes.

As a last resort, Pundit Madan Mohan Malaviya approached Maharaja Lakshmishwar Singh Bahadur of the princely state of Darbhanga, who needed little persuasion to buy the vast property. The December 1888 Indian National Congress session at Darbhanga Castle, under the presidentship of Sir George Yule, was a grand success. With well-equipped reception halls, conference rooms and dining areas, its vast grounds accommodated a beautiful 150 × 100 ft. pandal donated by a well-known Muslim raees of the city. The pandal held a small marketplace and some reading and meeting enclaves on the same stretch of land on which the Durga Puja pandal was now being installed. The grounds had thronged with people, European and Indian—the meetings, it is recorded, attended by eighty European memsahibs!

What may have been the reaction of the British administration just a lane away in Government House (present Medical College) is easy to speculate! As a child I remember going past the tall ochre pillar-gates of those premises, opposite the George Town Post Office (another truly period little 'dawk khana'), before they were demolished. The house had been the official bastion of the lieutenant governor of the North-Western Provinces of Agra and Oudh, when Allahabad was the capital.

It was a former occupant of the house, Sir William Muir, who had sanctioned the proposal for a high-profile college (later to be the launching pad of a possible university), and the site chosen for a temporary beginning was the former Lowther Castle. This was in accordance with the resolution that 'the Committee be authorised to take on lease a suitable building… for a certain period, say of three years, pending the completion of a building to be erected.'[2] At ₹250 a month Lowther Castle was rented by the Muir college, and the first lease agreement signed for three years. The college started functioning on 1 July 1872, exactly 101 years before I entered the University of Allahabad as a BA student.

Prior to the opening of the college—at a durbar held on 24 May 1869—Sir William Muir had expressed his identification with this region (located in the remote hinterland of imperial Calcutta) along with his vision of a college therein. He spelt out his hope that local citizens, which might include notables, men of letters, 'merchant princes' and all who held the interests of the city to heart, should come together as a think-tank, raise funds and formulate plans to translate this vision into reality.

It must be mentioned here that four universities already existed in India, in implementation of the British policy for generating local graduates—groomed in British mode—to man the assembly lines of an expanding imperial machinery. Located in the three presidency towns of Calcutta, Bombay and Madras, these universities also served to (partly in earnest and partly in tactical demonstration of paternalistic solicitude) initiate a culture of liberal dissemination of cosmopolitan knowledge. A fourth university, in Lahore, was the product of a somewhat different vision, with a far greater element of Indian initiative and resource in its creation.

As far as Allahabad was concerned, Sir William Muir's protestations of warm patronage that took up the cause of the entire North-Western Provinces—his special charge, as against the manifest progress of higher education in Bengal—do have that particular equivocacy that I may call 'the British attitudinal syndrome' towards India. It appears as a combination of sometimes honest humane commitment with a typically hard vein of pragmatic calculation. 'Belonging to you myself and not to Bengal,' avowed Sir William, 'I am jealous for your interests and your honour.'[3]

So, we are told that a group of Allahabad citizens came together at the house of the British commissioner, a certain Mr Court, whose claim to fame resides in his assertion that he had 'chiselled out a scheme for them'. This scheme would have the British architects of an educational system, with Mr Kempson—director of public instruction, who worked out the budget—enlist local craftsmen to 'chisel' out a splendid edifice. With our present-day penchant for ethnographic detail, I find the break-up of the committee's Indian members particularly revealing of those times. The names—Babu Peari Mohan Banerji, Lala Gaya Prashad, Rae Rameshwar Chaudhri, Maulvi Fariduddin and Maulvi Haidar Hussain—constitute a near-equal number of Hindu and Muslim members!

This brings me to the title I have chosen for this history of the Allahabad University: *Three Rivers and a Tree*. Every University buff is acquainted with the significance of its hoary bargad, or banyan, tree; yet it bears retelling here. The tree is believed to be an offspring of the legendary Akshaya-vat. The Akshaya-vat, whose stubborn existence exceeds the cosmic time grids spanned by srishti and pralaya (creation and destruction), is the indestructible survivor of another aeon of macro-temporality. It exists both in physical space, (located on a site now girdled by Akbar's fort) and in sacred mythology.

Our bargad, magnificently spreading its earth-brown shade of dense aerial roots, occupies an eminently visible area behind the imposing Senate Hall block. A stroke of inspiration it was that chose the tree as a symbol for the University, representing both the spread and transcendence of knowledge, as also an essential place identity. Conceived by J.G. Jennings, a principal of the Muir Central College, the logo, worded significantly in Latin as befitting a transplanted culture—'Quot Rami Tot Arbores' or 'As many branches, as many trees'—was also of Jennings's creation. It encapsulates a veritable grafting of spatial and mental environments in a city battle-scarred and reinvented after the upheaval of 1857. The banyan tree motif, executed by Asit Haldar and later stylistically modified by D.P. Dhulia, has, like its mythical original, survived the mutations of tranquil and turbulent times.

Most histories of the city and the University routinely refer to the Sanskrit passage in Kalidasa's *Raghuvamsa* that has Sri Rama flying Sita back from Lanka in a floral vehicle, pointing out the Akshaya-vat and the courses of the two rivers meeting at Prayag:

> O my beloved, thou with the shining limbs: below us is the great green banyan tree, with its red berries like little pieces of rubies scattered over a mound of emeralds. And there, my love, are the dark waves of the Jamuna mingling with the white waves of the Ganga. And at places it looks like blue sapphires in a necklace of pearls; or like a garland of blue and white lotuses; or even like the mingling of a

flock of blue geese with the white geese of Mansarovar; or the dappled play of moonlight through leafy shadows…

Near the junction of India's 'river of destiny' and 'river of romance', as R.N. Deb refers to the Ganga and the Yamuna respectively, stood the legendary tree; and somewhere thereabouts was the notional confluence of a third river, the Saraswati. More a tradition than a geographical reality, it is an inherited fable persisting in the intractable belief system of the Hindus. The legendary Saraswati was said to have vanished from its site in Punjab into the subterranean regions, and become the third invisible member of the trinity of rivers that gives Prayag the name Triveni. With a pithy relevance to the University, the name of Saraswati assumes an added dimension of significance, Saraswati being the Hindu goddess of scholarship and creative inspiration.

There is an engaging and little-known myth about the image of the goddess Saraswati that, in some rare icons, describes a tiny box placed beside her foot, in addition to her symbolic veena, swan and sheaf of neatly piled bark scripts. That box is supposed to carry her memories of the time when she was a river. I digress into this by-lane of my narrative in order to make a point. Allahabad's 'Ganga-Jamuni' culture of confluence has been an inherent aspect of the city's character, with the University likewise reflecting a healthy aloofness from sectional wranglings. If anything, it richly represents the wealth of both Indic and Islamic cultural traditions even in times of relative disturbance.

However, and notably, the third stream related to a race that belonged elsewhere, as the Saraswati did. It was a race that came with memories of another continent and cultural traditions, and which formed—and continued to do so for a long time—the impetus that gave the city and the University its unique character.

Some of the Englishmen who came, lived and taught in the early years, did not even know how to pronounce the name of the city. Some went back and wrote verses in its honour. A comic poem appeared in the very first issue of *The Allahabad University Magazine*, published in October 1922. It is tucked away between essays of commanding gravitas: the formal felicitation message from His Excellency Sir Harcourt Butler (KC, SI, CIE, LLD, DLitt, governor of the United Provinces, and chancellor of Allahabad University); a message from Claude de la Fosse (vice-chancellor); serious articles like 'The Subject Matter of Economics' by Prof. H.S. Jevons and 'The Scientific Quest of Ideals' by E.A. Wodehouse (yes, elder brother to the delightful P.G. Wodehouse!); a learned piece on Vyasa (the sixteenth-century Hindi poet) by Beni Prasad; 'Muhammad Tughlaq's Abilities as a Financier' by Ishwari Prasad; 'The Life and Work of Sri P.C. Ray' by Dr N.R. Dhar...the edifying list could go on and on.

But the poem I'm going to transcribe is a little gem authored by someone who obviously wished to remain anonymous till posterity, though he was, I'm sure, well known to his contemporaries. He signs as K.W.S.J., and the title of the poem is 'A Rose by any Other Name Would Smell as Sweet'. It has four stanzas:

> Now I wish to be sure of the way to pronounce
> The names of old India's turreted towns
> Yes, I think it's high time I began.
> It is easy to speak of Bombay or Calcutta,
> But others there are it is awkward to utter.
> I must learn ere I leave Hindustan.
> But desist! Oh my muse, you have plenty to learn
> The name of this land is pronounced Hindustan.
>
> I gather it's wrong, of scant culture the badge
> To observe: 'I've an auntie who dotes on the Taj
> With its *sweet* little tanks or canal.'
> You must quote her wise words with a mouth open large

And say: 'I've an auntie who dotes on the Taj
And *never*, please talk of Mahal.'

And when you relate how you had such a rag
Teasing turtles that roll in the river at Ag
At Agra, that place with the Fort
Remember: in 'Agra' the first letter 'A'
Is pronounced very long, the philologists say
And they know or think that they ought.

Then the name of this village is horribly hard
Should I rhyme it with 'mud' or say Allahabad?
A torturing problem, by God.
And my love (Oh! So great!) for this heavenly place
Would be more but for worry (It shows on my face
Which is nice but pathetically sad)
Should I talk (like the highbrows) of Ullahabad
Or say 'what's in a name?'—here I quote from the bard
William Shakespeare, a wonderful lad,
Though he never, so far as enquiry has got
Had the pleasure of living like us in the spot
Which I still shall call—Allahabad.[4]

I have read of the verbal doodlings of British civil servants and laughed over countless limericks written to relieve bureaucratic boredom. But this is the first time I came across that curiously British mode of self-entertainment in an academic.

Here is a verse by S.G. Dunn, professor and head of the English department, written in a more thoughtful vein:

My heart has for the home you gave to me
As many a hill man ties upon a tree
On some high pass, a votive rag to show,

> But this upon your tree of many stems,
> (Quot Rami, Tot Arbores), I shall never,
> Though many a sea and mountain us dissever,
> Forget you, Allahabad, Nor shall I fail
> Daily to pray that Love may yet prevail
> To make men know Earth's nations are but one,
> The meanest of her weakest tribes God's son;
> So shall we lift our learning to that sphere
> Where far and near are one Eternal Here.[5]

But why set up a university at Allahabad of all cities? A number of colleges had recently come up in the province: Canning College in Lucknow, Queen's College in Benaras, Christ Church College in Kanpur, St John's College in Agra and Bareilly College in Bareilly. A fierce debate ensued as to the claims of Benaras being the Oxford of the East against Allahabad that was, in the eyes of the Benarasi pundits, an upstart with a floating population devoid of any continuity of tradition, and never a stronghold of learning. But wait; I have fast-forwarded my account to a subsequent decade.

Back in 1872, the college had just opened in Lowther Castle, with funds being actively sought and collected for the permanent university, and a final site for the prospective high-profile institution undergoing careful consideration. The figure of ₹216,993 finds mention in the records, which included a ₹100,000 contribution by the Maharaja of Vizianagram, and the sum of ₹2,000 as a personal donation from Sir William Muir. A stretch of land called Clydesdale Lines—a name we have not come across in local history—was the initial site proposed. This stretch of land was rejected due to its somewhat sloping gradient, with even the level part being declared unsuitable. It may come as a bit of a surprise that Clydesdale Lines was the name first given to the site of the villages that were razed to the ground by British forces in the Uprising of 1857. The complex was later developed into the Alfred Park, and is currently known as Chandra Shekhar Azad Park.

The commander-in-chief, Lord Napier, had favoured the plot where the Swaroop Rani Medical College Hospital now stands (formerly the site of the Malacca Jail, or the Gora Hawalaat, as it was called). The final choice of the Muir College campus is credited to a certain Colonel Hutchinson whose words of 29 April 1871 have a quiet note of careful speculation, envisioning a green campus of pleasant aspect and commanding presence:

> The more I look at the site, the more do I think it a good one for the College. It would be well seen from the Alfred Park, from the City Road, the Cawnpore Road, and from the East side. I would bring up the Park to it, or, in other words, would lay out College grounds between the Thornhill Road and Katra, as a continuation of the Park, and then Katra should be made to put up a good front on the side next to the College.[6]

I am fascinated by the unknown names that played decisive roles in 'chiselling out schemes', and choosing sites. However, colleges are named after known personages, so Sir William Muir's name was obviously the most appropriate one. While Muir Central College had begun its classes in Lowther Castle, preparations were afoot to build the imposing structure we now know as the Muir College. The foundation stone was laid with full pomp and ceremony, and with all of the gracefully choreographed ritualism and protocol so dear to both British and Indian sensibilities. It is recorded that a silver trowel was specially ordered from the Calcutta firm of Messrs Hamilton and Company and on it was engraved: 'The Foundation-Stone of the Muir Central College, at Allahabad, was laid with this trowel by His Excellency the Right Honorable Thomas George Baring, Baron Northbrook of

Stratton, G.M.S.I., Viceroy and Governor-General of India, on the 9th day of December, 1873.'[7]

As an auspicious rite, it is customary to place money of some particular value and denomination in a vessel and lay it in the ground. Such coins as were needed were brought, fresh and gleaming, from the Calcutta Mint. A large assembly of Indian princes in full regalia, the important citizenry of Allahabad and the benevolent donors attended the ceremony. It was an imposing sight that was created by the locally stationed troops and the additional members of the Volunteer Corps, marching past in ceremonial and martial majesty in honour of the occasion. *The Pioneer* enthusiastically announced to its readers that: 'The Muir College...will be, we are assured, when completed, the finest structure in the N-W Provinces, excepting only the Taj. It was designed by Mr. W. Emerson, in a modified Saracenic style... It is hoped that by March, 1875, the College will be in a sufficiently advanced state to permit of classes being held in it.'[8]

Spectacle and scale were the defining qualities of imperial British architecture, while also conveying a political message as architecture often does. The towering extent of imperial power striking the indigenous viewer with awe, was carefully combined with the suggestion of a liberal readiness to assimilate local cultures within the larger vision of progress. This is also the reason why Indic and Islamic styles were blended. As Prof. Manas Mukul Das explained it:

> The Queen of England's government in India, through the architecture of its public buildings, was trying to speak to a nation that had only recently risen in revolt against the rule of the East India Company. Care had been taken not to disturb sentiments, to extend a gesture of goodwill, and to surpass the architectural grandeur of the past... By choosing the language of the Islamic tradition of architecture, William

Emerson erected a building that perhaps said more than he was aware of consciously. At the height of its glory, Islamic culture was a synthesis of Arab vigour and Persian grace. Rejecting the very thought that the splendour of Godhead can at all be represented through finite natural forms, Islam developed an abstract, austere art. The tower in Islamic architecture emphasized the gesture towards the Infinite, the upward thrust, the vertical axis connecting the human to the divine.... The dome was the perfect form symbolising harmony and grace.[9]

The college took twelve years to build. Modelled on the Al-Azhar University of Cairo, it was made of yellow stone from Mirzapur and white stone from Sheorajpur. It combined grandeur with a delicacy of design in the perfect tracery of its stonework, in its

Muir Central College from the drawing made by the architect W. Emerson

carved aerial galleries, in its elegant tiled dome (though Jennings later disapprovingly compared the pattern to something resembling a linoleum surface!), in its fine-wrought minaret—said to be second in height only to the Qutab Minar, and in the breathtaking loveliness of its Vizianagram Hall.

The colours of the Italian tiles were chosen for their symbolic association: blue representing the infinitude of the sky, and white for the clear purity of a seeking mind. These tiles were fired over and over again in different kilns, and repeatedly polished and luster-painted by a hundred and fifty artisans brought from Jaipur. They crafted the tiles for over six months, 'using only the whites of thirty thousand eggs while discarding the yolks that were mainly eaten by their family members'[10] camping on the site. This was a thousand-year-old art form that had migrated from Egypt and spread to Turkey, Iran, Anatolia, Syria, Central and West Asia and even Spain. It had been brought to India by the Mughals and adopted by expert craftsmen in Rajasthan.

Manas Mukul Das has traced the architectural symbolism of the long, broad verandas which 'over the centuries…surround(ed) an inner space that represented the cave of the heart, (and) have been used for reading, prayer and meditation while walking, (while) an inner courtyard, connected to the sky, invites the infinite to the centre of a community's dwelling place and all its activities.'[11] Spacious lecture rooms, reading halls with 'mahogany bookshelves fitted into notches carved for their support in the floral designs above stone pillars',[12] professors' rooms, a glorious curving arcade along a swirling driveway, a very interesting spiral staircase and a lush green quad were surrounded by ample grounds stretching from Thornhill Road on one side (named after Cadwent Bensley Thornhill, CSI) to the Katra Road on the other side and Colonelgunj on the third. (And, excitingly enough, was Colonel Hutchinson—the man who chose the Muir College

Inside Vizianagram Hall

site—the person after whom Colonelgunj is named?)

There are a few interesting scraps of lore about the Vizianagram tower—that due to the lasting insecurity of the British after the 1857 Uprising, the basement of the tower was a hidden armoury and 'was stocked with weapons in case the university came under attack in a future uprising.'[13]

The cost of the Muir College building was calculated at ₹889,627. Almost thirteen years after its foundation, the college was ceremonially inaugurated on 8 April 1886 in an event of regal formality, great spectacle and pageantry. Thus far, I have been dipping into former Vice Chancellor Amaranatha Jha's account among others, along with a running commentary of my own, but the inauguration event defies comment. Like Jha, I shall transcribe the account published in *The Pioneer*'s 'Extraordinary Supplement', devoted to 'The Opening of the Muir College' when Vizianagram Hall teemed with dignitaries, European and Indian:

> All day long, the flag flying from the stately central tower of the new building, above its gaily tinted domes, and the long line of fretted galleries and the unusual life and stir about the precincts of the College, had given index of some special cause of interest; and as the hour appointed for the ceremony drew near, a vast crowd of spectators gradually assembled. From gate to gate, along the well-kept lines of approach, through the spacious ground surrounding

the Muir College, an expected throng, many deep, were waiting, long before the cloud of dust in the far distance betokened the galloping approach of the cavalry escort, a smart detachment of the 7th B.C. By this time the Hall was entirely filled. Not one chair remained unoccupied.

Along the gallery above—thick as leaves clustered the alumni of the older College; while above all, the vaulted tracery of the roof, with its quaint hues of Eastern pottery and dainty arabesques, furnished a worthy frame to the picture spread below…

The ceremony was one which will not easily be forgotten. Shortly after 5 o'clock, His Excellency arrived together with Lady Dufferin, Sir Alfred Lyall, the Hon'ble Terence Blackwood, Mr. Mackenzie Wallace, the Hon'ble Miss Thyme, Lord William Beresford and Captain Gordon.

The Durham Light Infantry presented a Guard of Honour. Then the Hon. Justice Tyrell, chairman of the committee, read a formal address to the viceroy, followed—as Amaranatha Jha's recounting of the *Pioneer* article states—with a speech by Sir Alfred Lyall, the lieutenant governor. There is another oft-quoted speech and part of Allahabad University's founding vision:

> The building commemorates, my Lord, the liberality and public spirit of those who freely contributed to the original fund, and who spared no pains to promote the work. It also commemorates the firm, earnest, and statesman-like trust placed by Sir William Muir and other leading personages—the principal chiefs and the most enlightened representatives of different classes in our society—the trust placed by them in the sure and certain progress and spread of higher education in this part of India; their belief in its great public advantage, and in its promise and potency

> of future development. And if we may pretend to read a meaning in the style and proportion and design of the architecture of this College, we may say that it foreshadows and anticipates the speedy expansion of higher education under the combined impulses of Eastern and Western ideas and traditions and the advancement of learning to a greater dignity and more imposing position among us.
>
> Now that we have taken to erecting for our students a hall like this in which we are assembled, with cool colonnades, domes, and towers, spacious lecture rooms and libraries, we have set up an external visible sign of the spirit in which our generation regards education. We are having expression not only to the modern principle that we are all bound to aid, publicly and privately, in throwing open the Gates of the Temple of Knowledge, but also to the much more ancient feeling that architecture may play a great part in education, and that knowledge, like other powerful influences, should have a fitting seat and sanctuary.[14]

The resounding sonority of British oration still reaches us across a century and a quarter. Yet, given our current reflexes of postmodern scrutiny, 'we', that is members of academia in the year 2015, are amused by that use of the royal plural. It is inalienably associated with the bounteous benefactions of liberal imperialism in initiating the process of knowledge for those largely destitute of it. But in spite of our historical scepticisms and bifocalities, we are stirred by that ring of prophecy, that faith in the fusion of noble architecture with the lofty aspiration that the lieutenant governor's words evoke. That the prophecy was abundantly realized, at least in the first half-century of its history, constitutes the memory-bank energizing so many of our present realities. And the gallery of personalities that make up this reservoir still preserves, after more than 125 years, eminent candidates for our renewed acquaintance.

They were the stuff of legend, those teachers, and deservedly so, representing the best of British commitment in an apt response to Indian dependence—or subservience—which often did bring out a genuine protective chivalry in the British. Jennings explained it as 'the delightful old Indian sentiment of filial regard for preceptors (that) still lingered in the precincts of our Colleges and appealed to all that was best in the teachers.'[15] Their names make up a memorable roll call in

The Muir College quad and view of the Muir College dome and tower

the University's annals, and not all of them were European. Harrison, Cox, Thibaut, Gough, Hill, Linton, Buddon, Jennings, Bhattacharya, Zakaullah, Amjad Ali, Banerjee were amongst those written about fondly by students. In such vivid details were they remembered as to establish their personalities, for all time, in the histories of the University and the city. This memorabilia makes each one come alive and, having combed through many reminiscences, I have come to know those great teachers almost as intimately as if they were my own.

Some were brilliant eccentrics with amusing and endearing idiosyncrasies. First amongst them was Augustus Harrison who rode around the city on a large tricycle. He made a venerable figure, very neat in his dress, his long flowing beard and twinkling eyes earning him the affectionate nickname of 'Budhwa', which means 'oldie' in local dialect. His office peon was called Mangal, a coincidentally apposite name when linked to a popular Benaras fair called 'Budhwa-Mangal'. This earned the pair the same hyphenated moniker by the local populace—a joke the professor hugely enjoyed. Somewhere between a saintly patron and a rigorous academic, Harrison was the first principal of the Muir Central College. He taught, formally and informally, an amazing diversity of subjects—mathematics, English, astronomy, Latin and French!

That is the first thing that strikes us: the multifaceted nature of those teachers who were equally comfortable in such wide-ranging domains of knowledge. Harrison had been a class-fellow of the viceroy—Lord Ripon, so well-loved of Indians—and likewise a man of a catholic disposition. He had been transferred to Muir from the Bareilly College and had assumed the role of friend, philosopher, guide and guardian angel to the wide-eyed boys committed to his charge. A confirmed bachelor, he frequently declared that his students were his children; he proved to be no mere classroom presence but a pervasive force in the lives of his pupils. He greeted them, at all times, as 'my boy'; encouraging them to study beyond the formal requirements of examinations, and cultivating in them a sense of right living.

Statue of Augustus Harrison in Vizianagram Hall

Nor were those students an extraordinarily docile or diligent lot. It makes amusing

and heart-warming reading to come across such interesting data as I give below, from the Muir College Annual Reports:

> 1876: Sunder Lal failed in Persian, Sanwal Das... in English and Persian.
> 1878: At the FA Examination... Motilal Pundit failed in Mathematics.
> 1882: Motilal Pundit failed in English and was absent the remaining 5 days.
> 1883: Madan Mohan Malaviya failed in Mathematics and Satyendraprasad Sanyal in every subject.[16]

These celebrated and monolithic icons of history become humanized in our imagination, and rendered more accessible through these charmingly fallible human details, lending them a warm sense of everyday boyish reality! What's more, Muir College boys, well-spoken and well-behaved under watchful eyes, were known for their mischief in the absence of teachers! They would play 'pass-on-the-slap-on-the-pate'—a relay head-slapping game—in class, and throw paper pellets at each other in lecture rooms. They were also known to throw fried grams at teachers who were too gentle to retaliate, and to jeer at those who were unpopular.

Harrison, amused by harmless boyish pranks, could be severe with those he considered moral offenders. When a boy slyly picked up a discarded map thrown by another and attached it to his own answer script, Harrison 'thundered in rage: "We can put up with incompetent or lazy boys but not with dishonest ones!"'[17] Once, a student fared badly, so he banteringly compared him to a crab that moved backwards. If a student's reading of a passage from *The Merchant of Venice* (something that Harrison himself is admiringly remembered for) did not meet with his high standards of elocution, he would snap impatiently: 'That'll do! That'll do! Or rather that will not do!'[18]

Yet he took up the cause of students in trouble with the civic authorities. When a boy broke a bench in the Alfred Park and invited the wrath of Mr David, the garden in-charge, Harrison stoutly supported the student's case, preventing serious consequences for him. Again, when a student was ill and shifted from the hostel to a local guardian's home, Harrison sent the civil surgeon there for his treatment. He helped the poor ones with money from his own pocket and arranged job placements for them through his connections. Some of that solicitude and humorous radiance still seems to emanate from the marble bust that his devoted students installed in his honour in the Vizianagram Hall, after his death in 1885. It stands there, presiding over the silent hall tinted by glimmering shades of light that slant in through the lofty stained glass panels like a patriarch-philosopher espying generations of students in the empty spaces ahead.

Another unique specimen of genius was Homersham Cox. A typical abstracted mathematician-metaphysician, Cox was altruistic to a fault, absentminded and shy. A lovable and gifted eccentric, he had had a distinguished career at Cambridge University. The reflections of his students conjure up the image of a small, pale, thin man. In loose, ill-fitting trousers, baggy at the rear, he bore scant regard to the finer details of dressing—a coat buttoned to the neck to conceal a missing collar, a shirt front all awry, even sometimes a different shoe on each foot! We see a tiny form jump out of his gharry and go rushing class-wards, trying to step into the centre of each flagstone as he speeds along, childlike. Often, banging against a wall in his absentmindedness, or ramming headlong into a group of students, he would utter a polished apology, as befitted a scholar and a gentleman.

Dr Cox's abstraction was well known and to see his harried khansama, Lal Mohammad, racing after his gharry to remind his sahib that he had forgotten to eat his breakfast was no unfamiliar sight. His indifference to conventional behaviour was such that a student remembers being welcomed by him, freshly emerged from his bath in a state of engaging déshabillé, barefoot and clad only in his trousers. Quite oblivious of these circumstances, he carried out a chair for the student, himself proceeding to sit unceremoniously on a packing case. His students were welcome without any formality of prior appointment, and there is an unforgettable picture of Cox clad in a Kashmiri choga and cap, eating halwa in his chair and readily offering it to his visitor.

As a mathematician he was unexceptionable, though his methods were unorthodox and his style as eccentric as the rest of him. He would sit bent over his desk, working out problems at lightning speed, skipping over the steps—his students clustering around, baffled, and constrained to gather up the sheets of paper to construe later. Or he'd stand, pondering over a problem and tugging at his moustache in perplexity. How unorthodox he could be is borne out by the account of a boy who approached him with a request that a certain topic was too difficult to understand and would the professor provide him with some notes? Prof. Cox humbly agreed that the topic was a hard one but came up with a remarkable suggestion. He asked the student to go home and devote himself whole-heartedly to the topic and prepare some notes that he could then lend the professor to use in his teaching. The student agreed, requesting to be let off from classes for three weeks. The request was granted, and the student returned having mastered the subject!

Mastery of subject was what Cox and other teachers of the time emphasized over and above mere examination preparation—a difficult standard to measure up to. No wonder only a few—sometimes, just one—student(s) attended Cox's lectures. He didn't seem to notice or mind. And apart from his one and only textbook of arithmetic, he wrote monographs on metaphysical subjects. Persian and French literature were other interests with him, as much as were anatomy and physiology. He even coached a student on how to perform dissections, and an old student visiting him after many years found him poring over volumes of anthropology and ethnography!

Homersham Cox was a deeply sympathetic being who hired a bungalow next to his own dilapidated one to house impoverished urchins for whom he engaged a local teacher, and to whom he personally taught English. There is a picture of him in his carriage bound for college, with his servant's son sitting beside him, taking lessons from this round-the-clock teacher! And still another, with him surrendering meekly to riotous Holi revellers with the words, 'I am at your mercy', giving them ₹10 for sweets and placing his handkerchief on a stool for them to spray abir-gulal on.

He could appear in the examination hall to oversee the convenience of a single student, and he could close down a magazine on a whiff of seditious writing but refuse to disclose the name of the student to the paranoid authorities. And when a student fell ill, Cox visited him in his rented room in Colonelgunj every two or three days until he was well again. After more than a half-century of jaded cynicism and institutional decline it does one's heart good to make the acquaintance of Homersham Cox.

The name of G. Thibaut seemed to fall on my ears with a familiar ring until I discovered that it has sat on my family's bookshelves for years—to be precise, as the translator of volumes 34 and 35 of *The Vedanta Sutras* in *The Sacred Books of the East* series, edited by Max Muller. I open it and read: 'Sankara's Introduction—First Adhyaya: "Reverence To The August Vasudeva!" The opening para reads: 'It is a matter not requiring any proof that the object and the subject whose respective spheres are the notion of the *Thou* (the Non-Ego) and the *Ego*, and which are opposed to each other as much as darkness and light are, cannot be identified...' It is faultlessly translated, in two impressive tomes, by this sometime teacher and principal of Muir College. George Thibaut had studied Sanskrit intensively from a pundit in Benaras and was a scholar of international repute, his area being ancient Indian astronomy; he was also able to read with complete understanding a work on the subject written in Marathi. Hailing from an illustrious family of Heidelberg, he had been an assistant to Max Muller at Oxford. Short, grave, moving with slow deliberate steps, he could be a delightful, even humorous speaker on theoretical subjects. At the start of his talk he often caused his friends some moments of misgiving, for he hesitated, seemed tongue-tied and very diffident, before surprising everyone with a brilliant and confident discourse. Jennings provides us with a powerful visual image of George Thibaut:

> In appearance Dr. Thibaut was somewhat peculiar, though dignified and impressive. Out of doors he always wore a small hard black hat, such as I never saw worn by anyone else in India. Even in the hottest weather he favoured this headgear.... His forehead was high and massive, his eyes were marred by a slight defect, his nose though well-formed was tilted at an unusual angle, and his round and massive chin was characterized by a remarkable dimple. In manner he was reserved and shy....[19]

Dr Thibaut taught English and philosophy, but he was at all times ready to lecture on political economy, classical history and astronomy, and could even help out a weak student with mathematics. A German, he was an authority on the English language to boot, and other senior English teachers sought his guidance in points of language and literature, which he provided in his heavily accented German articulation. A pure intellectual, he stayed immersed in his books and papers, writing for prestigious encyclopaedias and journals on subjects of Indology. A very private person, he led a quiet existence in the city of Allahabad, living in a scantily furnished bungalow like a rishi, as perceptively recalled by a student.

The best anecdote about this scholar extraordinaire is supplied by Jennings again, who recounts how Dr Thibaut, though a willing borrower of books, was a refractory returner. This reputation had stuck so, that a boy—exasperated to the point of turgid outcry—demanded his book back, declaring: 'Sir, I cannot allow you to indulge your bibliophile propensities any longer at my expense.' For his own part, Jennings had devised an ingenious strategy for recovering his books. For each book lent to Dr Thibaut, he borrowed one from him and held it hostage, adding more to the number until half a dozen had collected. At this point, he tells us—and we can hear the chuckle in Jennings's voice even now after more than 125 years—'we would exchange our borrowings.'[20]

There are others whose personalities haunt the records: Archibald E. Gough, tall, trim, robust and well-dressed, of 'ruddy complexion and golden moustaches' who walked at such speed that it was hard keeping up with him. A professor of English and philosophy, he was, like many Muir College teachers of those times, a Sanskrit scholar besides being knowledgeable in Latin, Greek, German, French, Hebrew, Persian and Arabic. He was said to have read all the books in the college library and was in the habit of rushing out at short notice to look up a point in a book when he had to cite a reference. His students treasured his notes for years. Gough had been a popular principal, so well-loved by students that when he returned after a long period of leave and was sighted entering the college premises, boys ran out of their classes to welcome him, leaving nonplussed teachers behind. He was said to have sided with the students when the lieutenant governor, Sir Charles Crosthwaite, insisted that the FA (First Arts) class was an unruly lot, very noisy, and should not be allowed to attend the convocation. If he was a despot, he was a benevolent one whose severest punishment or threat was a fine of the astronomically high sum of ₹1. His talents as an administrator were questioned by some and because he fell foul of certain lobbies, had to seek early retirement, and typically, not everyone attended the farewell party held for him.

Then there was the meek, mild-mannered C.H. Linton who shrank from giving full marks to his own student out of courtesy to a student from another city for fear of seeming discourteous, and who bashfully munched on paan in deference to a student's wish. There was the generous S.A. Hill who freely paid the tuition and examination fees of a student who was hard-up, then gracefully returned the money which the boy's father had raised from loans—with some money added—as a graduation gift to the student. Such personal gestures of grace and kindliness that lie glowing in the recollections of nostalgic students surely ring more true than any suspect master narrative of colonial patronage.

Nor is this a record of the white man heroically hoisting his burden. There were Indian scholars of equal talent and popularity among the Muir College teachers. Mahamahopadhyaya Aditya Ram Bhattacharya—professor of Sanskrit but equally adept in English—in his long flowing choga and bushy beard lived an ascetic's life in his house in Daraganj on the banks of the Ganga. He would meditate on his connection with Kalidasa through the mediation of the Ganga, into which flowed the waters of the Shipra, which—when traced upstream—led backwards in space and time to Kalidasa's Ujjain.

Aditya Ram Bhattacharya was most certainly a being of

fulsome flights of imagination, as reflected by his enthusiastic reaction to the first phonograph recording he was told about. He exclaimed that if human invention could preserve voices in a mechanical device, then surely God or his angels must possess some device in which every thought and word in the universe is preserved! The professor had his share of absentminded quirkiness, and was known to stand lost in discourse with students in the verandah outside the lecture-room, forgetting all about his class. His insistence on the perfect pronunciation of Sanskrit words was well-known, and he was a great disciplinarian both in public and private life.

Although discipline and affection went hand-in-hand in terms of successful child rearing and youth motivation in those Victorian times, sometimes the discipline was excessive. But we are scarcely in a position to judge or dismiss that position, when in our times we have brought to bear the consequences of the polar opposite, or reverse theory, of liberal upbringing.

There was U.C. Ghosh, assistant professor of mathematics, whose classroom would be full even when Homersham Cox's was half-empty, for Ghosh was lucid and accessible to ordinary students where Cox's genius was cryptic and hard to decode. Ghosh's mathematics class was lively and his artistic handwriting on the blackboard an object of general admiration.

Then there was Prof. Zakaullah, learned and gentle, and the witty Amjad Ali. Persian and Arabic were subjects taught at par with Sanskrit and English and, together, this array of languages was richly representative of Allahabad's intellectual culture. Ali's quaint wordplay with his unique fusion of new and existing words, has found a place in Muir College history, especially his delightful 'ungetonable', by which he meant an absolutely impossible student with no hope of making any progress at all in class. There was also his mischievous quip regarding the Eid holiday that, in his words, 'depended on the eyesight of the moon'! Finally, the gifted Dwarkanath Banerji, whose initiatory lectures in law proved to be unforgettable revelations of essential principles for students who subsequently rose to great positions in the Bar and the Bench.

If we take an overview of the climate of education in practice at the time, we come away with a few striking impressions. The teachers were multi-focal, comfortable with several disciplines at the same time. Teaching often exceeded official timings and continued informally in the homes of teachers. It also exceeded the syllabus and the requirements of the examination. Teaching methods were often startlingly unorthodox. I've referred to the ingenious way Homersham Cox got a student to master a topic. There are other interesting vignettes, some very well-known but always eminently repeatable, being evergreen scraps of campus lore.

Shiva Adhar Pande narrates an amusing anecdote in the University's *70th Anniversary Souvenir*. The charming Mr French—'tall, smiling, amiable, very spruce'—would reassure the students that there was nothing threatening about the prose of Charles Lamb. He could hardly be expected to perceive what the students' problem was. The essay mentioned many unknown English card games! When a nervous student laid the matter before him, he laughed. The next day he brought along a pack of cards, asked the lads to open their books and feel free to ask for card game demonstrations. I can imagine what a fascinating English lesson that must have been.

And there is that utterly comic sequence of the soda-machine antics in the chemistry lab, narrated by the late Rai Bahadur L. Shyam Lal, and quoted in several volumes of University history. Its deadpan comedy cannot be captured in any voice other than the original narrator's so I reproduce it exactly as he wrote it in 1888:

I was once preparing lemonade in the Science Laboratory and to my surprise Mr. Hill happened to come in. I was in a fix. Mr. Hill asked me what I was doing. I said, 'To tell you frankly, I am preparing lemonade and want to see what will be its effect on stomach.' He smiled and said, 'This is a very interesting experiment and I would like to perform this experiment myself.' He took a bottle of the lemonade I had prepared and after tasting it (said) 'It does show a good chemical manipulation. I have got a hand soda-water machine at my bungalow; if you see it in this experiment you will succeed better.' Next day he brought the machine and gave it to me. From that day we used to perform this experiment at leisure time and Mr. Hill used to take part in it.[21]

No round-up of portraits of those early days can be complete without a better acquaintance with J.G. Jennings, who, as mentioned earlier, was the conceiver of the bargad symbol. He joined Muir College in 1895, teaching English and history, and later rose to the post of principal. Tall, imperious and exacting, Jennings maintained absolute order in the college. Students bowed deeply to him as he passed by; and if guilty of the lapse of not wishing him were made to retrace their steps and come past again, this time offering respectful salutations. If caught walking in the manicured lawns, students were asked to go immediately to the office and pay a fine of eight annas. At cricket matches he kept watch, walking through the crowds, making ironical jokes; and at convocations he saw to it that everyone sat in seats proper to their station.

He had a dreaded 'black book' in which were recorded the sayings and doings of students. By turn, every student had to meet him at his house once a year to face a lengthy interview. His word was law and that law was stern—yet there were mischievous students who tried out pranks. Shiva Adhar Pande shares a funny incident. When Jennings came to teach poetry to an MA (Previous) class for the very first time—the lesson on Tennyson's poem 'Break, break, break…'—the entire class of boys, by prior arrangement, partly through pure mischief as well as from some vague sense of nationalistic tokenism, appeared wearing dhotis. Jennings, always strict in matters of dress, preserved a stern expression and proceeded with the lecture, ignoring this singular provocation and making no comment.

This same Jennings was deeply immersed in poetry, stoic philosophy and Buddhism, and wrote with great feeling of his early days in Allahabad which influenced the rest of his life. Although he knew no Sanskrit, he produced a very respectable transcreation of Kalidasa's masterpiece, *Abhijnanasakuntalam*. A recast, yet

J.G. Jennings, principal, 1905–1913

something of Kalidasa breathes in the lines, like a fresh, fragrant breeze, with Sakuntala watering flowers and creepers, along with her friend Priyamvada, before Dushyanta ever came into her life:

> Set we to work
> Upon the task of love nearest our hands
> To fill the parching channels round our trees
> That these dear plants may drink.
> For Heaven has made
> The flowers and us kin. These are our sisters,
> Whom passion never soils, that never stray,
> Whose love estrangement never rends asunder.
> God is in all, all lives are God's alone,

> Whose sole life peopled all his worlds with lives,
> And some have soared, and some have climbed with pain
> Partly the distance back to Heaven's fond heart.
> And some have strayed, and lie apart; and some
> Like these fair flowers, have never left God's bosom...[22]

Who were these men who filled the ranks of the teaching community? Mostly they were members of the Imperial Educational Service, many of whom advanced from teaching assignments to administrative positions. In 1896, the service came to have an Indian offshoot and was subsequently called the Indian Educational Service. Later, a service for Indian candidates recruited in India was developed and called the Provincial Educational Service.

And who were the students? They were drawn from all over North India and even from provinces in Maharashtra and Rajasthan, after passing the matriculation examination from their local colleges. The class we now call the intermediate or plus two was then part of the university course and was called the FA (First Arts course). Students sat for an entrance examination conducted by Calcutta University, which controlled Muir, Canning, Christ Church, Queen's and other institutions in the North-West Provinces and Oudh until 1887. Admission to Muir was difficult.

Students from afar were initially lodged in old bungalows that served as hostels. One such bungalow was located in the area where the Swaroop Rani Medical College now stands. The residents of this bungalow were later moved to another in the grounds of Lowther Castle itself, and thereafter to a third in Colonelgunj close to the Bharadwaja Ashram hillock where, adjoining St Anthony's Convent, a park has been created. Life in those hostels has been described, in several depictions, with such warmth and feeling that even the voices of grumbling servants can reach us across more than a century. Kahars did the kitchen-work, and a chowkidar and sweeper completed the domestic staff.[23] Jokhu, the self-important kahar's words: '*Chouka main karoon, bartan main karoon, dhobi main, mehtar main…*' still amuse us with their perennial note of house-harried complaint!

Amongst other activities of the early days, cricket matches took place between the college boys and the Boys' High School students on the one side, and the soldiers of the resident British regiment on the other. A wrestler from Katra was brought in as a trainer in kushti. A college magazine had existed but was closed down by Cox when suspicious murmurs of sedition were levelled against it in the corridors of Government House. As for ragging, a very British inheritance, it simply wasn't there. There are—much later in the history of the University—references to fun on Introduction Night in Holland Hall. One anecdote describes (during the days of the First World War) a mock wedding procession with a 'bridegroom' riding a donkey down the hostel corridors, requisitioning freshers in a noisy celebration; but there was no trace of offence in it.

There was also an Honours list in Muslim Hostel, in which satirical and sometimes unpleasant nicknames were given to inmates, but that too was a very mild thing. Discipline was too firm, and the bonding between teachers and students much too strong and anchored in awe, to allow for any such incidents as ragging in its present sense. The boys came to study, to absorb the intellectual ambience, and to prepare for placements in the government's many expanding public services.

As for unions in their present avatar, this is Jennings's opinion:

> My desire was to follow the old ways and to permit the intimate study, but not the practice of politics…. I used to narrate to my students the fable of the sapling planted by the roadside and defended by a fence against the wayside

Muir College Staff, 1890

goats, who would otherwise have devoured the leaves and tender branches; and when the young tree had reached a sufficient height the fence was removed.[24]

That the college was young, a sapling, and needed protection, was Jennings's argument. The only form of politics prevalent was the simmer of unrest against the British sarkar and that too was something still tentative, timid and largely under wraps. As of then, the British sarkar created the colleges and offered placements in 'all branches of the public services'[25] if not in the British sarkar then the princely states.

When the Muirian passed out, he was certified pucca and dependable. No wonder so many of the alumni were men honoured with the Rai Bahadur or Rao Bahadur testimonial of dependable subjecthood to the Empire, from whom no threat or challenge could possibly be entertained. Bureaucrats, members of the High Court Bar and the Board of Revenue, and men who manned the assembly-lines of the Empire passed out of Muir. Some were to demonstrate their loyalty as subjects and some their innate impulse against the machinery that created them. It is possible to cite only a few names, though there are a great many more. Pundit Motilal Nehru, Pundit Madan Mohan Malaviya, Sunder Lal, Durga Charan Banerjee and later, Purushottam Das Tandon, are names that history has made visible in the multitude of well-spoken, well-read, well-groomed and loyal Muirians that the college produced. Muir proved to be a promising overture to the larger entity that would emerge as the Allahabad University by the Act of Incorporation, as it was called, in 1887.

2
ACT TWO

The name 'Allahabad University' dates from the Act of Incorporation, or Act XVIII, passed on 23 September 1887. It had entailed lengthy correspondence between the secretary of state for India, the Government of India—Home Department (Education)—and the Government of the North-West Provinces of Agra and Oudh. Here, the word 'incorporation' is employed in an erstwhile sense, a shade removed from its present connotation. To 'incorporate' was to give material or corporal substance to an idea, and Allahabad University, which was so far a notional possibility (although increasingly growing towards a certainty), was given concrete identity by this act.

K.K. Mehrotra's account states that 'the projected University of Allahabad' had already been voiced at the durbar mentioned in the previous chapter, held in Agra in 1869—three years before Muir College opened—during the visit of the duke of Edinburgh.[1] The college, also known as Allahabad College, was regarded as the nucleus of a future university, even though the Government of India had not spelt out when this would happen. The project found strong support from Sir Alfred Comyns Lyall, lieutenant governor of the North-West Provinces, who argued that the umbilical cord connecting remote colleges in North India with the parent university at Calcutta had to be severed sooner or later.

There were sound reasons for this, in which context Sir Lyall's words have become history:

> The mere distance of Calcutta from this part of India has always been a disadvantage; while differences of race, country and language always imply, and should be freely permitted to induce, a certain diversity of study and variety of intellectual development. Moreover, a University... should be in the midst of the people to whom it belongs; should be easy of personal access to students, to the members of the governing body, and to all representatives of the communities... We have to consider, gentlemen, the very considerable place that education is now occupying in these Provinces.[2]

The lieutenant governor's words argued not merely a contemporaneous principle, but were to prove worthy of far-reaching impact. For decentralization, whether of governance or of education, invokes a pragmatic law of expanding institutions. A spirited debate ensued before the act was passed, addressing two major issues: Why Allahabad and why not Lucknow, Benaras or Agra, when each had its contesting claims? And what was to be the educational philosophy underlying the character of the institution to be created?

The question 'Why Allahabad?' found two strong opponents: Sir Syed Ahmad Khan of Aligarh and Babu Bireshwar Mitter of Benaras. Indeed, both Aligarh and Benaras could boast of worthy cultural bloodlines, just as could Agra and Lucknow. But in the end, Allahabad was chosen simply because it was the new capital of the North-West Provinces and, being the seat of government, had a large number of qualified personnel to constitute a governing body. Also, the High Court, the Government Press, the *Pioneer* and other high-profile institutions had set up base in

Allahabad. The city had an appropriate venue in the impressive Muir Central College, and Allahabad loyalists advanced an enthusiastic argument, stating an intellectual bloodline of their own. Here are a few lines of support from a long poem written by Rai Bahadur A.C. Mukerji:

> Each foot of ground that thou dost tread
> Is hoary with antiquity,
> And hallowed by the memory
> Of heroes whose immortal name
> Sheds luster on the rolls of fame,
> But look. And mark how passing strange
> Has been the all-defacing change:
> The holy hermitage gone:
> The forest area built upon.
> A busy thoroughfare now runs
> Down where the Ganges gurgled once…
> …That holy saint whose presence blest
> This hallowed spot, has gone to rest…
> A greater university
> Than Bharadwaja could e'er foresee
> Now rears its domes and turrets where
> The incense-smoke perfumed the air;
> And hostels, playgrounds, libraries
> Have ousted those primeval trees…[3]

The idea took root, as did the bargad. Delivering a special convocation address in 1958, Jawaharlal Nehru expressed the same general idea:

> So, even though your University may be young, only seventy years old, it is built on a much older tradition which goes far, far back. And here, standing in this city of Allahabad or Prayag, my mind goes back, inevitably to another great

centre of learning, which existed here long years ago, not far from this place, in the Bharadwaj Ashram. And you, perhaps, you of the University of Allahabad might be justified, to some extent, in considering yourselves as the successors and inheritors of that great seat of learning which existed not far from this particular spot.[4]

This is a pleasant thought to lay against the heart!

Jawaharlal Nehru delivering the special convocation address. Also on the convocation dais are: (L–R) Dr Shri Ranjan and V.V. Giri

The second subject of intensive debate centred on the nature of education to be imparted. Was it to be founded on local culture and tradition, using local languages, or a European-style education based on what may roughly be defined as cosmopolitan knowledge? Benaras and Aligarh subsequently developed along the Anglo-Oriental model, but Allahabad adopted the cosmopolitan version while retaining essential regional and classical studies within dedicated departments of their own.

As necessary groundwork to the 'incorporation', it was decided that the first chancellor would be the lieutenant governor of the North-West Provinces and chief commissioner of Oudh—Sir Alfred Comyns Lyall—and the first vice chancellor, the Chief Justice of the High Court, North-West Provinces—Sir John Edge. Two governing bodies, the Senate and the Syndicate, were to be created. At first, the University was to be an examining body only, with an extensive catchment area including all of present-day Uttar Pradesh, Uttarakhand, Madhya Pradesh and Rajasthan.

The inaugural convocation of the University of Allahabad took place on 15 November 1887 at 3 p.m. in Vizianagram Hall—the venue for all formal meetings henceforth—with Sir Alfred Lyall presiding in his capacity as chancellor. The first Senate comprised Sir John Edge, vice chancellor, and the following members: Douglas Straight, W. Tyrrell, Syed Mahmud, Syed Ahmad Khan Bahadur, J. Woodburn, Ajudhia Nath Pandit, Colonel Forbes, E. White (surgeon), Major Cleghorn, Raja Shiv Prasad, A.E. Gough, Raja Jai Kishan Das, A.J. Lawrence, M.S. Howell, J. Nesfield, K. Deighton, W.C. Bennet, A. Thompson, Raja Uday Pratap Singh, Babu Pramoda Das Mitra, Pundit Babu Dev Sastri, W.H. Wright, W.N. Boutflower, Maulvi Zakaullah Khan Bahadur, S.A. Hill, C.H. Dodd, the Reverend Hewlett, Pundit Lakshmishankar Misra, Theodore Beck, Pundit Aditya Ram Bhattacharya, Munshi Nawal Kishore Bhargava, Babu Bireshwar Mitter, Dr Mukund Lal and Babu Ram Saran Das.

The second meeting, presided over by Sir John Edge, was held in February 1888 at an eight-hour sitting. It worked out the composition of the Syndicate, the body next in hierarchical authority to the Senate. In our times, the Senate and Syndicate would largely correspond to the University Court and the Executive Council respectively. The Syndicate was to house the executive governance of the new University. At this crucial meeting were chalked out certain guidelines: how the Syndicate was to be constituted, how its members would be elected, the rules to be followed in the proceedings, the frequency of meetings, the number of members allotted to each faculty and how they were to be chosen, and the duties and term of the office of the registrar. Most importantly, the process by which colleges were to be affiliated was also decided.

The system was firmed up in a series of subsequent meetings, and the first entrance examination was held in March 1888, for which candidates from places as far-flung as Ajmer, Dewas, Rewa, Jabhalpur, Patiala, Nasirabad, Satna and Jodhpur appeared.[5] Within five years, the Allahabad University's territorial stretch extended across what was, in the terms of those days, 'as comprising the United Provinces of Agra and Oudh, the Central Provinces (including Berar) and Ajmer-Merwara, and the States included in the Rajputana and Central India Agencies'. This covered an area of 452,830 square miles and a population of 9 crores, with undergraduate education being delivered in colleges scattered over this entire belt.

By 1902 Allahabad University had extended to seventeen first-grade and fifteen second-grade colleges. These were located in cities within the North-West Provinces such as Agra, Faizabad, Aligarh, Almora, Bareilly, Benaras, Gorakhpur, Kanpur, Lucknow, Mussoorie, Meerut, Nainital, and in other provinces at Ajmer, Gwalior, Jabalpur, Jaipur and Ujjain.

The number of students was growing rapidly and since law was an important career option, the Government of India—in the same year—urged the local governments to institute law colleges. This was the beginning of postgraduate courses in Allahabad University, and for which a new and appropriate infrastructure was needed. The Senate Hall campus owes its origin to this decision. 'This was the origin and the beginning of the present group of English and law departments, the Senate Hall and the library buildings."[6]

> The site on Church Road, now Pandit Moti Lal Nehru Road, was chosen in 1909. Sir Swinton Jacob was asked to draw up the plans. These were approved in 1910 and Sir John Hewett, the Chancellor, laid the foundation stone of the University Senate Hall on January 17, 1910. The approximate expenditure on the three buildings was over 10 lacs.[7]

Opening ceremony of the Senate House, 1912. Seen in the photo are (sitting; L–R): Dr Ganganatha Jha, Mr Jennings, Sir George Knox, Maharaja of Balrampur, Sir John Hewett, Sir Sunder Lal, Sir P.C. Banerji and Dr A.H. Ewing

The Senate House, the library building and the Law College/English department buildings were completed in 1912.

Professor Manas Mukul Das has commented on the complex with feeling and insight:

> The historic Senate House commands the Arts Campus. Built shortly before the First World War, when the British

empire was at the height of its power, it blended Islamic, Rajasthani, and English styles of architecture, to stand as an icon of order and imperial authority. The perfect symmetry of the consolidated design of three buildings in a row converges on a central clock-tower, which from its height sonorously and emphatically announced, not only the hours, but also the quarter, half, and three-quarters with rolling chimes.

In this complex of buildings, Sir Swinton Jacob, the architect, visualised a blending of space and time, a mingling of the symmetry of pattern with the regularity of rhythm. The order, repetition, and balance of motifs within a spatial design were being continually reinforced every quarter hour by the regularity and sequence of the beats and melody in the chimes of a hidden bell situated high in the centre of the tower. The symmetrical external form emblemised the perfect order in which an unseen centre held together its spacious domain.

Seen from inside—before the archways connecting the Central Hall to the North and South Halls of the main building were sealed—as they are now, the Senate House building was one integrated flowing space that provided a magnificent aspect of vistas within vistas of archways, halls, balconies, overhanging galleries, and connecting bridges with latticed stone railings, pillars and arches, deep verandahs, from which carved stone staircases ascended to the first floor, ceilings decorated with carved woodwork, light filtering through stained-glass designs set in huge skylights, polished red floors embellished with mosaic patterns and rows of tall, brass-fitted teakwood and ribbed-glass windows and doors opening onto a view of meadows, trees, paths, and adjoining peer buildings.

Looking at the changing vistas, through arches within arches within arches, one got the feeling that the domain of knowledge was the unknown, unfolding as one passed through the arches into a forever receding horizon. Today the chimes are silent, a number of arches sealed, the texture of stone and exposed brick surfaces hidden under coats of paint. Moulded plastic chairs are screwed onto the red floor. Wire mesh and asbestos partitions divide several halls into cubicles for the administrative staff. Still the desecrated buildings retain much of their grandeur.'[8]

A rare photograph of the Senate House shortly after completion

If the Muir Central College had a 'modified Saracenic' architecture, combining Indic and Islamic styles, the Senate Hall, designed by Sir Swinton Jacob, experimented with creating a synthesis of Hindu, Muslim and Western styles. R.N. Deb, with his artist's eye, admitted that the skyline had 'too many turrets and cupolas' and to the purist, the red tiled roof of the main hall 'is not an architectural triumph'. But the 'massivity of the structure and its magnificent proportions'⁹ has earned it a high place among the best university buildings in the country. Pavilions with chhatris and ornamental balconies, and a plentiful scattering of floral motifs arranged at various heights, convey the impression of a Rajasthan palace.

Today, the Law College holds the Department of English and Modern European Languages, and the library houses the registrar's and accounts offices.

The clock tower, till the late fifties, was said to be the highest in India and the clock itself the largest. With a story of its own, the sombre tunefulness of its chimes and the roll of its deep gong were said to have disturbed the sleep of a British magistrate's wife. Orders were sent to the University that the chimes be silenced, but such compliance was politely refused. Subsequently, we are told that the University tempered down its stubborn refusal and the chimes were reduced in volume. After Independence, a chain in the mechanism of the clock broke, and a certain Mr Michael, an employee of the University, undertook to repair it, but failed to do so. Ever since then, from time to time, the clock is repaired and the chimes are heard for brief intervals, but the structure of that clock clearly exceeds the technological comprehension of our digital age.

Among the tales about the University building there is yet another interesting one: that somewhere on the campus there is a secret hangar for a two-seater plane for the vice chancellor but till date no one knows where it is, not even the long line of successive vice chancellors![10]

This is, as stated at the very beginning, a storyteller's account of an institution's genesis, its growth, its lived realities, its personalities and its function as a sensor of a history of regional transformation. Yet, I must perforce make selective reference to those acts, ordinances and statutes that seem to be milestones in the University's progress (or, sadly, decline). The Universities Act, 1904, and its immediate sequel, The Indian Universities Act, 1905, are two such inescapable points that stirred up a veritable hornet's nest. These two acts, put simply, were moves to exercise greater control on universities, their Senates and Syndicates, and their affiliation of colleges.

Since, initially, there was no proper system of inspection, affiliation had come to be a random affair. The subjects taught, the nature of the management, the buildings, facilities and the financial state of the colleges, were frequently unreliable and liable to disaffiliation, for which suitable precedents did not exist. The Lt governor, Sir Ramfylde Fuller, proposed the disaffiliation of some Bengal colleges due to his alleged understanding of a steady growth of seditious activity; but upon failing to gain the assent of the Government of India, chose to resign.[11]

The Universities Act, 1904, sought to monitor the character and composition of the governing bodies; and to lay down rules, minimum fee requirements and defined course guidelines. The public viewed this as a highly imperialistic move, particularly the abolition of the second-grade colleges and the bureaucratization of Senates and Syndicates, turning them into organs of the government. The act had the potential to destroy indigenous unaided colleges—such as were founded and maintained by Indians—and to leave them out of the recognition circuit. There was even a feeling that only colleges headed by a European principal could hope to gain recognition. It was believed that, under the guise of reform, the government was transferring power to educationists of European origin and to missionary colleges, in a bid to stunt indigenous enterprise in higher education. Lord Curzon was accused of a deliberate move to strangle higher education in India.

Once the Universities Act, 1904, was enacted, a storm erupted, in which the most vocal and visible leaders were Annie

Besant, Gopal Krishna Gokhale and Sir Pherozeshah Mehta. The Indian National Congress strongly protested, the press raised an outcry of dissatisfaction, and both Surendranath Banerjea and Gokhale put their dissent on record. Moti Lal Ghose, the editor of Calcutta's *Amrita Bazar Patrika*, summed up the pernicious effects of the act in four lucid points: It would impose governmental control on the university system; the stipulated courses would give no useful knowledge to students other than what was needed to serve as cogs in the government's machinery; the insistence on a higher pass percentage in English would engender more failures; and finally, private colleges would be forced to close down.[12]

Whether Curzon honestly believed that he was improving the university system, or whether the dissemination of knowledge and freedom of expression needed to be contained before it became inconvenient, is open to debate. However, the sequel—the Indian Universities Act, 1905—decreed arbitrarily that, protest or no protest, 'all directions, declarations and orders made in pursuance of the authority of the Indian Universities Act, should be deemed to have been duly made....'[13]

We must at this point step back and consider the genuine dilemma of the situation in the eyes of the British administration. How much education was too much education for the Indians, and how much was just right? The old joke about teaching just enough English to the locals, in that 'Chatterjee should speak and Mukherjee should understand', has really more serious content than it seems to have. And what, in the eyes of the Government of British India, was the real goal? The education imparted was limited to a specific class designed for a specific function. Valentine Chirol wrote in *Indian Unrest*: 'The fundamental weakness of our Indian educational system is that the average Indian student cannot bring his education into any direct relation with the world in which, outside the class or lecture room, he continues to live.'[14] In the earnest declarations of faith and the personal commitment of great teachers is evident a genuine sense of mission. But in the wary perception of those whose first duty was to safeguard the interests of the Empire, the business of education had to be handled with caution. If we compare the ringing tones of the benefactors with the very perceptible discomfort of subsequent sceptics, developments like the acts of 1904 and 1905 fall into place.

Sir Alfred Comyns Lyall had spoken of an institution in which 'the combined impulses of eastern and western ideas' would enable 'the advancement of learning to a greater dignity.'[15] He had spoken of 'the importance of founding within these provinces some central institution for the encouragement and development of the highest kinds of learning and placing first-class teaching within the reach of students.'[16] In all fairness to him, he had espoused the cause of the vernaculars. At the November 1887 convocation, he had reiterated his belief that 'education had never had a clearer field, or more open ground, than in British India, to show what it could do for a people...'[17] Even as late as 1912 the king-emperor affirmed the avowed principle in his reply to the address of the Calcutta University: 'It is my wish that there may be spread over the land a network of schools and colleges, from which will go forth loyal and manly and useful citizens, able to hold their own in industries and agriculture and all the vocations of life...'[18]

But concurrently there was disquiet that unless the behemoth was controlled, higher education could pass into the hands of nationalist lobbies who might use it to further agendas injurious to the Empire. There is a tiny anecdote in Shiva Adhar Pande's reminiscences: Once, he saw Jennings pass a group of Indian students who were making a racket in the corridor and he heard Jennings strongly reprimanding them. Soon afterwards, at the same spot, he saw Jennings passing a group of Anglo-Indian students making a racket and he went past them without a word of reprimand. Pande plucked up courage to go up to Prof. Jennings and ask him the reason why he had not scolded the latter group of students. And Jennings's reply was cryptic. 'Well, that's life,' he had said with a shrug, possibly because even a dedicated scholar like him had no conscious or convincing answer. A revealing little incident, however trivial it may have been.

The British sarkar worked according to strictly preserved hierarchies. Within that frame they were liberal, fair and square. But once those hierarchies were seen to be at risk of being disturbed, more pressing agendas supervened, as was witnessed in the acts of 1904 and 1905. By linking jobs with the degrees awarded by universities and colleges, the system was kept under control.

The consequences of the Indian Universities Act, for Allahabad University, effected a reorganization of territory, and a reconstitution of the Senate and the Syndicate (amid angry murmurs about the European members outnumbering the Indians). More importantly, university and school became separate entities, with Intermediate (or FA) classes falling out of the University basket. This shift led to a fall in revenue at the University due to the loss of fees, and rendered it more dependent than ever before on government grants. There was talk of opening a medical college and an engineering college; so far medical instruction was imparted through a medical school in Agra, and a new one in Lucknow; the Thomason College of Civil Engineering at Roorkee supplied the necessary trained engineers to the region.

Changes had been afoot. The Benaras Hindu University was 'incorporated' at Benaras in 1915, followed by the Aligarh Muslim University at Aligarh. Under the patronage of HE Sir Harcourt

Butler, who loved Lucknow, a university came into being there as well, and two others arrived on the scene, at Nagpur and at Agra. Gradually Allahabad University's domains were diverted to those universities nearest the affiliated colleges. In 1917, Sir Michael Sadler, who conducted a survey of the educational field, advanced the suggestion that the time was ripe for the government to opt for what is referred to, as 'unitary, residential and teaching' universities, so that in the course of time the system of far-flung affiliations would fade away.

The Government of India had given a recurring grant of ₹45,000 and a non-recurring grant of ₹3 lakh to all universities. So far, the teaching staff of the new Allahabad University was a largely disorganized sector. The staff of the Muir Central College automatically migrated to the University. Distinguished lawyers and judges of the High Court conducted law classes. Other teachers belonged to the Imperial Educational Service and the Indian Educational Service. Now, with the arrival of the grant, chairs in modern Indian history, economics and law were created, followed by others, and a beginning was made in postgraduate teaching and research. Distinguished professors Dr Venis, Dr Weir, Prof. Rushbrook Williams and Prof. Stanley Jevons organized schools in their subjects—law, history, economics etc., and started a system of lectures too.

Paving the way for the Allahabad University Act of 1921, a slew of new reorganization regulations were passed, which included the birthing of the Board of High School and Intermediate Education to take care of secondary education. Although the reorganized university officially started in 1922, it wasn't till 1927 that the machinery began running smoothly. A sub-committee was appointed to choose sites and purchase buildings for the new, reorganized residential university of learning (as against its earlier status as a seat for examinations alone). Under the chairmanship of Prof. C. Weir, it made a series of recommendations:

The following sites were to be acquired, if and when necessary:

(a) The block of land lying between the Muir Central College, the law hostels and the road running through the Katra bazaar.
(b) The triangular block bounded by the Bank Road, Katra Road and the Prayag Road.
(c) The land bounded by Bank Road, Pioneer Road, Mr. Rattigan's compound, and the University compound, so far as not required for arts buildings. Eventually the rest of the land bounded by the Church Road, Phaphamau Road, and Bank Road might be acquired, if possible.
(d) Land in the neighbourhood of Trinity Church and along Church Road opposite the university.[19]

The committee further suggested that 'the apex of the triangle formed by the Church Road and the road running through Colonelgunj'[20] be taken over and cleared for construction right up to the older Colonelgunj police station. The Muir Central College buildings were assigned to the Science Faculty, and ideally, as per the recommendations of the committee, 'there ought not to be any roads with shops running through the site of the University.'[21] But, this could not be implemented, with the result that the University Road, with its students' bookshops, eateries and general market runs between the two campuses

Sir Claude de la Fosse

of Arts and Science.

In 1923 the government authorized the vice chancellor, Sir Claude de la Fosse, to acquire the Indian Press Property that lay adjacent to the Senate Hall block. It was bought for ₹700,000 and those buildings, the oldest on the Senate Hall campus, form the present departments of medieval and modern history, as also of philosophy and economics.

There was a somewhat unsavoury footnote to this deal when rumours began circulating that Fosse, the last European vice chancellor of Allahabad University, had taken a bribe from the owner of the Indian Press. It resulted in the filing of a defamation suit by the vice chancellor against three persons: Iqbal Narain Gurtu, Nanak Chand Sharma and Ishwari Prasad. The case was withdrawn after an apology was tendered, but Fosse chose to go on leave prior to his retirement, and the next vice chancellor, Ganganatha Jha, assumed office.

Muir College Staff, 1901

3
HIGH NOON

The period 1927 to 1957 is called Allahabad University's golden age. The times were inherently interesting and the institution was in a state of energetic and creative growth. If we pause at the year 1957 and look back, an avalanche of information inundates us. Thirty years in the life of an institution is long enough to delineate a substantive character, especially if those years happen to coincide with a definitive transformation in the history of a nation. In as early as the 1950s, R.N. Deb, in one of his essays, reacted defensively to a friend's comment describing Allahabad as a city of great memories alone, by speculating that such was not the case, and that there was a meaningful future ahead as well.[1]

Every generation defines meaning in its own way and against different standards of valuation. In 2012—half a century into that so-called 'meaningful' future—as I drive into the car park one morning, and walk towards my department, it is the scraps of history and the memories that assail me, giving sense and substance to what now seems anarchic. The car park, a fairly recent entity, is chock-a-block with gleaming vehicles of every make and price, although we haven't yet reached the BMW and Volkswagen slot. Some drivers lounge inside the cars, listening to music or catching up on their sleep.

I am reminded of an amusing account in Rajeshwar Dayal's profiles in which he mentions a time when 'the internal combustion engine was little known in the University precincts except for Dr M.U.S. Jung's ancient car, which was of rare vintage even for that time, and which used to proclaim its approach to the law department by a series of shattering explosions.'[2] A decade later there were so many more cars—one of the most individual being Amaranatha Jha's in which, we are told, he kept flowers, aesthete that he was, to perfume the enclosed air! '*1924 model Ford Car from Gilbert, the motor dealer. Paid ₹2000/- for it*' records his diary.[3] And, still later, there was S.C. Deb's car, black as his dress, his hair, his stick and his glasses.

As I take the metalled road curving past the accounts office block, I remember that it had been a gracious old library, as sacrosanct in its cloistered silence as it is noisy and crowded now. The road turns into a spacious square. I can't say when the road was first metalled—records mention that they were all re-surfaced with asphalt around 1955–56—but it has always, in the thirty-five years that I have walked it, been in good repair.

To my right is an extensive green stretch of lawn, no longer well-groomed, despite obvious and ongoing efforts to restore to it a semblance of presentability. And I think of how it must have been, resplendent with colourful tents in which the country's greatest maestros of music were housed, during the mammoth All India Music Conferences of the 1930s and '40s held in the Senate Hall. The massive boom of Faiyaz Khan's voice resounding far beyond the stone walls of the hall, reaching the ears of eager students who could not find a place within. And how, when a celebrity performer did not show up, Ustad Alauddin Khan, present for his own performance, requested D.R. Bhattacharya, one of the organizers, to give an opportunity to a new boy in his entourage named Ravi Shankar. 'He's a promising lad. Let him fill this empty slot in the programme. You can give him fifty rupees for it,' suggested the ustad. That was 1941, and one of Ravi Shankar's first public performances.[4] The rest of the year those manicured lawns were kept scrupulously untrodden by reckless feet, 'Keep-Off-The-Grass' signs posted in little placards along the edges and a fine of eight annas imposed on those who broke the rule.

Muir College lawns, likewise, were famous, and the favourite venue for national tennis and hockey celebrities like E.V. Bobb, D.N. Kapoor, P.L. Mehta and Ahad Hussain, who, after graduating from the University, returned regularly to play with the students. To my left looms the clock tower, its hands frozen in a halted instant of time, the same clock whose noisy ticking and tuneful chimes had kept a magistrate's wife awake. I walk through the portico and recall that this was where the Prince of Wales's car drove up at exactly 9.30 a.m. on a cold December morning in 1921. The prince had emerged along with his ADC, Lord Mountbatten, and his private secretary, Earl Rowland Cromer, and moved briskly up the stairs into the Senate Hall.

Turning the corner of the North Hall and beneath the grand old tree that casts its generous shade across a wide expanse of road, I think of old Dr C.A.R. Janvier cycling down 'at remarkable speed all the distance of about four miles to teach…Milton's "Paradise Lost".'[5] Imagining Ganganatha Jha's horse carriage driving up to the vice chancellor's chamber reminds me of a passage in *The Allahabad University Magazine* of December 1932, by D.B. Dhanapal[6], an MA student, which evokes a strong image of the University awaking to a morning's round of duties:

> As the hour approaches ten in the morning, a mass of youthful humanity surges onwards through the portals of the University of Allahabad. Bicycles meander (in) with many motions. Motor bicycles rush through with a roar.

> Lady students arrive most elegantly in tongas. Soon the soft whir of high-powered cars is heard. And one by one, the professors swerve through the big gates, some rolling in sedan cars, one of which…is upholstered in red plush. There also arrives one of those curious contrivances, now fast disappearing, looking like a darkly painted Nice biscuit tin on four wheels drawn by two shaggy ponies.
>
> Inside this most unimportant-looking carriage sits the most important man of the University—the Vice Chancellor, Mahamahopadhyaya, Dr. Ganganatha Jha. Dressed in almost rustic artlessness, steeped in a sense of silence and slow time, with an intent gaze into the blue beyond, Dr. Ganga Nath Jha for ten years has lived an exile in his own University. In a modern Indian Institution like Allahabad where most professors look like Western fashion plates in the flesh, where most students have the air of American millionaires on holiday, he seems to be a stranger in a strange land, strayed in by mistake… He looks a fortunate misfit—an epic among parodies, among pharisees a prophet.

Dhanapal's innocently affected and self-conscious passage has caught the mood of elite posture and style that coexisted with real grace and quality in the University's ambience, though I find it hard to imagine that bit about American millionaires on holiday! I find it easier to relocate my imagination to the fifties and see Harivansh Rai Bachchan pedalling his bicycle slowly down the same road, also at 9.30 in the morning.

But this is memory time I recall—not real time, fixed, even at its most fluid—as I make it to the English department building, which looks more like an imposing Rajasthani palace than a university site. Records state that by 1910 the Oudh Bar Association had collected and donated the funds for constructing and furnishing this majestic structure that started functioning in 2012.⁷ Its façade bears the words 'Law College' because for a long time the building was shared between the departments of English and law. It was an arrangement convenient enough since eminent lawyers and judges, after their court duties, conducted several law classes in the late afternoon and evening.

Kailash Nath Katju has spelt out the organic connection between the University and the High Court:

> In the sphere of national service, the association of the Allahabad High Court, with the Allahabad University has been of the closest. The old boys of the University have, by their legal learning and forensic ability produced a strong Bench and Bar, and they in their turn have served the University with singular zeal and devotion. Pundit Sunderlal, the leader of the Allahabad High Court Bar, served the University as a Vice Chancellor and in other capacities for many years, and Pundit Madan Mohan Malaviya loved it exceedingly...⁸

Before the Law College premises were built, law classes were held in the Muir College building including in its Vizianagram Hall. Students, who were later to occupy positions of great eminence, fondly remember the gentle Professor (later Sir) J.C. Weir, a King's Counsel and a puisne judge at the High Court, as well as the head of the law department in 1921. A teacher so kindly that he once cancelled an important extra class when he learnt that the students had planned a picnic at Shivkuti on that day, postponing the class till the picnic was over, even when it meant changing a personal schedule and taking an inconvenient night train.

The great old halls of the Law College have resounded with the voices of Tej Bahadur Sapru, Motilal Nehru and the effervescent R.K. Sorabjee, whose vivacity kept a class of 150 law students spellbound. Sir Tej was, in fact, the first student who enrolled for the LLD degree in 1909.⁹ Dr S.C. Banerjee, Dr S.N. Sen, Dr Kailash Nath Katju and Justice Walliullah followed him, and in the 1960s the honorary degree was awarded to Sri Sunder Lal and to Chief Justice Das of the Supreme Court. The centenary souvenir lists an impressive gallery of alumni from the law department—bureaucrats, governors, judges, advocates, ministers, ambassadors and diplomats. There have been law ministers like S.N. Kakkar and Shanti Bhushan, and certain faculty members have gone on to become Supreme Court judges. Chief Justices of India include Chief Justice M.H. Beg, Justice Iqbal Ahmad, Justice P.N. Sapru, Justice S.N. Katju, Justice R.S. Pathak, Justice V.N. Khare, Justice J.S. Verma—all products of the department's golden era.

Nor was it all solemn study and no mischief. Here is a lovely little account of a hilarious classroom prank in a law class, hatched and executed by a future vice chancellor of the Benaras Sanskrit University. The account, T.N. Kaul's; the year, 1934.

> It was a hot day in April, we all wanted to take it easy, but Dr. M.U.S. Jung had to lecture on 'Roman Law'. Aditya Jha and I took it upon ourselves to hide Chaturvedi under the platform on which was placed Dr. Jung's chair. As soon as Dr. Jung mounted the platform and took the chair, young Chaturvedi beat his hands on the platform from inside and the whole class laughed. Dr. Jung was puzzled for a moment, but soon realised the mischief and sat determinedly on the chair...[10]

No Caesar ever sat so imperious on his throne than did this professor of Roman law! The culprits 'got worried lest young Chaturvedi should suffocate. We went up to Dr. Jung, confessed our doing and begged him to release Chaturvedi[11]'. The teacher sat firm as a rock, registering no appeals to his mercy. The students grew shamefaced though continuing to plead. What young Chaturvedi underwent, positioned beneath the professor's rostrum, is best left to our imagination. We are told, though, that he emerged a hero subsequently, but only after the professor rose in a huff, 'feigning displeasure', and strode out of the class.

When the reorganized University started out as a 'unitary, residential, teaching' institution it had fourteen departments, some of which soon enough parented other departments. Sanskrit, which had been a subject intensively taught by Mahamahopadhyaya Aditya Ram Bhattacharya in the Muir College days, now found a patron in the vice chancellor, Mahamahopadhyaya Ganganatha Jha. The department had a composite name—the Oriental department, which included the study of Sanskrit, Hindi, Urdu, Arabic and Persian.

Later, when these broke away into separate departments, the Sankrit department came to be known as the Department of Sanskrit and Prakrit Languages. It was headed by the well-known Sanskrit scholar, Dr P.K. Acharya, a sound authority in the fields of archaeology and architecture as well. The department had names like Dr Babu Ram Saxena, Pundit Khetresh Chattopadhyaya, Dr Umesh Mishra and Pundit R.M. Shastri. The subjects taught included the Ved, Sahitya Darsana, epigraphy and Pali Prakrit. To Dr Acharya's credit may also be ascribed the very first classes in ancient Indian history that Allahabad University held under the aegis of the Department of Medieval and Modern History.

The Sanskrit department gave rise to its promising offspring, the Hindi department, later to become a legendary nucleus of literary activity. Starting out in 1924 with just one teacher, Dr Dhirendra Varma, and five students, the Hindi department was to evolve exponentially. The range of subjects covered a detailed study of Tulsidas, Surdas, Kashavadas and Prasad, and specialized study of Sanskrit and Pali, Prakrit and Apabhransa, textual criticism, contemporary literature and criticism, and folk literature. Two more teachers were appointed soon after the commencement of the department: Pundit Devi Prasad Shukla and Miss Chandravati Tripathi.

The character of the department was chalked out in consultation with famous scholars like Pundit Shyam Behari Mishra, Lala Sitaram, and Babu Shyam Sunder Das, as also with in-house scholars like Babu Ram Saxena of Sanskrit and P.E. Dustoor of English. Between 1929 and 1960, the Hindi department witnessed the appointment of stalwarts such as Dr Ram Kumar Varma, Dr Ramshankar Shukla, Dr Mata Prasad Gupta, Dr Uday Narain Tewari, Dr Lakshmisagar Varshneya, Dr Hardev Bahri, Dr Raghuvansh, Dr Jagdish Gupta, Dr Dharmveer Bharti, Dr Ramswroop Chaturvedi, Dr Keshavchandra Sinha, Dr Paras Nath Tiwari and Dr Mohan Avasthi. Some were acclaimed poets, others novelists, critics, historians, linguists, folk litterateurs and even painters. Together they nurtured a creatively dynamic and innovative department, which proved to be the invigorating centre for the great Hindi efflorescence still known as Prayagvad in Hindi literature. Bengali, Marathi, Telugu and even Chinese were taught as diploma courses by the Hindi department!

The other offshoots of the original Oriental department were the departments of Urdu, Arabic and Persian. In the Muir days, the first head of the Arabic and Persian department was Maulvi Zakaullah, who belonged to Delhi and came from a family of hereditary scholars who were, according to tradition, tutors to the Mughal princes for several generations.[12] Gifted in the fields of mathematics and science, he had also authored, it is said, one hundred and forty-three books on an assortment of subjects, apart from publications in Oriental languages. Maulvi Amjad Ali and Maulvi Mohammad Ali Nami were other distinguished Arabic and Persian scholars of the time. The University of Allahabad conferred the degrees of Maulvi, Alim, Fazil, Munshi and Kamil before the UP government took over the function. Following this, the University began awarding the BA and MA degree certificates, and provision was made for courses and research along contemporary lines. The prominent teachers of the time were Dr A.S. Siddiqi, Dr Zubaid Ahmad and Prof. Naimurrahman.

As for Urdu, it started out independently at the same time as the Hindi department with only one teacher, the dynamic Prof. Zamin Ali; MA classes in Urdu began in 1928. The staff now included two part-time members, Dr Tara Chand—who later joined the Department of Medieval and Modern History, distinguishing himself as an iconic historian—and Prof. Ajmal Khan—who went on to become secretary to Maulana Abul Kalam Azad.[13] As the years progressed, Dr M. Hafiz Syed, Syed Aejaz Husain, Amarnath Baijal, Mrs F.F. Naseer, Vishnu Gopal, Dr Rafiq Hussain and Masihuzzaman also joined the staff.

The Partition of India led to the migration of a good number of the Urdu department's scholarly alumni, who later earned eminence in Pakistan in the field of Urdu letters. Among these were Dr Hamid Hasan Bilgrami, Prof. Mumtaz Husain, Prof. Vaqar Azim, Prof. Mujtaba Husain and Mustafa Zaidi. The year 1954 saw the appointment of the illustrious Dr Aejaz Husain as head of the department. His name as a historian of Urdu literature and as a litterateur is well-established, as is that of Prof. Ehtesham Husain, the famous Lucknawi scholar who joined the department as professor. The Urdu department was a popular haunt of intellectuals from all over the University, drawn to its plays and mushairas.

The Department of English and Modern European Languages, headed by Prof. S.G. Dunn, was the largest in the University—with English literature a compulsory subject for all students and English the medium of instruction and of examinations. When the department took off, as one alumnus, V.G. Oak, put it:

It was ten years after the end of the First World War. Hitler was not much of a force in Europe yet. The international scene appeared peaceful. The civil disobedience movement in India had not yet started. Most people were convinced that British administration in India was going to last till eternity. That was the year 1928.[14]

The under-construction English department

But in 1937, no doubt in resonance with the political zeitgeist, English literature ceased to be a compulsory subject and was made optional like any other. Instead, a BA in English was introduced, divided into compulsory and optional components. It is interesting to recall that immediately after 1947, motivated by a high-minded patriotic impulse, there was a noticeable decline in the number of students opting for English. This stood at odds with the publication of the Radhakrishnan Commission Report of 1949 that proposed a sensible approach to English, the vehicle of internationalism in all areas of modern knowledge. English was also declared as the official language of India for the next fifteen years by the Constituent Assembly.

A resurgence in numbers followed—the department, even

with twenty-nine teachers, the largest in the University—struggling to cope with well over 4,000 students belonging to all three faculties. In spite of this overload, its alumni distinguished themselves in the ICS, IAS and other competitive examinations, and in the academic and creative fields, becoming writers and critics of note in English, Hindi, Urdu, Bengali and Maithili. S.G. Dunn, E.A. Wodehouse, Amaranatha Jha, Shiva Adhar Pande, S.C. Deb, Raghupati Sahai Firaq, P.E. Dustoor, K.K. Mehrotra—these are names which belong to an iconic lineage.

Many others served for short periods before taking up prestigious assignments elsewhere. Bhagwat Dayal became the Indian ambassador to Indonesia and Afghanistan. Bhawani Shankar served as principal of the Joint Services Wing at the National Defence Academy, Dehradun. Dr Harivansh Rai Bachchan joined the Ministry of External Affairs. Ahmed Ali, the famous Urdu writer who also wrote in English, had taught in the department too. The names of P.C. Gupta and R.N. Deb belong to this era as well. Diploma courses in French, Italian, German and Russian under Prof. Benoit, Dr L. Patech, Dr J.C. Manry and Miss Kemp, respectively, were begun, but the Italian classes were discontinued when Italy became an antagonist to Britain in the Second World War. In many ways the English department could claim to be one of the nerve centres of the campus, feted for its clubs, theatricals, personalities and memorable teaching.

The philosophy department traces its heritage to the time of Prof. Gough and Prof. G. Thibaut, whose engagements eminently represented the interface between philosophy and science. Those Muir days are claimed by the department as its first chapter. After reorganization, a separate Department of Philosophy started with twelve students in the MA class and as many as a hundred students in the BA class. There were only five teachers—

professors P.S. Burrel, H.N. Randle, Ranade, A.C. Mukerjee and R.N. Kaul.

The second chapter in the philosophy department's history is the Ranade–Mukerjee period just before Independence. The learned Prof. Ranade with his 'scholarly stoop and golden turban' was a sage-like spectacle as he arrived in the department, always carrying a change of clothes in a small suitcase. It was he who initiated the prestigious *Review of Philosophy and Religion* that enjoyed high respect between 1936 and 1948. It was also Professor Ranade who helped found the Indian Philosophical Congress in 1925. The department was strong both in the area of Indian philosophy and Western, Advaita and Immanuel Kant being the most prominent subjects of study.

Other branches of study were ethics, social philosophy, Western and Indian epistemology and metaphysics. Both Prof. Ranade and Prof. A.C. Mukerjee made significant contributions to contemporary Indian thought, with the department, in the era before Independence, supplying large numbers of successful candidates for the Civil Services. In 1949, the Radhakrishnan University Commission Report gave its stamp of approval to the department in recognition of its strength and distinct identity in the field of metaphysics.

The department was also the foster parent of the psychology stream, which was to branch out independently in the early 1960s. Issues of the nature of knowledge and knowing straddle the borders between the two disciplines, and the philosophy department was open to investigations on the nature of the mind, and even paranormal phenomena like hypnosis. An alumnus recalls that 'a former teacher, who went off to teach in Dacca University, wrote a highly popular book, *How To Hypnotize and Cure*, published by Kitabistan. At a talk held in the large Lecture Theatre, this Professor hypnotised a student, then got him to deliver a speech in the voice and style of Muhammad Ali Jinnah!'[15] Freud's Unconscious and the Indian concept of the Superconscious, both came in for research under the aegis of the philosophy department, at a time when the combination of conservative philosophical thought and avant garde areas of investigation were still new in many academic circles.

Among the oldest and most celebrated departments was that of modern and medieval history, with the lofty and acerbic Sir Shafaat Ahmad Khan as its professor and head in 1922. There are several striking anecdotes about him; he could dismiss a student's essay with the words 'jejune, superficial, and perfunctory,'[16] and he once threw away his wristwatch because a plebian dared to ask him the time! While the University was still a fledgling in the throes of reorganization, the history department had in its professorial chair Prof. Rushbrook Williams, former Fellow of All Souls' College, Oxford, and member of the American Historical Society.

Williams's general lectures, to which not only students but all interested people were welcome, were announced in the pages of *The Leader* as early as 1915. To him may be ascribed the selection of an impressive body of scholars whose names brought lustre to the history department: R.P. Tripathi, Ishwari Prasad, Beni Prasad, Bisheshwar Prasad, Tara Chand and Banarasi Prasad Saxena. Followed by O.P. Bhatnagar, D.N. Shukla and C.B. Tripathi, collectively they brought into existence what was known—in the thirty years of the great era—as the Allahabad School of History. The distinctive qualities of this school were the application of meticulous methodologies for the authentication of historical evidence, the broadening of the nature and range of sources, the analysis of the personal element in history in collusion with the structures of given societies, and the building of a consistent and larger perspective of history. A detailed knowledge of Indian history as well as a firm grounding in world history was provided to the students.

The Department of Medieval and Modern History gave rise to its noteworthy offspring, the political science department, originally christened, in 1927, the Department of Civics and Politics. For a considerable length of time the two departments shared the valuable services of the iconic teachers Dr Beni Prasad, Dr Tara Chand and Dr Ishwari Prasad, each one a legend in his own right with a cult following. The political science department also ran two diploma courses, one in local self-government and the other in village uplift. Jurisprudence, international law, public administration, diplomacy and international affairs were some of the popular papers chosen by students.

The history-political combination became a highly preferred option for the Civil Services well into the 1970s and '80s.

The other prominent spinoff of the Department of Medieval and Modern History was the Department of Ancient History, Culture and Archaeology, inaugurated in 1956. In the early days its teachers were scholars like Prof. Acharya and Prof. Khetresh Chattopadhyaya of the Sanskrit department, and Dr Beni Prasad of the history department. But once established, under the leadership of brilliant scholars like Dr G.C. Pande, J.S Negi, Lallanji Gopal and B.N.S. Yadav, the department took great strides of its own.

One of the special strengths of this department was its archaeology stream. As early as the era under consideration, excavations at Kaushambi and its vicinity revealed a wealth of information about a highly developed civilization in the Gangetic plain contemporaneous with the age of the Buddha. The Saka-Parthian presence, the connection between the Harappan and the Vedic civilizations and the investigation of prehistoric sites in Mirzapur and Banda have been some of the department's achievements. At a later stage, Prof. G.R. Sharma, Prof. Mandal and Prof. S. Bhattacharya ably carried on this work, especially so Prof. Mandal and his team. Weeks spent day and night on the site by this team, unearthed archaelogical riches of enormous interest, the discovery of which radically transformed the portrayal of hitherto scripted Indian history.

The relatively newer departments on the Senate Hall campus established between 1927 and 1957 were those of geography, education and music. Geography in its commercial and economic aspects was taught in the commerce and economics departments since 1926, but it was only in 1937 that it was flagged off as a separate department. Its first head was Dr R.N. Dubey and there were two other teachers, M.N. Khan and R.N. Singh. It was only a decade later that MA classes in geography were added and became a popular choice for students. As an interdisciplinary and field science, geography has shared frontiers with subjects like sociology, anthropology, environmental studies and even political science. The department, in its early days, interpreted the subject in its descriptive aspect and evolved to a scientific and analytical mode over the years as the horizon of enquiry changed.

Education started with the introduction of an MEd course, conducted under the patronage of the philosophy department, and later evolving into an independent entity under the headship of the well-known psychologist, Col Sohan Lal. The department, in course of time, came to have the services of D.N. Mukherjee, Dr Rajdan, Prof. P.S. Naidu and Dr S.B. Adaval. BA classes began in 1945, and after 1955 further expansion provided the department with its own library and educational laboratory.

Music started as a two-year diploma course, with classes held in the galleries of the Vizianagram Hall and in extra rooms of the Women's College. The idea of a Sangeet Parishad was fostered, in 1926, by certain senior members of the University—Dr Tara Chand, who became its president; Dr D.R. Bhattacharya, its vice president; Dr Amaranatha Jha; and Maj. Ranjeet Singh. Teachers' names included Pundit B.S. Pathak, Pundit S.R. Mavlankar and Pundit N.R. Joshi. Later Pundit B.A. Kashalkar, Pundit B.N. Thakkar and the famous violin maestro, Gagan Babu, were appointed. Tabla and pakhavaj were taken by Pundit Radheshyam Bhatt and Pundit Ram Dev Tiwari.

During the 1930s, as mentioned earlier, the Sangeet Parishad organized the annual All India Music Conference in the Senate Hall, which was later shared by the Prayag Sangeet Samiti, and subsequently held on alternate years. Funds for a prospective music department were raised by these events and Amaranatha Jha laid its foundation stone in 1947. Vocal and instrumental music and painting were included in the BSc Home Science syllabus in 1945. An endowment of ₹15,000 provided for the creation of a chair in music, to which Prof. U.S. Kochak was appointed. He was to head the Department of Music and Fine Arts for thirty years. By 1950 the department building was complete, music was made a degree course and two more teachers were appointed—P.R. Bhattacharya to teach sitar and Mahesh Narayan Saxena for vocal music.

Painting was a diploma course attached to the Department of Music, and classes were held in one of the upper halls of the Old Library, the present-day accounts office. The initiation of this course in 1942 was marked by the appointment of the famous painter, Kshitindranath Majumdar, who was a disciple of Abanindranath Tagore. Two years later, D.P. Dhulia joined the department, later moving to Gorakhpur University; and in 1958, Pundit Shambhu Nath Mishra was appointed. A class for photography was also initiated with a studio and four dark rooms built for the purpose.

Within the older set of departments fall the illustrious ones of physics and chemistry, piloted by stalwarts of the stature of Meghnad Saha and Neel Ratan Dhar respectively. Prof. Saha, whose ionization formula in astrophysics put Allahabad University on the world map, headed the physics department from 1923 till 1937. It is said that when he was made a Fellow of the Royal Society, for his work on thermal ionization, Ganganatha Jha came to him to see what an FRS looked like! Under Prof. Saha's guidance, the department's laboratory was built into an internationally recognized entity, known for its brilliant spectroscopic work. After leaving Allahabad University, the professor engaged himself with nuclear physics and was succeeded by K.S. Krishnan, also a Fellow of the Royal Society and a student and associate of C.V. Raman.

Prof. Rajendra Singh (Rajju Bhaiyya), who studied under Prof. Krishnan in 1939, mentions the visits of C.V. Raman and Homi Bhabha. The latter, it is recalled, did not like the laboratory so decided against joining the department as professor. As for C.V. Raman—the high point of Prof. Rajendra Singh's memories of the physics department was about the time when he had to demonstrate the Raman Effect to none other than C.V. Raman himself, who had come as an examiner.[17]

The department was known for its eminent physicists like Dr R.N. Ghosh, Dr G.B. Deodhar, Dr K. Majumdar and Dr B. Dayal. Together they helped create strength in the fields of electronics, acoustics, astrophysics, quantum statistics, wireless and ionospheric investigations, ultrasonics and crystallography. The department also had people like Prof. K. Banerjee, Dr R.K. Sen, S.C. Chakravarty and Dr B.V.R. Murty. Later, in the 1940s, Prof. Krishnaji made great contributions towards microwave research, and designed and invented his own instruments in the departmental workshop.[18] Towards the end of the so-called golden era of the Allahabad University, Prof. Bipin Kumar Agarwal had already begun researches into particle physics, then an area little explored in Indian universities.

The business house of the J.K. Singhanias of Kanpur, along with the Government of India, funded the creation of the JK Institute of Applied Physics, inaugurated in 1956 by Jawaharlal Nehru. Headed by Prof. S.N. Sen, the objectives of this department were to extend the reaches of conservative physics to include frontline areas like space physics and technology, computer science, and new branches of physics. Living up to its goals, its workshop created complex instruments, electronic devices, and even a room-sized computer. The department conducted a BTech and an MTech course with specialization in radiowave propagation, control engineering, radiating systems, microwaves, communication and space electronics, solid-state electronics and microcomputers.

The Department of Chemistry combined the physical and biological science groups and was developed around the original chemistry laboratories of the Muir Central College where Hill had taught. Under the brilliant leadership of Prof. Neel Ratan Dhar, who was attached to the Muir Central College as a member of the Indian Educational Service, the department grew to impressive dimensions, especially in the soil sciences, Dhar's special area of interest. His own work, though, was on the 'Induced and Photochemical Reactions and Colloids'. Under his leadership the physical, organic and inorganic branches of chemistry were all made into fields for teaching and research. Stereochemistry, the colour and chemical constitution and chemistry of medicinal plants, chemical kinetics, coordination and analytical chemistry were slowly included within the ambit of study as the department grew in size and stature.

One of the first to engage in the research of organic chemistry was Prof. S. Dutta, in 1925, while plant chemistry was the area of professors J.D. Tiwari and R.D. Tiwari. Chemical kinetics was the domain of Prof. S. Ghosh, and later of professors Bal Krishna and M.P. Singh. Prof. Krishna did cutting-edge research in dielectric properties and molecular structure. Prof. K.L. Yadav is to be credited with developing an original electro-kinetic technique to study quick reactions of up to thirty to forty seconds, as also with the modification of the electrophortic technique. Coordination chemistry employed the expertise of professors A.K. Dey and H.L. Nigam.

The Sheila Dhar Institute of Soil Science was the result of a large endowment from Prof. N.R. Dhar himself. Created in 1946, the institute had an advanced laboratory equipped for research in soil science, agricultural chemistry and biochemistry. The history of the institute as one man's gift to the University, created out of his lifetime's savings, after having lived a life of extraordinary austerity, makes for inspiring reading. The *Centenary Souvenir* of 1987 provides one of the clearest accounts:

> Prof. Dhar, after constructing his residential building on Beli Road, Allahabad, in 1927 also constructed another huge building on the same land, on the pattern of a Research Institute consisting of two big laboratories, one large central hall, one office room and half a dozen small rooms to be used as stores and staff rooms. The construction was completed in 1934 and was properly equipped in 1935, and was named the Indian Institute of Soil Science, but after the demise of his wife, Mrs. Sheila Dhar, in January 1949 (who was a distinguished Physical Chemist) Prof. Dhar, on the advice of his favourite pupil Dr. Iqbal Krishna Taimini..., a great theosophist and Reader in the Chemistry Department, renamed the Institute the Sheila Dhar Institute

of Soil Science and donated it to the University on the condition that the Institute would be an integral part of the Chemistry Department of the University, and Prof. Dhar the Honorary Life Director. He also donated a large amount of money to the University for the creation of N.R. Dhar Endowment Fund.[19]

With the help of a substantial University Grants Commission (UGC) grant, sanctioned by D.S. Kothari, chairman of the UGC and a past student of N.R. Dhar, extensions were added to the building including a greenhouse in the agricultural farm. With a further land donation from Professor Dhar and a cash donation to go with it, a hostel was built. The key focus of the institute's research was to investigate how soil humus and organic matter increased nitrogen content in the soil, through atmospheric nitrogen fixation, as a result of sunlight-induced acceleration of oxidation of organic matter. The institute is a striking example of one man's dedication to the science that was his life's calling and passion.

The Department of Mathematics has a singularly legendary record. In the Muir days it had been dignified by the presence of teachers like Homersham Cox, Prof. Elliot, Prof. W.N. Boutflower and the interesting J.R. Holl, ICS. Holl's fondness for mathematics was such that students 'used to catch him walking on the road and he used to solve Mathematical problems for us sitting on a culvert first smoothing the dust on the putri of the road and writing on it with his stick'.[20] Later, he returned to England and became the librarian of the Bodleian Library at Oxford. Among Homersham Cox's students was the famous Ganesh Prasad, who was often the only one who hung around in the classroom, closely following the teacher's calculations. There was also Prof. R.H. Moody.

The mathematics department made Allahabad University a well-known centre for mathematical study. Dr Ganesh Prasad's eminent pupils, Dr Gorakh Prasad, Prof. B.N. Prasad and P. Mohan carried on the noble lineage. In 1929, Prof. A.C. Banerjee, a Cambridge Wrangler, became head of the department that also came to include Dr P.L. Srivastava and R.N. Chaudhuri, MA (Cantab.). All iconic names: Srivastava had done his PhD under the famous scholar G.H. Hardy, at Oxford; and B.N. Prasad did his under Hardy's famous pupil, E.C. Titchmarsh, and later also studied under Prof. A. Denjoy, the eminent mathematician, in Paris.

The Allahabad School of Analysis, as it was called, became a prominent hub. By the end of the golden era, many more names lent lustre to the department: R.S. Varma, P.L. Bhatnagar, M.L. Misra, H.K. Sen, S.K. Roy, U.N. Singh, J.A. Siddiqi and R.S. Kushwaha. In the 1950s, a whole crop of eminent students passed out of the department, of whom, newly appointed members like professors T. Pati, H.C. Khare and P. Srivastava were to continue the tradition of quality and excellence into the subsequent 1960s.

Prof. Rajendra Singh recalls his student days when he became the close friend of Harish Chandra, who was to become a scientist of world repute and to occupy the chair of professor of mathematics—formerly Einstein's—at the Institute of Advanced Studies, Princeton, USA. Although mathematics was more of a private interest for Harish Chandra in the early years of his phenomenal career, Prof. Singh narrates the most striking anecdote about him in that connection. He recounts an incident when Harish Chandra lay ill, running a temperature of 104 degrees, but engaged in solving abstruse mathematical problems nevertheless. When asked to rest, he explained that mathematics made him feel better and kept his mind diverted from his physical discomfort![21]

The Department of Botany separated from the old biology department in 1923. Its first professor and head was Julian H.

Mitter, and it enjoyed the services of prominent botanists like Dr Winfield Dudgeon and Prof. P. Maheshwari, FRS. Other well-known figures were the Drs S. Ranjan, R.K. Saksena, R.N. Tandon, D.D. Pant and B.S. Mehrotra. Senior alumnus Bishan Tandon writes of the warm friendships between members of the old botany department staff under Prof. Julian Mitter, the constant comings and goings to one another's homes, and the midday tea break attended by all, even visitors. In those days, the department had a wide range of subjects for specialization and research—plant physiology, mycology, plant pathology, cytogenetics, systematic botany, ecology, algology, palaeobotany and bryology. It also had a well-qualified staff and the names of A.K. Mittra, S.P. Naithani, G.D. Srivastava and N.S. Parihar belong to this select group. Agricultural botany was a subject begun under Dr Ranjan's initiative before he became vice chancellor.

Zoology was part of the old biology department as well, but as early as 1906 the vice chancellor, Claude de la Fosse, had also laid the foundation for the future independent Department of Zoology, with its first head being Prof. F.M. Howlett.

The long galleries of the science faculty

The erstwhile composite Department of Botany and Zoology (then called the Department of Biology) lasted until 1914, with the famous zoologist A.D. Imms holding a professorial chair between 1907 and 1910. When he left—to become forest entomologist, and subsequently professor of entomology, in Cambridge—he was succeeded by Captain Parker and Maj. Cunningham, and then by another famous zoologist, Prof. W.N.F. Woodland.

With a staff of distinguished experts, most of who ended up in other positions and universities, the Department of Zoology's special area was cytology and helminthology. A great deal of original work was done in the area of fisheries, while fish morphology, entomology and agricultural zoology were other areas of departmental expertise. Dr D.R. Bhattacharya remained head from 1922 till 1947, and under him cytology and cytogenetics research made still greater strides. Prof. H.R. Mehra succeeded him, after whom came Prof. M.D.L. Srivastava. Dr D.R. Bhattacharya, who became vice chancellor in 1948, conducted a survey of the fish fauna in Chilka Lake.

Between 1937 and 1945, two new departments were instituted in the Science Faculty. The experience of the Second World War brought home the realization that military science, as a field of study, was of critical value and was therefore made a specialized subject. Strategy and tactics, the science and economy of war, its administration and organization, military law, the psychology of fighting men and their management, the great world chronicles of war—all these proved to be potentially promising areas for academic attention. Accordingly, defence studies as an optional subject for undergraduate students was launched, and made a subject for postgraduate study and research only in the 1960s.

Regarding girl students, it was only in 1927 that they made their first appearance in the newly introduced co-ed English literature class—'five shy girls used to huddle together on one bench usually meant for three!'[22] The chemistry department was thrown into a state of violent excitement when the first girl, the only one, appeared in N.R. Dhar's lecture class, the professor protectively escorting her in and out of the classroom every time. Girls formed only between 4–5 per cent of the total number of students in 1940, the exact number in the entire University being 108. It may be mentioned, in passing, that initially classes for girls were held in the Crosthwaite College premises, and it was only in 1938 that the Women's College was built. By the end of the thirty-years' golden era the number was 888, that is 13 per cent.

It is an unwitting revelation that the Department of Home Science, started in 1945, was meant specifically for girl students. Women being considered in the primary role of homemakers, it was thought that their proper vocation might possibly be improved by knowledge of chemistry, biochemistry, hygiene, nutrition and dietetics. Vocal and instrumental music, painting, home decoration and home economics were included in the course. Child psychology was also a subject (in fact, experimental psychology and child psychology were subjects initially intended for girls!).

In 1932, Prof. V.N. Mehta had argued the cause of introducing subjects of practical commercial applicability such as advertising, copy editing and feature writing, practical poultry raising, newspaper reporting, cookery, etc. He relied, for his argument, on data gathered from a study of certain European and American universities. As we no doubt perceive, all these areas have currently positioned themselves in clear-cut disciplines, much sought after by students aspiring after careers in them; but in 1932 the idea was too progressive to be accepted.

So, even though plans were afoot—as early as in the latter years of the 'golden era'—to set up an Institute of Business

Administration with the awarding of a masters in business administration (MBA) degree, commerce continued to be taught like any other purely theoretical subject.

Although the Department of Commerce started in 1926–27, it took some time registering commerce as a viable subject with the University authorities. At one point of time it was even proposed that the department be closed down because it had only two students.

However, better judgment prevailed, and the apprehensions of naysayers belied by the steady rise in numbers, as awareness of the importance of the science of business grew. Prof. M.K. Ghosh and Dr A.N. Agarwala were two of its early figures of distinction.

Economics had been a popular subject even in the Muir College days when J.G. Jennings and W.J. Goodrich had taught it, and it continued to be so when the University was reorganized. In 1914, the department brought out the first journal of economics in India. It had the privilege of having H.S. Jevons in its professorial chair, and his open lectures (like those of Rushbrook Williams) were events of high-level discussions. They were held in the lecture rooms of the Old Library building (those halls have been turned into office cabins now).

Dr Jevons's voice—in a high profile lecture series on public finance, territorial development and irrigation in the Indian context, between 1916 and 1917—reaches us even today. He had summed up the subject matter of economics in the amplest and clearest definition possible: 'Economics, as developed during the past fifty years, has become essentially a study of the welfare of man in relation to material things. Economics is primarily concerned with the satisfaction of wants—how they arise and how they are satisfied. Economics is necessarily a psychological science...'[23] Mahatma Gandhi, too, lectured on the subject:

'Does Economic Progress Clash with Spiritual Progress?' at the economics department venue in December 1916.

With an ambience of committed research, of particular significance was a successful experiment carried out by the economics department in 1930, during the Great Depression. In a time of large-scale recession and unemployment in the Western world, an effort was made to delink the mental processes of Indian students from Western habits of thought. An essay paper in Hindi and Urdu was introduced to foster independence of expression in indigenous languages, an experiment way ahead of the age, and prefiguring some theories of higher education still half a century ahead in the future.

The department was fortunate to have distinguished teachers like Sam Higginbottom, Prof. A.R. Burnett Hurst, C.D. Thomson, S.K. Rudra, N.S. Subba Rao, Maheshwar Dayal, B.R. Adarkar and J.K. Mehta. Of these the most legendary is the name of J.K. Mehta who is credited with giving the subject a philosophic dimension, creating what is often referred to as 'rhyme, rhythm and truth' in the hitherto 'dismal science'.[24]

By the end of the 1950s there were twenty-one departments. As a 'unitary, teaching and residential' institution, the Allahabad University had earned a position of prestige and

A statue of the famous Hindi poet, Suryakant Tripathi Nirala, in front of the library building

distinction in the country.

But, what of the 'residential' aspect? Ideally the University aspired to be completely residential, students living in close contact with teachers in an engaged intellectual community. Practically speaking, the numbers pouring in every year from all over North India and even further afield made this goal difficult, with only four blocks of rooms for students existing in the Muir campus, referred to in the old records, as government hostels. The names of the University's early hostels and the order in which they came up reveal the sectional character of the province in which a composite culture existed alongside inter-dining and inter-marriage taboos.

The first separate hostel to come up was the Muslim Hostel, the brainchild of Maulana Samiullah Khan Jang Bahadur who helped raise funds and acquire land within the Muir campus itself. The first wing was built in 1892, and later additions were completed in 1898. The hostel received grants from both, the government and the state of Bhopal. The Muslim Hostel predates the Anthony Macdonnel Hindu Hostel. There are some interesting little facts recorded in the Muir College records. I quote a random selection from the principal's reports:

> The new Muhammadan Boarding House has made a further advance towards completion. The private rooms which suffice for about twenty boarders are very practically arranged and when the Library and the Dining Room are finished, nothing will be wanting to make this boarding house comfortable, attractive, and fully suited to its purpose…I should be glad to be able to give an equally favourable account of the Boarding House for Hindu students… But the two old bungalows in which the Hindu boarders reside are neither roomy enough, nor in any way specially

> adapted to our requirements. Some of the rooms are too small for even one student; others are excessively dark; others so big that, considering the general insufficiency of accommodation, they must be utilised for harbouring three or more students...[25]

This was the academic session 1895–96. The need for a boarding house for students was a pressing one. Plague was raging in Benaras and students flocked to Allahabad. By 1899–1900 the principal recorded: 'I understand that certain influential members of the Hindu community... have recently taken up the question of the establishment of a really suitable and sufficiently roomy Boarding House. I can only express a hope that active steps will be taken without much further delay to supply a long-felt want...'[26] Around this time Pundit Madan Mohan Malaviya started raising funds for the Hindu Hostel and there are many stories buried in Allahabad's narrations, of the people who provided him with the resources, often under a pledge of secrecy.

In 1901, the principal's report reads:

> A Hostel for students of all denominations, reading in any of the colleges of Allahabad, was opened by the Church Missionary Society... But for obvious reasons a considerable section of our students are reluctant to avail themselves of the advantages, undeniable in many respects, of this excellent institution, and hence the establishment of a suitable general Hindu Boarding House remains an urgent want.[27]

This hostel sponsored by the Church Mission Society appears to be the ancestor of Holland Hall, earlier known as the Oxford and Cambridge Hostel.

1901 witnessed the opening of the Macdonnel University Hindu Boarding House Society, named after the lieutenant governor of the United Provinces. After reorganization of the University, and the increase in students following the Second World War, extensions were built to the Hindu Hostel. In 1946, following Pundit Madan Mohan Malaviya's death, it was deemed a university college in keeping with its 'unitary, teaching and residential' status due to its in-house undergraduate tutorials.

But although the first hostels were organized along sectional lines, there were others of a completely secular character with repeated references to the existence of 'two government hostels' located in dilapidated bungalows. The principal's report of 1909–10 states: 'I am grateful that Government has sanctioned a new Government Hostel for 60 students at a cost of ₹60,000/-. One of the two ancient bungalows, hitherto dignified by the name of Government Hostels, has partly fallen down, and has since been condemned, and dismantled.'[28] A new Government Hostel was opened in 1911, later to become Ganganatha Jha Hostel in 1927. Two other hostels, originally called Law Hostels and reserved for law students, later began admitting students from other disciplines as well. Eventually, these two hostels were named Sir Sunder Lal Hostel and P.C. Banerjee Hostel.

Meanwhile the Kayastha Pathshala Trust, established by Munshi Kali Prasad Kulbhaskar, built its own hostel in 1925. It formed one of the three university colleges, with Macdonnel Hindu Hostel and Holland Hall, in that it provided facilities for residence as well as undergraduate tutorial classes. The old block of the Muir Hostel was extended in 1928, and the Sarojini Naidu Hostel for women came up in 1939, a year after the opening of the Women's College. Muir Hostel was renamed the Amaranatha Jha Hostel, after the charismatic Amaranatha Jha who had been its warden and guiding spirit from 1928 till he left, in 1947. It enjoyed the highest profile amongst the University's hostels, mainly on account of the large numbers of civil servants it supplied; Sir

Sunder Lal, P.C. Banerjee and G.N. Jha hostels were just a small step behind.

Prime Minister Jawaharlal Nehru at the AJ Hostel Variety Entertainment. Also seen are (L–R): Lal Bahadur Shastri, Dr Homi J. Bhabha and Dr Shri Ranjan

In 1947, when the University celebrated its diamond jubilee, a hostel of that same name was built. Like the other hostels, it soon came to have its own register of the Who's Who and its own legendry. The funniest story is that of an inmate once daring to flout discipline by singing aloud with full-throated fervour: '*Awaara hoon, main gardish mein hoon aasman ka tara hoon*' in joyous celebration of Raj Kapoor's recently released film, when a stern voice came booming from the other end of the hostel: '*Awaara ho to hostel se bahar nikal jao. Yahan awaaron ka kaam nahin hai. Yeh Diamond Jubilee Hostel hai!*'[29]

Each hostel had its celebrity list comprising bureaucrats, political figures, scientists, explorers, academicians, writers and diplomats. The list can run on for several pages. Allahabad University hostel alumni filled the corridors of power, the creative fields, the sciences and administrative services so extensively that a veritable Allahabad identity-field was generated. A shared culture of in-house anecdotage and memory reserves cemented connections for several decades, only to dissipate slowly as the state of UP lost its political primacy, and various educational centres in other parts of the country emerged.

Each hostel has its history but that of Holland Hall is perhaps the most interesting and unusual. Established by Anglican missionaries, it was originally called the Oxford and Cambridge Hostel, with two blocks: the Oxford Court and the Cambridge Court. The latter was constructed first, and work on the Oxford Court was held up for want of adequate funds. It goes to the credit of the Reverend W.E.S. Holland, the warden, to think of an ingenious method for raising money. Taking advantage of the great exhibition of 1911, at which the first Humber Biplane was on display, the Reverend Holland, with the help of Sir Walter Windham, set up a novel scheme for the world's very first aerial postal delivery! For two days, the hostel functioned as a busy general post office, receiving mail with an enclosed donation of 6 annas, addressed to various destinations around the world, but sent 'Care of the Warden'.

The special postmark for the first air mail courier service

A special postmark with a particular magenta dye was used; it contained a line drawing of an aircraft and the words 'First Aerial Post, 1911, UP Exhibition, Allahabad.' Watched by hundreds of people, the French pilot, Henri Pequet, took off and flew six miles across the river Yamuna to Naini, where he handed over the mailbag. The postal department then sent the letters to their intended destinations and their recipients had the satisfaction of receiving a letter that had actually, for the first time in history, flown through the air! The hostel earned about ₹2500 from the donations, and the Oxford wing saw its completion, leaving the name of William Holland as an exceptional legacy to the hostel.

Caste and food habits being sensitive issues then, the earlier hostels did not have a common mess. Students got together and organized their own separate messes; the Bengalis had theirs, so did the Paharis, and the most rigidly orthodox too. Reading accounts of the religious, ethnic and caste-specific observances, we come across some illuminating details. For Holland Hall's annual dinner, orthodox Hindu students sitting on the floor, Indian style—so as to keep their purity unstained by any mlechh proximity—refused to eat in the same row as the English warden, Mr Shaw, and his lady, who were seated at a separate table.

These were, however, tolerantly accepted lines of division, and a harmonious coexistence prevailed, with due concession being made to taboos and obligatory observances of different sectional groups. Religion and caste were core realities of the province, then as now, but their identity as bitterly contesting bastions had not yet become as intensive and unifocal as at present. In fact there is a peculiar paragraph written in the principal's report in 1908-1909 which provides some food for thought concerning British policy:

> While religious feeling appears to be increasing in the educated West, it is sad to observe the apparent growth

of irreligion in the educated East. The policy of religious neutrality must doubtless still be preserved in Government institutions, but it should be clear that whilst neutrality implies a large-minded tolerance, it is by no means the same thing as indifference. It appears to me that College addresses by members of the staff interested in this matter might possibly prove useful in this direction.[30]

This administrative dismay had arisen because the warden of the Muslim hostel had reported that attendance of Muslim boys in the hostel mosque (with a permanent pesh imam to conduct prayers), had dwindled except during Ramzan. One wonders why the British principal wanted to ensure that religious identities be preserved in a state of sectarian separateness, piously advancing the merit of religion, rather than allow students the freedom to do as they thought fit. These are the small giveaway details that stud historical accounts. Some years down the line we saw the consequences. This entry, incidentally, was made just four years after the Partition of Bengal.

If we consider the denominational lines along which some hostels and colleges arose, this perennial character of the province reveals itself. The Jain Boarding House, Kayastha Pathshala and the Ishwar Saran Hostel, started in 1951, all with an overtly sectional character. Despite this, if we glance through the round-up of hostel activities printed in the early issues of *The Allahabad University Magazine*, we get the feel of a whirl of exciting activities. Exceeding sectarian considerations, these activities included literary gatherings, picnics, sports events, dramatics and debates. Also, a wholesome secularity was noticeable in hostels like Muir, Sir Sunder Lal, P.C. Banerjee and G.N. Jha.

Each hostel had its library and its magazine. The annual functions of the Muir and Sarojini Naidu Hostels were keenly awaited University events. The mock-parliament sessions of

Holland Hall were likewise a highlight of that hostel. A popular feature of the 1930s ragging would have the girls of Sarojini Naidu Hostel take position on their terrace to enjoy watching the parade of the Holland Hall freshmen march up to their hostel. They would laugh at the comedy, wave and applaud as the boys bowed and saluted them three times, and then march back to Holland Hall in true military style. This was no doubt an annual entertainment much anticipated and discussed.[31]

By the 1950s, ragging in its harsher forms had started making its appearance. There are at least two references to this in the recordings of alumni. One states: 'P.C.B. was not very notorious for ragging. News of blue faces, swollen eyes and bleeding noses came to us freshers from other hostels...'[32] Another writes: 'The life of a fresher was on expected lines, as we were subjected to the "affectionate attention" of our seniors year in and year out. The midnight drenchings of broken surahis, the obligatory farshis to seniors, the nights spent out in Alfred Park in desperate attempt to escape; all of these were common occurrences.'[33] Ragging continued to grow in intensity in all the hostels until by the end of the century it had assumed very serious proportions, causing grave injury and pain to new entrants, and becoming an exercise of collective cruelty rather than an ice-breaking exercise for new students.

The University did its level best to provide alternative living accommodation to students, by hiring 'lodges'—usually large, old private bungalows. The names of some of these lodges crop up in records: Colonelgunj lodge, Allengunj lodge, Roanoke lodge, Bank Road lodge, Dilkusha lodge, and later, Mumfordgunj lodge. Partly to solve the problem of accommodation, a Delegacy Lodging Houses Bureau had been established in 1941. The Delegacy had other facilities for students who lived with their families or relatives, or in hired independent accommodation. To begin with, there were just two: the North and East Delegacies. By

1957, the city had been divided into twelve Delegacy circles, each under the supervision of a teacher. Concurrently there was a zonal division of each Delegacy, with sports and other competitive co-curricular activities organized between the five zones. There was also a book banking system to lend textbooks to poor students, and a separate Delegacy for girl students that later expanded to two units. A Delegacy building (now the Nirala Art Gallery), was constructed to handle Delegacy matters. By the centenary year there were twenty-three circles.

The tutorial system died out as the number of students soared, which was a loss because, as D.D. Khanna commented in his remembrances: 'The seminar classes in the University provided... opportunity for students to receive personal attention by teachers. (The) classes were of 8 to 10 students only. A student could freely interact with the teacher and may develop a lifetime relationship and seek guidance as and when necessary.'[34] It is an intriguing thought that its place appears to have been taken by the scores of coaching institutes that have mushroomed in the city. Cities and institutions morph and mutate into strange incarnations of their earlier selves in response to shifting demands.

And in spite of the addition to the number of hostels, large areas of the city seem to have been colonized by students, rooming singly or in groups. They study in the University proper, or in the multiple coaching institutes that groom them for entrance to various professional careers, or for the University examinations themselves. This is alongside the bizarre reality of University hostels being routinely occupied by students whose legitimate academic terms of stay are long over—and even by outsiders! The law-and-order situation that invites regular raids and police intervention had, if not anticipated, at least introduced a note of foreboding in the remarks of the then vice chancellor, Dr Tara Chand, as early as in1946–47. He stated that with the number of students accelerating at a rapid pace, discipline was turning into a problem.

The congregation of vast numbers of young students in overcrowded areas, in circumstances of a bitterly competitive struggle for employment, they also have little assurance of transparency or justice in selection. Further, condemned to inhale the noxious fumes of large-scale corruption, nepotism and sectarian prejudice, it is not to be wondered that for our students the system has veered out of control. Hence, the vision of making Allahabad an educational centre stands countered, and supplanted by other cities in India with better facilities and more progressive cultures of discipline.

But if the fissures were visible even during the golden era, they were easily counterweighed by the positive energies animating the institution. When we sift through the records, we find that the laboratories and libraries of the time, though under-equipped by international standards, were still spaces for original work and dedicated study. The laboratory of the Sheila Dhar Institute of Soil Science, developed under the guidance of N.R. Dhar, was at par with the best in the country, highly capable of its research enterprises in photochemistry, colloids, stereochemistry etc. The physics laboratories, although hampered by the cost of equipment during the Second World War, nonetheless developed a modern X-ray lab, which had a powerful electron microscope and diffraction unit. The J.K. Institute of Applied Physics had an advanced course in radio physics and Electronics, and possessed a closed circuit television set (in the 1950s!). It also owned lab apparatus related to atomic, nuclear and molecular physics, and para-magnetic resonance spectroscopy. The zoology and botany labs, however, did not quite keep pace with the high levels of research being done in their departments, and had felt the need for better facilities.

What laboratories are to the sciences, libraries are to the humanities, and from its early days the Muir College library was a space precious and memorable to students. Shiva Adhar Pande, writing about the library as it was in 1905, has this to say:

> After a lecture, we were told to go to the Library. Very few books had been taught in class and from the start we were encouraged to behave like graduates, and to shift for ourselves. If we had a book in the course, we got out the books of the author, read what pleased us, then read his biography, then tackled all his masterpieces, and whatever criticism we could get. We thus luckily escaped the lop-sided reading in fashion later on. In 1905, the Muir College Library was in Vizianagram Hall—tiers on tiers of books right up to the escutcheons, lanes on lanes of bookcases all over the Hall—the librarian and the peon tucked away invisible at a small table in the door at the North-Eastern corner. It was the biggest library in the province, and it had the atmosphere of a library. Queen's College might have *more* books but they were sprawling in its corridors, right up to the steps! They did not know what is due to a *Library*.[35]

(There was fierce rivalry between the students of Muir Allahabad and those of Queen's College Benaras—an Oxford and Cambridge situation!)

But already in 1906 the hallowed silence, the sacred aura had changed. Shiva Adhar Pande recounts how the library was shifted to a larger room in the Muir College, a room where the boys sat chatting around the students' table, and the peon sat watching a cricket match being played outside. You could not browse and pick up a book—you had to write down the name and hand the slip to the peon, Shiv Nath, who is described as 'perennial'.[36]

Later, when the Senate Hall complex was built, the library was moved to what is our present registrar and accounts office. It had a large central hall, with a long table running down its length, and the scholarly hush and whisper special to libraries. We are told that in 1937, it had 96,191 books, subscribed to 282 international journals, and received plenty more gratis. Between 1937 and 1957, the number of books rose to over a lakh, purchased with the help of government grants and a handsome donation from the Maharaja of Darbhanga. In 1939, the Darbhanga Reading Room was inaugurated (one of the halls partitioned into office cabins now). French, Italian and German books were received as gifts from those governments; to books in English and the Indian languages were added manuscripts in Sanskrit, Persian, Arabic and Urdu. The Provincial Government Museum of Lucknow contributed valuable additions to the Allahabad University library's stock of rare coins. The library also received—'for custody'—eight boxes of rare books and manuscripts from The Royal Asiatic Society of Bengal.

The chief librarian was usually a senior member of the teaching staff, and Mr Parmanand, R.P. Tripathi, P.E. Dustoor—all served the library in this capacity. By 1947, however, the need for more professional guidance was felt towards improving library conditions, so Rao Sahib S.R. Ranganathan, librarian of the Benaras Hindu University, was invited to offer inputs to enhance efficiency. His report, among other suggestions, emphasized the need for a larger building and better finances. The 1953 Enquiry Committee suggested the construction of a new building, and the creation of an independent post of librarian of the same rank and remuneration as a professor.

Following this, the University Grants Commission sanctioned a sum of ₹10,000 for the creation of an all-new central library. Even so, the increase in the number of students quite outpaced the rate of growing resources and despite all grants and endowments a general inadequacy was experienced. The year 1942 was widely felt to have been the turning point from sufficiency to insufficiency, financially, and consequently in other areas. All the same, compared to the present, the library then—even with its relative insufficiencies—was used with proper diligence, another feature meriting identification of that period with terms such as 'heyday' and 'golden era'.

Quite apart from the infrastructural facilities provided by the institution, there was a driving energy that fuelled the intellectual life of the campuses in the form of the many associations, groups, study circles, clubs and a variety of lively activities. Of these, the foremost was the Students' Union. As early as the Muir College era a Students' Representative Council had existed, as it was resolved—after much deliberation by S.G. Dunn and his colleagues—that it was desirable to promote such an initiative. 'In order to further the co-operation of students in the organisation of the College, and to promote unity and corporate life among them, a Council should be formed, representative of students of every status.'[37] (In fact, in an enlightening essay that appeared in the December 1923 issue of *The Allahabad University Magazine*, Dunn traces the origin of medieval universities to guilds or unions of scholars.)

That was October 1914, and those are the words Amaranatha Jha cites.[38] 'Corporate activity' was stressed, though the shape of this activity was to undergo basic transformation over the decades. Initially Jha tells us: 'This Council was to meet the Principal from time to time and consult with him in all matters which might affect their fellow(s) and the well-being of the College as a whole.'[39] The first objective was to work for the celebrations on Foundation Day, and their hard work won the members badges with the words 'Duty Our Watchword' inscribed on them. The following year, Jha relates, they got 'beautifully coloured turbans and silk badges with S.R.C. embroidered thereon'[40]—turbans that were later converted into silk kurtas by some members.

When the University was reorganized, the existence of a Students' Union was considered necessary, along the lines of the unions at the Universities of Oxford and Cambridge. In 1923, a meeting of the University's leading members took place in the Lecture Theatre (of what is the medieval and modern history department) and a decision was taken to create a university union. The vice chancellor, Claude de la Fosse, was made chairperson, and Bhola Nath Jha was elected to the office of temporary president. The first elections took place soon afterwards, in the same year, and the first office bearers were S.G. Tiwari, P.D. Awasthi and P.N. Singh elected to the positions of president, vice president and secretary respectively.

The vice chancellor, Ganganatha Jha, who succeeded Fosse after the scandal previously described, inaugurated this first union, which within a month created its constitution. The main features were, that principal office bearers be student-members, that elections take place each term i.e., three times per session, the position of librarian and treasurer be held by graduates of at least four years standing, and their terms continue for the entire session. A Working Committee was constituted of one member from each hostel, and one representative of the faculty, to assist the office bearers in matters relating to the budget and other specific decisions.[41]

Ganganatha Jha

For a period of time the Union lived up to its models at Oxford and Cambridge, as a place of intellectual discourse and debate. If we skim through the accounts of alumni, we come across abundant references to the active intellectual profile of the Allahabad University Students' Union. I have chosen three random references by P.C. Gupta, H.S. Saxena and V. Rajamani, which give us a vivid picture:

P.C. Gupta: 'The debates in the Union used to draw big crowds. They were held in the Vizianagram Hall or the Large Lecture Theatre. Distinguished persons like the late Chintamani, Mr. Kunzru, Mr. P.N. Sapru or Dr. Katju came and participated along with students in these debates. Lectures and debates were the core of the Union activities in those days...'[42]

Pundit Govind Ballabh Pant laid the foundation stone of the union building on 9 August 1939. H.S. Saxena recalls: 'There was a comfortable restaurant in the Union building and a reading room where students read newspapers and periodicals in their vacant periods.'[43]

V. Rajamani gives us an even livelier picture:

> The Allahabad University Union has a place for itself in the campus. Both during university hours and long after, it may be seen sizzling with activity. The Union Café is the favourite centre of those in search of gossip and a cup of tea! The Union building attracts all kinds of students—both present and prospective student leaders, lobby-men, loungers, debaters, enthusiasts and aimless wanderers. The Union provides a platform for visiting V.I.P.s to address the students. The Union Executive seeks to ventilate the grievances of students and to bring about a semblance of order into what would otherwise be a babel of voices.[44]

The Allahabad University Students' Union was intimately associated with the freedom movement in the city, as will be described in the next chapter. Perhaps the involvement of university students in the Indian National Movement unwittingly admitted a new and dangerous element into the DNA of the university union, something which persisted after Independence and mutated to unanticipated proportions. I shall write about the University's interface with the freedom movement presently, but for now it is sufficient to mention that the engagement of youth in a country's freedom struggle may have been an exciting and meaningful chapter in their—and the country's—history. It may even have provided valuable apprenticeship, in the practice of politics and pressure lobbying, to many eminent future members of Parliament and the Legislative Assembly, but it left some precedents, which, over the long haul, were to prove pernicious.

Fasts, lockouts, noisy demonstrations, the strangle-hold of state and national political party affiliations, and a trade-union style of combative bargaining—most of these are the residual sediment of tactics learnt in the 1920s, '30s and '40s. They worked towards paralysing British administration then, and they work towards paralysing institutional administration now. The step from civil disobedience to uncivil disobedience is a small one. The University, which P.C. Gupta's telling lines so movingly qualify when he writes: 'There was an air of quiet tranquility about these Halls and an aura of learning and distinction...'[45] turned into a playground of politics and remains so till date.

This is indeed a far cry from the brilliant mock-parliaments and mock-sessions of the UN that were organized by the Allahabad University Students' Union. There would be intensive rehearsals, and on the final day intellectuals from all over the city attended. Prof. Dhanesh Mandal writes with awe-struck nostalgia of a particular mock-session of Parliament in which the Kashmir issue was discussed. It lasted seven hours, and the principal student-discussants were R.R. Chari, Gopi Arora and Otima Mukherjee, each with their own distinctive style. Chari enacted Krishna Menon's personality with such finesse that he seemed to be Menon himself! The other two went on to become prominent bureaucrats.

Mandal, himself a left-winger, mentions others of that ilk in the Students' Union—G.R. Sharma, Nurul Hasan, Asif Ansari and the brilliant maverick O.P. Mehrotra. So it must not be imagined that Congress proximity dominated the prevalent ideological tone of the Union. In the early 1950s, under the guidance of P.C. Joshi, the Allahabad University had a strong communist presence. Mandal recalls that a massive strike took place, spearheaded by left-wing leaders like Vir Bhadra Pratap Singh, O.P. Mehrotra, Kedarnath Singh, Mirza Muhammad Islam, Ali Beg Changezi and G.P. Singh (many of whom were rusticated). It was against Chancellor K.M. Munshi's move to remodel the writing of history so as to transform our composite culture portraits. Mandal writes feelingly of the left-wing arm of the Students' Union, many of whose members lived in Dilkusha Park. The names of friends he mentions—and not all were left-wing—send many bells ringing in our mind: Kripalani, Vidya Niwas Mishra, Negi, Janeshwar Misra.[46]

As the learnt methods of democratic expression gained strength, H.S. Saxena recalls that by the 1950s, 'agitations and hunger strikes were becoming an annual feature, (but) life in the campus became normal after the Dussehra vacations.'[47] The spirited demonstrations were not without their little comedies, as he recounts:

> Two students AA and RKG went on a hunger strike which continued for about two weeks. Dr. P.E. Dustoor was the proctor. He was very strict and would not compromise or give in to pressure tactics. AA and RKG had become very weak and the doctors gave alarming medical reports. I do not exactly remember how the strike ended but AA and

RKG hosted a dinner at Royal Hotel to celebrate the event. …A table was laid with spotless damask cloth, expensive crockery and gleaming silver.

Summan, the headwaiter, was supervising all the arrangements… Dr. P.E. Dustoor was the chief guest. There was a menu card on a stand and it was mouth-watering: tomato soup, fish mayonnaise, chicken and baked vegetables, pea polao, and pudding. Next day Dr. Dustoor told us about this dinner. AA and RKG had gone to Dr. Dustoor with the request, 'Sir, you have seen us starving, now we want you to see us eat.' There was no ill feeling when the strike was over. Dr. Dustoor was touched by this gesture. Later, AA became the President of the Union, joined the bar of the Allahabad High Court, and ultimately became a High Court Judge. RKG became a leading advocate of the Supreme Court.[48]

But besides the Union, there were as many as eighty-three listed associations in the year 1957. Some of them had been around for a long time. Some had piquant names. I mention only a handful: The Alphabets, The Afro-Asian Friendship Society, Akhil Bhartiya Darshan Parishad, All Flags Club, the Archaeological Society, Business Bureau, Busy Bees, Crescent Club, Conversazione, Clearing House, Clio, Elysium, Friday Club, Thursday Club, Golden Gang, Hindi Parishad, Good Companions, Hilful Arab, Indo-Bulgarian Friendship Society, Revellers, Mathematical Association, Mountaineering Club, Music Association, Painting Association, Progressive Club, Philosophy Academy, Social Service League, Three Colours and Five Stars, Union For The Study Of Great Religions, United Nations Students Association of India, World University Service Committee, Zoological Society—a list from A to Z with many omissions in between.

There were rules for membership to these clubs, which included the assent of all the existing members. V. Rajamani gives us a lucid account of the times:

> ...Education in the true sense begins after classes are over. The Allahabad University campus provides numerous opportunities to students to imbibe education in this sense. The large number of organisations devoted to co-curricular activities spring into activity immediately after the classes have dispersed. There is never a day when some Association or Society or Circle or Club or Committee is not holding one meeting or the other in the Campus, from which the eager student can derive both recreation and benefit.[49]

Every department had its association where papers were read and discussed, and lectures delivered by eminent visitors. There were common interest student groups and social clubs where, apart from discussions and readings, cultural activities and informal interactions took place with celebrity visitors. A quick glance at some instances leaves the reader refreshed and impressed. The Art and Culture Society, for example, awarded 'Aesthetic Sense' prizes to students, and organized garden competitions between hostels. The Assam Association, the Punjabi Association, the Bengali Literary Union and the Bundelkhand Parishad sought to promote and celebrate the cultures of their provinces through lectures, music programmes, poetry competitions and plays. The Delegacy—both the men's and women's wings—had lending libraries, subsidized lodges and organized sports and athletics. The Women's Delegacy's annual dramatic show and annual social were prominent events.

The Bharat Yuvak Sangh was an apolitical group of students interested in the problems of value-based nation-building and social service. Clearing House was an association of the

Commerce Faculty that awarded a silver medal for the best paper read. The Elysium had brainstorming sessions on various issues three times a month, and published an annual magazine. The Hindi Parishad published a literary magazine named *Kaumudi*. The famous Hindi writer, Amarkant, writes about how—as a BA student—he and a few others started a handwritten literary journal under the influence of Babu Ganesh Prasad, which carried pieces by students who were to become well-known writers in the future. The International Club organized paper readings by students of the politics department, followed by what the records call an 'intense discussion'.

The French Circle held an exhibition of the reproductions of paintings by French masters, and organized lectures on Baudelaire and Flaubert. The Friday Club staged widely attended plays: Shakespeare's *Twelfth Night* and *A Midsummer Night's Dream*, Bernard Shaw's *Arms and the Man*, John Galsworthy's *The Silver Box*, Oscar Wilde's *The Importance of Being Earnest*, W.B. Yeats's *The Land of Heart's Desire*, W.W. Jacob's *Monkey's Paw* and Kalidasa's *Abhijnana Shakuntalam*. (It is a nice little detail that in the Muir College days Purushottam Das Tandon acted as Bottom, the clown, in *A Midsummer Night's Dream*, and Madan Mohan Malaviya as Shakuntala; the narrator, Amaranatha Jha, coyly refuses to say as much but, tongue-in-cheek, drops hints enough.[50])

Later in 1944–45, as Bishan Tandon's writings reveal, Hindi plays were staged by a group of friends: Prasad's *Chandragupta*, Jagdish Mathur's *Bhor Ka Tara* and the play *Aurangzeb Ki Antim Ratri*.[51] The Hindi Parishad published an annual magazine and played host to guests of the stature of Jawaharlal Nehru, Sarojini Naidu, Acharya Kripalani and Sumitranandan Pant. The Thursday Club of the Urdu department organized high-class mushairas, and the Urdu Association staged one-act plays like *Ananas aur Atom Bomb*, *Batua*, *Akbar Allahabadi* and *Majaz*.

The Mountaineering Club organized Himalayan expeditions to the Pindari and Kaphini Glaciers, the Rupkund Lake and the extensive Milan Glacier near the Indo-Tibetan border. The Physics Society hosted many foreign scientists, and held debates on nuclear fission and the problems of cosmology and cosmogany, the formation of matter and the origin of the continents and oceans. The Research Study Circle held a lecture series on research methodology, and the World University Service collected funds for providing X-ray equipment to the University dispensary.

V. Rajamani put it succinctly when he wrote: 'Co-curricular organisations are the salt of any university; their influence is much deeper and wider than they ever suspect.... So much activity is centred in one place and a freshman not too enamoured of study is apt to drop in at one meeting after another because he is passing a door and sees a crowd going in.'[52]

There was a sense of busy involvement, a vibrant creative charge in the air, and an intimacy of connection that spilt out of the campus and pervaded the bookshops and cafes on University Road, and even beyond. H.S. Saxena has written warmly about Students' Friends, Friends' Book Depot, Central Book Depot and Jagati Restaurant. Jagati is also fondly remembered by other alumni as a favourite haunt of intellectuals and loungers, and famous for its cutlets: 'Jagati's Restaurant was already famous, as Bhagwati Charan Verma had dedicated his popular novel *Teen Varsh* to Manohar Lal Sah Jagati, the proprietor of the restaurant... The novel opens with a brief description of the University Road.'[53]

It is an endearing little touch, so much so that students who had read that description decided to visit the restaurant, as did the author of the article too.

> Out of curiosity, therefore, we went there for a pot of tea.
> Tea was served in a teapot and along with it there was a

strainer, a sugar pot and a jug of milk. There were normally two cups of tea in a pot. One could get refills of boiling water free. After the first cup of strong tea, which gave the initial impetus to the intellect, conversation was later sustained by progressively weaker and weaker cups of tea, hot water being readily supplied by the ever-obliging waiter... Later some of these intellectuals shifted to the coffee house in Civil Lines.[54]

But that is another story.

'There was another restaurant, "The University Restaurant", which was patronised by sportsmen. They used to frequent this restaurant in their blue and pink blazers. Chairs and tables were sometimes arranged on the pavement and one could enjoy his tea in the open watching other students strolling on the road.'[55]

Saxena writes of Subol Babu of Students' Friends, who knew 'each and every student here', for Students' Friends 'was a friendly shop and lived up to its name.' Prominently displayed in the shop was a framed certificate from Amaranatha Jha; visitors paused to admire 'the beautiful hand-written certificate.'[56] Saxena also mentions, in passing, that there were no general merchant shops on University Road in the 1940s. 'The town had not impinged upon the gown,'[57] as he puts it.

Advertisements in *The Allahabad University Magazine* dating to a couple of decades earlier make us smile, and it will be worth preserving their quaint language and persuasive marketing tactics in this volume. I quote two delightful examples from the same firm, it appears—that of 'Seyne And Company, George Town, Allahabad.' Amusingly, the two ads offer entirely different things. One is a book of love poems; the other is about tailoring services. I quote from the first:

A BOOK OF CHARMS FOR ALL BOOK-LOVERS
A BOUQUET OF KISSES

A NOVEL COLLECTION OF LOVE-POEMS IN ENGLISH
FROM
THE EASTERN AND WESTERN POETS
Arranged and edited
By A.K. SEYNE

All lovers of the beautiful in literature should have a copy of this publication

SELECT OPINIONS

Sir Henry Richards, Kt., Ex-Chief Justice of the Allahabad High Court writes:
It displays wonderful knowledge of the language and poetic feeling.
Hon. Sir William Tudball, Allahabad, writes: I am sending it home to my wife who I am sure will like to have it.
Prof. S.G. Dunn, M.A., University of Allahabad writes: The bouquet is indeed a fragrant one.
The Indian Review says: A handsome prize book for boys and girls in quest of love.
The Hindustan Review says: It is a collection of great charm and interest and should have a large circulation.
The Leader says: We are sure the book will have a large circulation. It is very attractively got-up.

The printed half-page ad assures the targeted romantic buyer that:

the get-up is lovely and picturesque—The text is printed with artistic border in red.
The price of the book is Re. 1/-
TO BE HAD FROM M. SEYNE, 49, GEORGE TOWN, ALLAHABAD.

That the enterprising Seyne undertook to appropriately equip the

University student for heady campus romance is evident from the second ad, which goes like this:

SEYNE & CO.

MODERN TAILORS

GEORGE TOWN MARKET, ALLAHABAD

For good materials, good Tailoring, moderate prices and Quick service combined with attention, we invite you to try our Tailoring Department. Excellent workmanship and the acme of perfection in fit, we guarantee. Perfectly cut men's Shirts, Soft Collars and Ties always in stock

PRICES TO SUIT ALL POCKETS

If you come once, you will come always.

No doubt the book sold well and the firm prospered because, by December 1923, the company had shifted to University Road and further refined its ads. The location now given is the site 'formerly occupied by Messrs Don and Company' and the persuasion has grown more discursive:

'We need not tell you that good tailoring is a Fine Art,' explains the ad. 'We are artists, desiring to have more models to make a suit or a shirt.' It then goes on to detail its strengths:

Measurement of each individual is taken with great care—all clothes are cut in the latest style by a cutter of great distinction, the greatest care is taken that your suit will fit and please you in every respect. We invite you to compare our workmanship with any of the reputed European firms. Suits are not our only speciality. Breeches, Sherwani or Turkish Coats done by us will give you the greatest satisfaction.

The ad ends with a rhymed couplet:

> Works we turn out on due date;
> Our charges are most moderate.[58]

This is 1923. Reading this appealing ad, I begin to make sense of the remark cited at the beginning of this chapter, about some University students looking like American millionaires on holiday! Romance on the campus is a theme pervading much of the literature of the times.

That little reference to sportsmen, in their blue and pink blazers, haunting the University Restaurant, brings me to the sports and athletics scenario in the campus. Rajamani creates the ambience of 'most evenings (when) one may see the athletic-minded at their track and field training. The University and hostel teams in various games are active throughout the session. Their friends and supporters are always present to cheer them from the sidelines. The laurels won by university sportsmen and athletes are recounted in the report of the Athletic Association.'[59]

It had been decided that undergraduate students should take part in some kind of physical activity. There was an array of games and sports, including swimming, on offer. In the Muir days cricket was the only game played, and Mr Buddon, who was the butt of much criticism on the academic front, tried his best to organize some forms of sport in the college. Later, when the University was reorganized, and the Athletic Association founded, considerable attention was given to providing suitable infrastructure for the advancement of sports in the campus. Tennis, hockey, badminton, and volleyball—in addition to cricket—came to be popular games. When the golden jubilee was celebrated in 1937, the universities of Lucknow, Benaras and Aligarh sent their teams to participate in the golden jubilee sports.

1938 and '39 saw the construction of the stadium and a

cemented hard court in the Muir College; also an electrified pavilion and a regular office for the Athletic Association. A swimming pool, funded by the Raja Sir Maharaj Singh (a former commissioner fond of visiting the University with his wife), came up in 1941, and it was to become the venue for the University's aquatic meets. A squash court and a physical training programme were introduced for students. 1941 to 1942 saw great activity with Allahabad University teams going on frequent tours to outstation destinations to participate and win.

Under Prof. S.K. Rudra, this activity grew to unprecedented proportions and new features were added: a best physique contest, a weightlifting contest, wrestling, boxing and kabaddi. The selection of 'Mr University' was quite an event. The house of the Singhanias, the JKs, sponsored the construction of two permanent stadia and a Mrs Rathore of Delhi proved to be the fairy godmother of the Athletics Association, donating to it many shields, cups and trophies between 1949 and 1953. Under the aegis of the Raj Kumari Amrit Kaur Sports Coaching Scheme, special coaching was provided for staff members to guide the students.

Inter-university and state meets enabled matches in cricket, football, tennis, volleyball, badminton, boxing and aquatics. The brisk and busy 1950s were full of sports events, some students representing India even in prestigious events like the Asian Games in Tokyo, and the Empire Games in Cardiff. This credit goes to W.N. Usmani and Jagjit Singh. Buddy Malvea represented India at the World Youth Festival in Budapest; Khurshid Ahmad in the Asian Games; Girish Verma, Dina Nath Tewari and Meenakshi Choudhary in Russia; Deep Narain, Ahmad Sultan, Anand Singh and O.N. Tresler in Kabul. Allahabad University teams participated in all-important tournaments at the national, state, district and local levels. Women athletes such as Raj Mohini

Kataria, Harbhajan Kaur, Surjeet Kaur, Anashi Minz, N. Navlekar, S. Lawrence and Renu Simlai made their mark as well.

Among the most sought after co-curricular activities was the UOTC (University Officers' Training Corps) that later morphed into the National Cadet Corps. Started during the First World War years, the University Corps became a permanent part of University life. It is recorded that the UOTC included members of the teaching staff, university functionaries and students in various military ranks—commandant, commissioned officers and non-commissioned officers. There were sixteen British instructors permanently appointed to impart training.

Rajeshwar Dayal recalls his days as a member of the UOTC:

> I join (ed) the University Training Corps of which Dr. Amaranatha Jha was the Officer Commanding, and ended my 4 years of glorious service with the rank of Lance Corporal. We paraded with dummy muskets and in oversize uniforms that were probably relics of the First World War. It was a particular treat to go on route marches with the pipe band playing Scottish airs. As a mark of special favour, we occasionally presented a guard of honour at Government House.[60]

Another lively account of this 'playing-at-soldiers' is in a 1925 issue of *The Allahabad University Magazine*:[61]

> About 75 of us were present...and we all marched together with our rifles on our shoulders, led by Lieutenant Karwal, our Company Commander. We reached the Camp at about 10.30 a.m. Our kits were taken away on lorries... We were allotted a row of tents with one N.C.O. in each tent... Regular work began from the next day and Reveille sounded at 5 in the morning. Everyone had to get up at that time. We had to place everything outside the tent

that was left quite empty for cleaning before we went on parade. The next bugle sounded at 6 when we were called for tea. After that we had to run for the first drill at 6.30 a.m., which lasted an hour. From 7.30 to 8 we were free to prepare for the next parade from 8 to 9. After another rest of half an hour we had the last morning parade from 9.30 to 10.30.

After these parades we had to prepare for the lines inspection… After the Adjutant's inspection the breakfast bugle sounded at 11.30 a.m. The number of men was so large… that we had to form a Queue in order that every one of us might get his share. The 'touchables' and the 'untouchables' all took their food in the same way and there was no distinction between the two…. After dinner we were free till 1 p.m., when we had another parade for an hour.' The rigour of the discipline is quite astounding. Defaulters had to do extra work, 'either fatigue duty or extra parades'. There was excitement as well. 'Absolute silence and darkness reigned after the bugle at 10 p.m. Only shouts of 'Halt, who comes here?' were heard now and then near the Guard room.

There are boyish truancies that make us smile. 'The regimental doctor attended us every morning and a large number of men gave their names for the "Sick- List" in order to free themselves from parade… The number of "sick-men" increased every day.'

There is mention of sports events at the camp.

There was a fairly big crowd of spectators including a large number of guests, with a fair sprinkling of ladies. "A" Company (i.e. Allahabad) fared well in all the sports. We won the Football Cup, but lost the Hockey Cup… The Cross-Country Race was an easy victory for us. In

> shooting as well as in Tug-of-War we got the Second prizes... Among the items that were of special interest was the Officers' Race. The competitors in this race included Major-General Nightingale and Major Ranjit Singh, O.B.E., I.M.S., who came out first and second respectively. Major-General M.R.W. Nightingale C.B., C.M.G., C.I.E., D.S.O., gave away the prizes. The Queen's furnished the band for the evening.
>
> Besides the above sports we had concerts by A, B and C Companies, that of A Company being much appreciated by all. All the members of the A Company were photographed on the 14th morning...

After parting from new friends from Benaras, Roorkee, Aligarh, Meerut and Lucknow: 'We marched back to Muir College where we were dismissed. This Camp, though it took much of our time, gave us an idea of military and camp life.'[62]

It continues to do that after almost a century. There was a severity and simplicity of discipline in the account, which arouses nostalgia for a possibly more wholesome time. There was a bond of solidarity as well, that endured for years, as Jagat Mehta's recollections so interestingly show:

> Some years ago I was (in) a foreign capital waiting for a lift in a hotel. A tall handsome gentleman looked at me (up and down) and then came forward. "Are you not Jagat?"
>
> "*Aray Sergeant Sahib, aap humko bhool gaye—Company Teesri Platoon. Aapne toh pardesh mein hamara kaafi paseena nikala tha. Ab kyon sharma rahe hain?* I am Noor, retired Brigadier in the Pakistan Army: Fought against you four times and now Director of Strategic Studies in Islamabad." After all, he added, "UP was my birthplace and Allahabad University my alma mater. Cancel whatever formal dinner

you are going to. Let us have a drink, spend the evening together and talk of old days."

(Mehta goes on to reveal still more breathtaking facts: 'In at least two sets of difficult negotiations with Pakistan, I believe that the successful outcome was, at least in part, because of Agha Shahi, the then Foreign Secretary and my opposite number. He was a contemporary of mine in the Muir Hostel.')

Officers of the University Officers' Training Corps

But the ties of the old UOTC demonstrated their strength in even more dramatic circumstances when Mehta, as foreign secretary, went to call on the law minister, Shanti Bhushan. Mehta writes of the incident:

> The Janata Government had just come to power. Since I had been appointed by the previous Government, I introduced myself with some formality and trepidation. Shri Shanti Bhushan got up from his desk, stood to attention, gave me an impressive salute correctly (the

longest way round and the shortest way down)... I may have muttered that as a mere sergeant I was not entitled to a salute, but in any case, I betrayed my fear that a Minister in the Central Government would not want to recall being a raw recruit. I had overlooked that the bonds of Allahabad do not get loosened even after 33 years and divergent paths of life.[63]

On the 15 July 1948, the UOTC was disbanded and its new avatar—the National Cadet Corps—was established the following day. In its post-Independence incarnation it continued to be active: Allahabad University cadets representing the 8th UP Battery, NCC, at the Republic Day parade in Delhi in 1953, and the Eastern Command Tattoo at Lucknow. A girls' division was created in 1955–56. The number of battalions was increased and the NCC continued to be a popular choice for students, although by the 1960s some complaining voices against compulsory NCC membership lie preserved in records.

The experience of browsing through old issues of *The Allahabad University Magazine* conveys the sense of a coherent, energetic, engaged community—physically and intellectually robust, and overflowing with purpose. There is an atmosphere of sufficiency and focus—the feeling of a complete world anchored in a cosmopolitan ambience without losing a quaint, polished localism all its own. It is not the positions in life that the staff and students subsequently rose to—though that is resoundingly impressive enough—it is the concentration of vitality, and the currents of creative interaction and expression that have an authentic ring. Nothing conveys this better than a quick browse through the antique pages of *The Allahabad University Magazine*. As Claude de la Fosse, introducing the magazine's very first issue in October 1922, wrote:

> [...a University magazine] is the chronicle of its life and an essential part of its corporate existence.... Future generations are sure to turn over the pages of its earliest numbers with more than ordinary curiosity, to learn how we, who worked together to build up a teaching and residential university at Allahabad, thought and acted in these early days...

The pages are brittle and crack easily. The animated voices that leap out of them are electrified with exuberant ideas.

The old yardstick to measure the University's stature was the number of bureaucrats it produced. In fact, after the ICS examination was instituted in India, (following the Second World War), Amaranatha Jha proposed to the Government of India that the Allahabad University could competently run an ICS training camp. Although his proposal could not be accepted, a statement is recorded in the home department's correspondence that the Allahabad University could well conduct the said task expertly.[64]

In the 1960s, Prof. T. Pati of the mathematics department would harangue students on this point. The University, he declared, was not a factory to produce civil servants. Its function was to produce excellent academics, writers, historians and scientists, dedicated to making the University a centre of high learning. But, in all fairness to the University, it must be said that it fulfilled this function, too, in those pro-active days. If we run through the guest list alone, there are names that leave a powerful resonance: Gardner Murphy, Norman Marshall, Dr A.L. Basham, Prof. and Mrs Julian Huxley, Sarojini Naidu, I.A. Richards, Eleanor Roosevelt, A.R. Todd, Edmund Blunden. These are among scores of other international figures.

Convocation Banquet. Jawaharlal Nehru, Lal Bahadur Shastri, V.V. Giri, Dr Zakir Husain, Maithili Sharan Gupta and Kamalapati Tripathi can be seen in the photo

If we leaf through heritage photographs, we see the iconic personalities of the time, ranged around tables at convocation banquets or alumni meets: Jawaharlal Nehru, Lal Bahadur Shastri, V.V. Giri, Zakir Hussain and Dr Sampurnanand—all in the same photograph! The convocation addresses, aside from the charged hyper-rhetoric of a soon-to-be—or newly independent—country still throb with the pulse of true idealism poised to deliver a message of genuine inspiration which, even to our ears debased by decades of cynicism, is sterling.

The fact that an international physicist of the stature of Shroedinger readily accepted the offer of a professorial chair in the physics department, after the departure of Meghnad Saha (though the outbreak of the Second World War prevented his coming), is another indicator that the Allahabad University enjoyed a widely known and respected presence.

We may be intrigued, when we go through records of the times, by the proud announcement that the University Dispensary has introduced the new injection therapy, and has started inoculating students against diseases. And that the dispensary kitchen has now got electricity, and the first computer is being planned—but we can only envy the palpable truth of the institution's in-dwelling well-being when we scan those thirty years between 1927 and 1957. Here is a 1932 poem written by a witty and scientifically disposed future vice chancellor in comic mode. It is called 'Biological Musings', and appears to maintain perfect fidelity to the facts of biological life:

> There was a little blastula
> No bigger than a germ
> Who performed invagination
> In his mother's mesoderm
> And then his nascent cilia
> With joy began to squirm
> In ecstasy supreme…
> "Oh mother dear," he cried in grief
> "Come quickly now and try
> To heal my little ectoderm
> Or I shall have to die."
> But mother dear was sessile
> And could only sit and cry…
> Now every night within the deep
> His little ghost is found
> Lamenting to the Annelids
> That burrow in the ground
> The hyroids wave their tentacles
> And shudder at the sound…

This sprightly allegory, penned by our local Lewis Caroll, D.R. Bhattacharya, seems to be about the tragically brief life story of a micro-organism, accompanied with a rousing chorus that goes like this:

> Oh! The joys of locomotion
> Down within the depths of ocean
> Oh! To feel the great commotion
> Within each blastomere.

This sense of creative adventure pervades many other writings and it is a joy to read them. True to the period they were written in, and full of a sense of exploration, these pieces convey the intellectual charge in the air. I have chosen just a few. A student ponders, tongue-in-cheek: 'Is there life on earth?' purporting to be Dr Michadi, director of the Wukov Observatory of Mars.[65] Another student speculates, with complete scientific gravity, on how the recent 'talkies', only just terminating the era of the silent film, could be made three-dimensional, thereby erasing the line between reality and illusion.[66] Yet another predicts the speed of flying in the future and designs his own aircraft (!):

> The main difficulty is that of starting and landing: If the plane descends in air at this high speed (i.e. 15,000 miles per hour) friction will turn it white-hot; if it lands at this high speed, it will be torn to atoms. To meet these problems the plane will be made entirely of metal. It will be started from some sort of projecting engine. For a minute or two it will travel with its wings till it reaches the stratosphere when the wings will be drawn inside. The explosive rockets will begin their work, then the plane will fly at the estimated speed. For landing, rockets discharged from the nose of the plane will act as brakes. The wings again will help the plane to make a nice landing.

The solemn scientist closes his prophetic piece with a word of caution: 'Whatever the prospects of aeronautics may be, and whatever success it may achieve, its future will remain uncertain, unless interest in aerodynamics shifts—like wireless—from the engineer to the physicist.'[67]

I used a phrase 'quaint localism' in reference to the University's ambience, and this is demonstrated by writings that could only be produced in a bustling provincial University town. For example, there is a poem about the Curzon Bridge. And an even jauntier essay on an ekka-wallah who can

> ...talk on a large variety of subjects: he will discourse on the Civil Disobedience, its results, or causes.... He gently whips his ass, or horse... He urges him by his peculiar ejaculations in the form of 'Tcha...tcha...' The whip is being circulated over the head of his ass...and he is controlling the reins, and he is asking 'the man in the street' to get aside, and he is talking to you, and he is smoking, and he is on the look-out for new customers, and he is cursing the horse... He appears to be a man of multifarious activities.[68]

Yet another precocious scholar tries his hand at writing a Greek play entitled *Apollo and Marsyas*. And a future ICS officer of well-connected lineage muses, mock-seriously, on the plight of being 'detained' as: refused permission to write the examination due to short attendance.[69] I close this chapter with a student's perky little essay, jocular and clumsy, but overflowing with fun and observation. Written in 1932, it unlocks a period, and is evidence enough of the University's vivacious intellectual climate in a particular era of its history. The student calls himself 'Amiya' and the title of the essay is 'The University Student':

> A university student is essentially precocious, full of doubts, romantic and ambitious. He walks in the air. He is Mr.

> Somebody in particular. He has the synopsis of all the modern novels by heart—six-penny series from "Kitabistan" he reads vociferously. Science also he dabbles in but with caution and care, lest you see through him. If science be his choice, a Saha or Raman he pretends to be. "The Spin of Light" or "The Theory of Relativity" are the topics he must talk about. But he is a politician too. The "Leader" with the morning tea helps him there. Some have the "Pioneer" and the "Times"; for they must appear in the competitives. Others are communists in the morning, socialists at teatime, democrats in classrooms, and aristocrats everywhere. Congressites too are not rare, but wicked people whisper about romance and rebuffs...
>
> In the matter of tastes there are as many genera as there are species though sometimes they cross each other. Some like smoking, others boating and a few prefer to gossip by conviction. Cards are common too, and music always welcome. But it is the talkies that are the favourites of all. To talk of the latest picture, to sing the latest song of Jeanette or Maurice—that is an achievement!

Could this be Maurice Chevalier the young man is referring to? In that case he is pretty up-to-date. I continue with his lively piece.

> Activities too are many and varied. But tea at restaurants, games and sports and U.T.C. in the Muir College, and meetings in the Union Hall are the most important. And only one purpose runs through them all. It is bravado and gasconade. Sometimes romance also peeps in. For a university student, you should know, must needs have some affairs; and he must talk of them with bated breath and burning sigh. And how can he help it? That brilliant kick of his in the football match, that excellent hit on the

hockey field, that graceful drive in the "All India," or at least that startling speech of his in the Union, must have pierced the heart of some dame—beautiful and modern. But please dare not question him. He must be, like Caesar's wife, above suspicion. That he dresses so carefully while going to the talkies is ample proof of it. If you still have your doubts, follow him stealthily. Or you may try to overhear the confidential talks that he has with his friends...

Some of course there are who are neither fish nor flesh though they may be quite good red herrings. They go to the clubs—Friday, Saturday, Monday, Tuesday—whatever it be. A very few—rigorously selected—belong to the Broken Hearted's Den. But let us not talk of them. They are Olympian Devas and Adityas and are better left with the University Blighters. But lest you forget that this is a residential university, try also to peep into the relations that exist between the teachers and the taught. And what a spectacle would you discover!

The students, you will find, vie with one another to catch a glimpse or a smile of the august Professors. And, oh, what a vieying it is! Trojans did not spend such restless hours for fair Helen's hand, nor did Ravan adopt subtler strategies to capture Sita. But, as is natural, it is only the chosen few that succeed. Those that fail try their skill with the "Readers", and failing them, with the "Lecturers". If all of them disappoint, there is yet one consolation—the departmental Clerks are there. Yet some are always left who survive all these. They move and shine and boast everywhere. The Proctor they claim to be their personal friend and the Professors to be their companions. Even the Vice-Chancellor, they declare, would respond to every beck and call of theirs. If you disbelieve them, you must do so at your own risk. But not even the stoutest amongst these will dare claim to know Dr. Khan or Prof. Ranade more than casually.

Yet the university student is not a mere frivolous coxcomb. Romance and ambition is his natural share. He must have them. He reads Stevenson, so he must needs wink at somebody. Novels and periodicals make life attractive. He cannot forget that Omar Khayyam teaches him to realise life like a young man. And down he bows to the commands of the old Epicurian. This may be wrong or this may be right. Who knows? But it is well that a young student does not sit tight and cut a long figure like an oracle. For, they say 'Art is long and time is fleeting.'

If this was a typical student in the 1930s, we can picture him swaggering down Lovers' Lane, self-consciously parading his amusing and bookish pomposities, in the endearing excesses of a language learnt from teachers who were figures of awe and glamorous erudition—in an age when erudition was glamorous.

'We were proud of our teachers,' wrote one of my teachers, H.S. Saxena, describing the campus where, in his words—if you threw a stone, you were sure to hit a celebrity.[70]

In the high noon of the Allahabad University, teachers were the celebrities.

4
TIDAL WAVE

In terms of location, if the Indian National Movement had a shifting centre of gravity, the city of Allahabad—with its fortuitous position as the headquarters of the All India Congress Committee—might well claim to have been one of them. Due to its politically high-profile leadership, active intelligentsia and culture of defiance against authority, the city acquired a centrality that makes for a particularly distinguished chapter in its history. Furthermore, the Allahabad University—by reason of its physical proximity to the centres of activism, and as a valuable resource for informed and impassioned youth power—supplied one of the many memorable subplots in the great saga of the freedom movement.

The nationalist impulse was slow to build up. We first hear its muted murmur in the chance reference to Augustus Harrison's friendship with the viceroy, Lord Ripon—loved by Indians (as mentioned in Chapter 1) after his sympathetic stance in the Ilbert Bill crisis. Those of us for whom the Ilbert Bill has receded into pre-history might be reminded that it involved the question of whether an Indian judge could try a European accused; in a 'High Court city' like Allahabad, the issue was surely of burning interest. Rai Bahadur Pundit Kanhaiya Lal's memoirs, in Amaranatha Jha's

History of the Muir Central College, specifically mentions Lord Ripon's visit to the city: 'During the Ilbert Bill controversy the students joined in giving a public reception to Lord Ripon when he visited Allahabad, but in other respects the students devoted their entire time and attention to their studies and took little interest, when studying, in other public affairs.'[1]

In the principal's report of 1906–07, a stray line appears: 'Political agitation among students is a phenomenon which has appeared among us for the first time this year.'[2] Considering the fact that the Partition of Bengal had already taken place and there was much disaffection in the air, it is hardly surprising. What is indeed surprising is the guarded and wary note in the official University record of a discussion held as late as in 1920–21, (a very eventful one politically, as we shall presently see): 'The students of the College made a serious effort to decide on the merits of the non-cooperation movement and did not allow themselves to be carried away by others. Their conduct was strictly proper....'[3]

A century later that extremely colonial phrase about strictly 'propah' conduct amuses, rather than provokes us. We must remember that this was an 'on-the-records' instance. The private communication from the lieutenant governor, in 1915, to the British district magistrate, S.M. Freemantle, is much more forthcoming with its true Brit wryness in saying that the band was 'tuning up already'. This was in connection with events unfolding in the real world, which were rather different from reports in the registers of official academic records.

All along there are hints and whispers. Much before the Indian Universities Act and the Partition of Bengal, colleges had been at risk of disaffiliation due to the suspicion of their having turned into 'nurseries of sedition'. Even in the time of Homersham Cox, a student's essay on his native state—Maharashtra—and its valiant history, had raised imperial eyebrows in Government

House. Enquiries commenced, and a harmless college magazine was closed down. It was not the student alone who was of concern; it was the looming shadows of Gokhale, of Tilak and of newly risen threat perceptions in the corridors of power.

In Cox's refusal to reveal the name of the student (mentioned in Chapter 1), M.V. Kibe, we see yet another instance of the white man divided against himself. But we are also told, in passing, that Jennings was strictly opposed to anybody who was 'agin the British.'[4] That said, he did what he considered fair and appropriate, as students were quick to realize, even when considerations of discipline compelled arbitrary measures. For example, he detained Govind Ballabh Pant, a Muir College student, from sitting for the examinations due to his nationalist speech at the 1906 Kumbh Mela in Allahabad. Even so, later, because of the intervention of Madan Mohan Malaviya, the orders were revoked and the penalty reduced to temporary expulsion from his accommodation at the Macdonnel Hindu Boarding House.

The 'band tuning up' was a particularly good metaphor to describe the warming up of a mood, coined with specific reference to Annie Besant's visit to Allahabad. As in the case of the fourth All India Congress Session, technical bureaucratic objections cropped up on 5 December 1915, regarding a public meeting at Mayo Hall where Annie Besant was to address the Allahabad University students. The application was politely refused, so the lecture was held at the Hardinge Theatre in Bahadurganj instead. The venue overflowed with students and public personalities like Tej Bahadur Sapru, Narain Prasad Asthana, Sachchidanand Sinha, C.Y. Chintamani and Ishvar Saran were also in attendance. In the city's annals it is recorded that crowds of students drew Mrs Besant's carriage. That should give us an indication that publicly, if not privately, the authorities were in a state of rehearsed denial and it was a matter of official policy to ignore the disturbing vibrations quickening in the air.

The times are described vividly in the recollections of two veteran alumni, B.N. Lahiri and Shiva Adhar Pande. For the purposes of this book it will be better to transcribe their accounts exactly as they set them down, aglow with the energy of personal recall.

B.N. Lahiri describes how as students 'we…turned out in a body to hear her (Annie Besant) speech and in doing so we felt like truants doing something on the sly.'[5]

Shiva Adhar Pande refers to

> […] the electricity in the air—the tense political atmosphere. 1905 was the year of the Partition of Bengal. Every Bengali felt that he had been stabbed to the heart, and Indians resented bitterly the stain on Indian honour, the wounding of the national pride. The brilliancy of the Proconsul Curzon added insult to injury and the country was seething with indignation. The slogans that flew about were Swadeshi and Boycott. Malaviyaji, with his instinctive repugnance to bitterness and animosity, advocated the former, and summoned Gopal Krishna Gokhale to his aid. Gokhale lectured in the Kayastha Pathshala Hall, which was packed to overflowing. Malaviyaji followed his line of sweet reasonableness, and high Indian rectitude; but Gokhale went right out with facts and figures, and advanced cogent arguments in support of his thesis. He was in the prime of his life, and it was a speech that would have done any statesman credit in Parliament, or out of it. But people were emotional; and most of it fell flat. It left the listeners cold. They admired these two veterans but did not ditto their sentiments.
>
> Then came Bal Gangadhar Tilak. He could not get

a hall, and so lectured inside a private compound in the Civil Lines.[6] Tilak, with his Maratha turban and his white Indian clothes, was beloved of the young. He stood like a statue, calm, unmoved, without a smile or a sneer; but the words that he uttered were winged. The whole audience was laughing or crying or shouting at his will in a storm of passion. It was a great speech. His features were immobile, but his words were biting and hitting and stinging like hail. He held up the honour of India to its height; its flag flew in the heavens, and its unity and solidarity was made patent to all gods and men. And there was a note of danger as well...

Next came Bipin Chandra Pal. His lecture was also in a private compound. The audience in both these lectures cannot have exceeded five thousand. The shouts of *Vande Mataram* filled the air... Bipin Babu pivoted and pirouetted on his small dais, to right and left. His long chudder flew all round in a whirl of hot anger. A flood of words swept over the crowd, a torrent of violent speech, raging and tearing, full of fire and fury, white-hot and red-hot, with tongues lambent, greenish and purple. I have heard Sarojini Naidu later in the Senate Hall; I have heard the leonine roars of Surendranath in the 1911 Allahabad Congress, but the palm went easily to Bipin Pal, for his eloquence was fortified by its substance, his matter was as good as his manner. He failed because his opinions failed to convince his compeers, and he was outmoded. His manner also became a mannerism. The worst enemies of Tilak could not say that about him. In 1905 however, at Allahabad, Bipin Babu totally carried the day; later he had differences with Anand Bhavan.

But the matter was clinched and the controversy ended when Lajpat Rai was invited to Allahabad, and he lectured on the Ramlila ground near the Muslim hostel. He used no claptrap, no gestures and he did not range widely among the passions; nor did he hunt for arguments. He caught the public voice fully, because he represented it so fully, so plainly and simply himself. Allahabad had felt the political storm.

Most people took up Swadeshi. Some shops and firms were established. Many people tried boycotting to some extent or other. But the wind did not create any whirlwind. Sunderlal, who was in the Hindu Boarding House, and busy with the programs, found that Mr. Jennings was fed up with him. He came seriously to grief some time after. Some others were shrewder and escaped. One even out-generalled Mr. Jennings with the aid of Homersham Cox and Satischandra Banerji. I cannot say that Jennings showed any personal animus at any time. He did what he thought to be his duty. This was not what happened in Durack's [a principal of Muir College] time...[7]

J.J. Durack's time was 1921, when the conduct of students was reported to be 'strictly proper'. As a matter of fact, strict action was taken against students involved in the non-cooperation movement. The Sunderlal mentioned was to be the fiery author of *Bharat Mein Angrezi Raj* in the future. The book, that was to be confiscated and banned by the authorities even before it was released in 1929, had already reached a large readership. Senior alumni of the University remember reading it by torchlight, hidden beneath a blanket. The authorities kept a keen watch on the Macdonnel Hindu Boarding House, for it was known to harbour persons of extremist leanings. In fact, as local memory has it, even the chooranwalas at the gates carried secret messages in and out of the hostel.

For many of those ignorant of local history, it may be clarified that Allahabad University had two celebrated Sunderlals: a Sir

Sunder Lal, the vice chancellor, and a Pundit Sunderlal, a freedom activist-historian. In fact, it was Sir Sunder Lal who began calling the student-activist by the name 'Pundit' Sunderlal, later followed by others like Sir Tej and Gandhi himself. *Bharat Mein Angrezi Raj* became an iconic book, proscribed and seized wherever seen, but recommended by Gandhi to all who valued freedom, urging them to keep and distribute copies even if it involved arrest and jail.

There is a thrilling episode between the two Sunderlals of the University. 'Pundit' Sunderlal, while still a law student and a resident at the Macdonnel Hindu Boarding House, had been exceedingly active as a volunteer during the visits of Gokhale, Tilak, Pal and Lajpat Rai. For this, he was expelled from the University and his belongings thrown out from his room during his absence. He found himself irredeemably disgraced and his student life came to an end. The expulsion order came from Sir Sunder Lal, who summoned the obdurate student to his chamber, promising to revoke the order and take a sympathetic view of the matter should an assurance be given of complete withdrawal from nationalistic activism. Said Sunderlal to Sunder Lal something along the following lines: 'I regret having to decline your kind offer but I cannot accept your conditions, sir. I've decided to work for the country and my mind is made up.'

Gandhi's very first visit to Allahabad in 1896 happened by pure accident. He alighted from a train, dressed European-style; a barrister newly arrived in India. The train was the Howrah–Bombay Mail, the date 5 July, and the time approximately 11 a.m. The halt at Allahabad was for about 45 minutes so, typically, Gandhi thought it long enough to explore a bit of the city and pick up some medicines. He rode out of the station in a tonga towards Johnstongunj. The expected happened—he missed the train. The station master had—out of respect—kept the train waiting an extra minute, after which he had ordered the missing passenger's luggage offloaded, and the train flagged off. All this we learn from Gandhi's own records.

To my mind it seems to be the city's cultural, if unknowing, answer to the Pietermaritzburg incident. On this first visit Gandhi merely broke journey, stayed at the Kelner's Hotel, visited the office of the *Pioneer*, met its editor and explained his South Africa agitation. Later he took a dip in the Ganga at the Sangam before proceeding to Rajkot the next day to collect his family and take them back to South Africa. His second visit was in 1916, when he was invited by the Economics Society of the Muir College to lecture on the subject—once again true to character—of the role of ethics and spirituality in economic progress. This time he stayed in Madan Mohan Malaviya's bungalow on Hamilton Road. The visit was a highly publicized one, and in the nature of a directly interactive session with students and local citizenry. It was 22 December, quite chilly as an Allahabad December tends to be, but Gandhi was dressed like a peasant, in his short dhoti, a small shirtlet, a Gujarati turban and no footwear. He walked at great speed, barefoot, up the Hamilton Road and all the way to the Physics Lecture Theatre at Muir College, accompanied by students and a crowd of people, who had trouble keeping up with him, so brisk was his pace. All along he carried on a lively exchange with the students, speaking typically of democracy, self-government, Annie Besant, Lloyd George and brahmacharya, punctuated by humorous remarks that set his companions laughing.

The lecture was classic Gandhi, beginning with his inimitable and disarming confession of personal ignorance; then an acute, original and extremely practical analysis of the subject in hand; ending with a discourse on his inner life, the role of conscience in the life of an individual and a society; and the importance of persistence in what one knows to be ethically right. The lecture had an inspirational appeal for students, and was printed in the next day's *Leader* by C.Y. Chintamani. It is recorded in Amaranatha Jha's diary that once the proofs were corrected by Gandhi, Jha begged leave to keep the original draft, which Gandhi laughingly granted, saying that it did not deserve to sit on its claimant's desk—a wastepaper basket might suit it better. Jha adds: 'I took his paper from him which was written on sheets on which was printed his South African address, "Tolstoy Farm, Johannesburg".'[8]

Already the differences between Gandhi's and Besant's views were obvious, as graphically described in Amaranatha Jha's diary entry of 6 February 1916, a few months before the economics department lecture:

> In the afternoon lectures by Mrs. Besant and Mr. Gandhi...
> In the middle of Mr. Gandhi's speech Mrs. Besant stood up, and said, 'Mr. President, I appeal to you to stop this most injurious conversation with students. It is most objectionable.' Mr. Gandhi said: 'If the President thinks my speech objectionable, I shall sit down. This is not the first time that I have been interrupted in my speech. I await your orders, Mr. President.' The students shouted, 'Go on.' 'No,' said Mr. Gandhi, 'No one but the President. I shall obey only the President.' The President said, 'Please explain your meaning.' Mr. Gandhi, 'Yes, I am explaining my meaning. Mrs. Besant has interrupted me because of her intense love for India. (Mrs. Besant—'Hear, hear!') But I love India as I shall allow no one else to love her.'[9]

This interface with Allahabad University students, who obviously chose Gandhi over Besant, was one among many subsequent visits. The youth formed a major focus of Gandhi's programmes, and the scenes that were to unfold presently in and around the campus, amply fulfilled his remarkable agenda. When Gandhi came again, four years later in November 1920, the collective campus mind was primed up and ready for his mode of activism. 10,000 people received him—a group that included villagers and students alike. Besides Gandhi, there were speakers like Abul Kalam Azad, Shaukat Ali and Motilal Nehru.

It was here that Gandhi used the strong phrase 'satanic government', and asserted the moral duty of resistance through non-cooperation. He spoke of swaraj and swadeshi. In the context of the University, he appealed to students to stop being members of a government institution, and this appeal actually motivated some students to have their names cancelled from the University's rolls. Records mention three names, students of KPUC—Guru Narain Lal, Mangal Prasad Srivastava and Tribum Prasad Sinha—who were the first to quit.

In January, the Duke of Connaught came to India, but by then a resolution had been passed at the Nagpur session of the Congress that nobody should participate in any official functions in honour of the royal guest. Fearing disturbance, the government took pre-emptive action and arrested fifty-five Congressmen during a meeting in Allahabad. This prepared the ground for further resistance, which played out in December 1921, at the visit of the Prince of Wales. Again there were pre-emptive arrests. The prince visited the Benaras Hindu University, but was seriously concerned to see that very few students showed up at the official function. The Lucknow visit, equally under-attended, was a lacklustre affair. His visit to the Allahabad University was a complete disaster. The prince was scheduled to preside over the sports event but the plan had to be cancelled.

The most graphic account of this episode is the prince's own, published in his book, *King's Story* (1951). This is what he writes:

> When on the appointed day I emerged from the train, in full-dress uniform, and started off from the railway station

in a state carriage, it was to be met in the native city by shuttered windows and ominous silence along troop-lined, deserted streets. It was a spooky experience. I attempted to maintain a rigid and majestic pose in the carriage in order to show that I had risen above the insult. But curiosity got the better of me; and, peeping up the empty side-streets, I was gratified to see peeking furtively round the corners of the blocks the heads of many Indians.[10]

B.N. Lahiri gives us a greenroom perspective:

His Royal Highness, the Prince of Wales...was to have presided over our College Sports. What actually happened was that a day or two before his arrival, word quietly went round among the students that he should be boycotted. The authorities came to know about this and so, as a precautionary measure, it was settled by them at the eleventh hour that he should visit the Senate Hall instead, to receive an address of welcome. At the same time it was given out that such of the students as were desirous of coming to this function would be welcome. But the most noticeable thing was that in spite of this open invitation very few of them turned out. I happened to be a junior member of the staff at the time and that is how I had occasion to witness the scene which ensued.[11]

Lahiri's account recreates the events in some detail:

Exactly on the stroke of nine, the Prince's car drew up in the front porch where he was received by the Governor, Sir Harcourt Butler and the Vice Chancellor, Mr. Justice Gokal Prasad. He then walked across the hall and as he emerged into view on the other side of it, he looked, in his light grey suit, extremely youthful and without a care in the world. The next thing he did was to sit down in the chair meant for him, while the Vice Chancellor read out his address. Meanwhile the Prince's Private Secretary, Earl Cromer and his A.D.C., Lord Mountbatten, stood at attention behind him. The reading of the address being over, the Prince turned towards Earl Cromer who stepped forward to make a deep obeisance before handing him his written reply that the Prince read out with much gusto. Thereafter, the Vice Chancellor sought the permission of the Prince to introduce the Executive Councillors who filed past him in a single row; as each of them did so, the Prince shook hands with him.[12]

There is a comic footnote to this solemn protocol-pressured fiasco. Lahiri has recorded it, tongue-in-cheek:

The function was, on the whole, a brief one and dull except for an interesting colloquy at its close, between the Prince and a student named Bindeswari Prasad, which ran something like this:

Bindeswari Prasad: We want a week's holiday.

The Prince: What?

Bindeswari Prasad: We want a week's holiday.

The Prince to the Vice Chancellor: May they have a week's holiday?

The Vice Chancellor to the Prince: Yes, certainly, Your Royal Highness.

The Prince to Bindeswari Prasad: Your Vice Chancellor says you *can* have a week's holiday.[13]

Lahiri writes:

The proceedings which had so long been going somewhat cheerlessly, were at this stage enlivened by the students present breaking into three cheers for the Prince who then went away. But despite this holiday windfall, so strong was the feeling in the hostels against those who went to the reception, that when they returned they were received with boos and even the cooks and kahars refused to serve them their meal that day.' Lahiri does not tell us whether the University did stay closed for a week, or whether those students who had patriotically boycotted the Prince also boycotted the holiday! He does, however, tell us something of the antecedent reasons for the rage that had filtered down even to the cooks and kahars.

This political consciousness of ours which had its first awakening in 1916 or so, had taken strong root in us by 1921 when many of us left our studies in the wake of the Non-cooperation movement launched by Mahatma Gandhi—Lalji Mehrotra of our hostel, who is today our High Commissioner in Burma, being one of them. If I am not mistaken it was in October that year that the news of Pandit Motilal Nehru's impending arrest went round the hostels like wildfire and we all flocked to his residence out of regard for him. I remember the first thing that greeted our eyes there was the sight of the old man himself sitting majestically on a chair on an open terrace outside his house, with the City Kotwal by his side. With his white hair and serene countenance he reminded one of a Himalayan snow peak standing firm and four square to the winds. The atmosphere seemed to be charged with electricity and a remarkable thing was that there was pin-drop silence till he went away.[14]

In Lucknow, C.R. Das had been likewise arrested. That 'pin-drop silence' lay behind the empty streets, the resistance politics of absence. The Allahabad papers made big headlines of the great boycott. The British papers raised a possibly bigger outcry. A correspondent of the London *Times*, who was present in the city as an 'embedded journalist' described the protesters as 'the most determined and hard-fibred people in the world'[15]— qualities which did greater credit to us then rather than now. The Prince of Wales later observed that his visit had provoked the unforeseen fallout of giving Gandhi greater visibility. The 'hartals', the picketing of shops selling foreign cloth, the khaddar campaign with the symbolism of the charkha, all belong to the period immediately following the prince's visit.

Student participation, even though contained and responsible, was considerable. Between 1923 and 1926, the Allahabad University Students' Union engaged itself in the issues of the time, first through debates, such as that of 19 December 1923, entitled: 'The Non-cooperation Movement has substantially accelerated India's progress towards Swaraj'. (Uma Nehru and Shriprakash, editor of the paper *Aaj*, supported the motion). Then, by declaring their solidarity with Mahatma Gandhi, in 1924, through a telegram to him: 'The members of the Allahabad University Union respectfully greet you on your unconditional release, pray for your speedy recovery and welcome you back to Indian public life.'[16] Mr Arundale spoke on Swarajya, and Annie Besant on 'Citizenship of Students' in 1926. Sir Tej Bahadur Sapru became the first associate member of the Allahabad University Students' Union.[17]

One of the reasons for this convergence of energies was the centrality of Anand Bhavan (home of the Nehru family) both physically and ideologically. Differences did, however, exist between its occupants and Gandhi, on the basic principles of non-cooperation and passive resistance—as Sunderlal found to his discomfiture. Bipin Chandra Pal too fell out with Anand Bhavan, but for the campus at large, the leadership at Anand Bhavan fuelled the engines of the nationalist movement. We are told that Motilal Nehru often invited students to tea parties at his house, the most especial occasioned on Jawaharlal's return from England.

The great Holi bonfire of foreign clothes on the vast lawns of the Swaraj Bhavan, headquarters of the All India Congress Committee, must surely have captured the students' imagination. And Jawaharlal, at a special convocation address in 1958, said:

> I did not have the opportunity and the privilege of studying at this University, but, many years ago, you were good enough to invite me to join your fraternity, and so in a sense, and in a close sense, I am one of you. But, whether I have studied in this University or not, I was born and bred up, to a considerable extent, under the shadow of this University.[18]

The Nehrus made themselves extremely accessible to students of the University. H.S. Saxena, a veteran teacher, remembers his impromptu visit to Jawaharlal Nehru while still a BA student: 'In August 1946 I purchased a copy of *The Discovery of India* and then, on an impulse, walked to Anand Bhavan to get it autographed by Pandit Nehru. Panditji was in a good mood and signed both in Hindi and in English.'[19] The detail about Nehru being in a 'good mood' that day is extremely telling, since he often lost his temper when mobbed by University students. The Congress dispensary, just adjacent to Swaraj Bhavan, Motilal Nehru's house, set up to attend to freedom activists hurt in public protests, was always open to students. Saxena recollects his visit to it—sick with fever just before an examination—with the uplifting words of the idealistic Dr Mittra, and the free treatment he received.[20]

But political ideologies of other stripes also had a presence in Allahabad University and which influenced students, as has already been mentioned in a previous chapter. Gangeya Mukherji describes the left-wing presence at Allahabad thus:

> The CPI had considerable influence over the Allahabad University Students' Union. The old CPI office in Johnstongunj, under which a couple of cycle shops have opened, is even today called Subhash Hall in memory of one of its Allahabad members who was killed in police firing in Ballia in 1950, while participating in a protest rally organised by the Party...[21]

An old party member, G.P. Singh, recalls how he was initiated into Marxism while a student of the Eweing Christian College in Allahabad:

> With the Party being banned, copies of the Party organ, *Crossroads*, used to be pasted on the walls of a building across the road at night, and the young students would feel a thrill of adventure as they came out of their hostels to read the pages early the next morning. Eric Higgins, a handsome young teacher...made Goldsmith come alive in the classroom, while in the evenings a handful of students would gather in the coffee house of the school to hear him quietly expound Marxism to them. Later, while a student of Holland Hall, of the University, Singh would meet with other students after dinner in a house called Gulab Bhavan, to listen to night-long lectures on social philosophy by the brilliant Marxist, P.C. Joshi.[22]

(P.C. Gupta of the English department was also a man of Marxist leanings, and in the early '50s OPM or Om Prakash Mehrotra, Communist student leader, and later president of the Students' Union, would be friend-philosopher-guide to academics like Prof. Dhanesh Mandal.)

Earlier, there had been a youth body named the UP Young

Comrades' League that, on Nehru's suggestion, was rechristened the Allahabad Youth League. This was a body, moderately left-wing, dedicated to a theoretical understanding of Marxism, and of practical contact programmes with the masses. In retrospect, its composite ideology came close to Nehru's own. G.S.L. Srivastava recalls how

> Pundit Nehru used to give a discourse on every Saturday, except when out of Allahabad in the Swaraj Bhavan to students under the auspices of the Indian Youth League... Kamla Nehru Ji used to attend and sometimes her daughter Indira, then aged about thirteen years... Pundit Ji's sister Krishna was at that time very closely associated with the students, in the activities relating to the freedom struggle.[23]

When the Simon Commission boycott occurred, Nehru described the Allahabad scene in a letter to *The Leader* of 6 February 1928. In it is a line about the young comrades who 'without any outside pressure or inducement decided to take a full part in the national demonstration and almost in a body left the University for a day.'[24] The vice chancellor was then Ganganatha Jha, who was to play a prudent and extremely tactful role during the unfolding scenes. On 17 November 1929, Gandhi, accompanied by Jawaharlal Nehru, honoured the Students' Union by accepting its address of welcome. The following year, it was resolved by the union that the National Flag would be hoisted on the union building, and that the union would appeal to all teachers, students and staff, to wear khaddar (the original form of khadi). The flag issue would prove an explosive one some years down the line.

After the historic Lahore Session of the Congress, and the declaration of the Independence Pledge, the collective political drive in the student community gathered further momentum. The practice of satyagraha—its inner spirit and outward execution—

came in for deep analysis. Both, Motilal and Jawaharlal Nehru, directed their appeals to students, elucidating the spirit of the movement and exhorting them to join it, but always insisting on disciplined civil disobedience. The Muir Hostel Literary Union held a meeting, presided over by Jawaharlal Nehru, in which Ishwari Prasad lectured on the pros and cons of complete independence as against dominion status.[25]

The summer vacation of 1930 was, by Jawaharlal's suggestion, to be a time of reflection for the Allahabad University students, on the ways in which they could assist the satyagraha programme. Gandhi, however, was for a more action-driven approach and his satyagraha call to students at that same time urged them to leave their colleges and universities and plunge into the movement. Gandhi's impact on them can be gauged by the little detail that G.S.L. Srivastava provides: 'Mahatma Gandhi once came to the University...and delivered a lecture in the Senate Hall. He had a narrow escape when students in large numbers made an effort to touch his feet.'[26]

An album full of images crowds the historian's pages—students hoisting the Indian tricolour at the Muir College, flouting the vice chancellor's orders, collecting near Senate Hall and, led by Jawaharlal, marching to Purushottam Das Tandon Park holding aloft the flag. Others show students circulating copies of proscribed leaflets like the 'Satyagraha Samachar', and papers such as *The Independent*, sometimes cyclostyled in secret, following police crackdowns. G.S.L. Srivastava remembers how, in the New Hostel (now GN Jha Hostel), 'every early morning there used to be group prayer in the courtyard starting with the words: "*Vardan hamen do, he Bhagwan, Bharat Mata (ka) dukh dur Karen*".'[27] A quick succession of events—the making of salt in the presence of massive crowds, policemen standing by, the auctioning of the salt, the highest bid of ₹500—reached its climax with a swift crackdown, and Nehru being arrested.

Four days later, salt-making resumed under the leadership of Jawaharlal's mother, Swaroop Rani—the lanes of Lawrencegunj with its several student lodges, Colonelgunj and Katra being the convenient sites of this symbolic law-breaking. I lived in that area as a child and have heard vivid descriptions of the salt-making from my mother and her siblings. Old houses in the lanes had crumbling walls, the powdery dust of which—when rubbed for a long time—yielded salt. Situated close to the Anand and Swaraj Bhavans and just beyond the University areas, it was also uncomfortably close to the Colonelgunj Police Station. The women of the Nehru family, Krishna, Uma, Kamla and young Indira, actively engaged in carrying forward the movement, Kamla, Indira and Vijaya Lakshmi going from room to room in the University hostels, selling flags and badges.

Salt was definitely the flavour of the season until the movement was voluntarily ended after seventeen days with the onset of the summer vacations. July saw a resumption of the agitation, the Allahabad University Students' Union playing an exceedingly active role in the demonstrations. In a special meeting on 26 March 1931, the union passed a resolution condemning the execution of Bhagat Singh, Comrade Rajguru and Sukhdev.[28] An event of overwhelming impact on the mood of the city, the shooting of Chandra Shekhar Azad has found a graphic description in the reflections of G.S.L. Srivastava:

> Once while attending Mathematics class in Muir Central College, sounds of firing of shots were heard from the side of the Alfred Park. There was a commotion. I and other students of my class went, out of curiosity, to Alfred Park where we noticed a robust young man lying dead, cordoned off by the police. We were told that he was Chandra Shekhar

Azad, and that he and his two companions who were having consultations, had been spotted by the police. The force was led by Knot-Bower and a D.S.P., Bisheshwar Singh. The companions of Azad succeeded in fleeing away but Azad was cornered and exchange of fire started from both sides. He could be shot dead only when the ammunition with him had exhausted. Bisheshwar Singh's lower lip had been injured by a shot and he had been taken to hospital, but Knot-Bower was present after a total providential escape. I had heard about Chandra Shekhar Azad as a revolutionary but had not seen him before. With tears in our eyes we returned after staying at the place for about half an hour.[29]

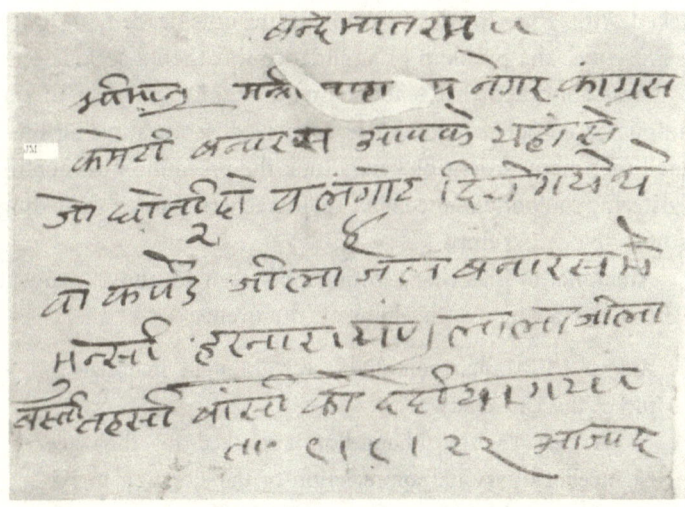

A note written by Chandra Shekhar Azad

If burning foreign clothes and donning khaddar was a symbolic act, and if making muddy salt out of old wall scrapings a symbolic defiance, then hoisting the tricolour was the strongest symbolic challenge. All over the country, students were mischievously, adventurously, emotionally or recklessly courting the exciting risk of scrambling up tower-stairs, domes or tiled roofs, reaching flagstaffs, wrenching off the Union Jack and hoisting the tricolour in its place. This became a major issue and remained one for a long time.

At a convocation the astute Ganganatha Jha calmed frayed tempers by quietly reasoning with the Students' Union leaders that, since the University was a dependent of the British government, he had no option but to let the Union Jack fly atop the Senate Hall. He allowed them the freedom to fly the tricolour at their hostels. At yet another time, the student body—urged by the Congress leaders—picketed the University. This meant that all gates were locked, with large crowds of patriots sitting outside, denying entry to everyone. The problem of attendance was then a serious one, so it was conceded that teachers living within ten miles of the campus could act as attendance keepers. It is an amusing little detail that many ardent picketers took the precaution of secretly registering their attendance with their teachers before proceeding to noisy picketing duty.

Amaranatha Jha's diary jottings, between 13 and 27 August 1930, throw an interesting light on the events:

> August 13 Women volunteers were brought in today to picket the University.
>
> August 15 The Chancellor has asked for the Vice Chancellor's personal appreciation of the situation in the University and said that government will have to consider if it can continue to pay for students who are not able to receive education.
>
> August 23 About 200 students—calling themselves 'anti-picketers'—forced their way into the University and attended lectures.

August 27 Dr. Katju and Krishna Kant Malviya came to settle details for the calling off of the pickets.[30]

By orders of the authorities, the police sought to disperse the crowds at the gates, violently beating them with lathis or trampling them under the hoofs of charging horses ridden by mounted police called sowars. The vice chancellor, Ganganatha Jha, strategically ordered the tall railings on the University walls removed, enabling escaping students to scale them with ease and seek shelter within the University campus.

In 1932, the Students' Union held a meeting to express its opinion on an imminent fast by Gandhi. At the same meeting, thirty-two members were appointed to devote their energies to the upliftment of the 'Untouchables'.[31] Then in 1936, another address of welcome was presented to Pundit Jawaharlal Nehru in the Senate Hall. Those present were Dr K.N. Katju, J.B. Kripalani, Sajjad Zahir, Dr Ram Manohar Lohia, Dr and Mrs Z.A. Ahmad, Purnima Banerjee, and Miss S.K. Nehru. Jawaharlal Nehru was made honorary member of the Union.[32]

Some years down the line, in November 1939, the flag issue arose again at a University convocation, this time in a different hue. The governor, Sir Maurice Hallet, refused to deliver the convocation address because the Union Jack was *not* in place. Amaranatha Jha simply took the microphone and delivered a most eloquent convocation address extempore! 1939 also witnessed the visit of Subhas Chandra Bose to the Union. His rousing appeal to the youth and his call for action met with great enthusiasm, and he was presented an address of welcome placed in a beautiful silver casket.[33] Between 1940 and 1942 both Maulana Abul Kalam Azad and Purushottam Das Tandon addressed the students. The title of Tandon's address was: 'What Students Should Do'. When Jawaharlal was arrested, the Students' Union called for a day's protest strike.

The flag issue came to a head during the Quit India movement, with the gunning down of a young BA (Part One) boy from Rewa, Lal Padmadhar. Aged twenty-one, thin, slightly built, usually dressed very formally, he had scrambled on to the roof of the collectorate and successfully hoisted the tricolour on the flag-mast when he was instantly shot dead. It was a time when the city was under Section 144 of the Indian Penal Code, under which processions or assemblies of people in public spaces were not allowed, and police firing was repeatedly resorted to in cases of defiance. The day Lal Padmadhar was killed—12 August 1942—all hell broke loose and the University was closed sine die. Processions erupted and military police jeeps came roaring down the streets, manned by American 'tommies' (present in large numbers due to the Second World War) with rifles at the ready.

Many stories lie untold in the private legends of old Allahabad families, my own included. I remember my father telling me how he and a friend, both University students, were walking down to their Colonelgunj lodge from the University at an hour when curfew had been imposed and everyone ordered to stay indoors. As they walked down the footpath lining the road where the Diamond Jubilee Hostel now stands, an engine roar was heard in the far distance behind them. There were 'shoot-at-sight' orders in place, especially in the case of students hanging about in the vicinity of the University. My father told me how, in the urgency of self-preservation, his friend and he decided to slacken their brisk pace to a lazy, aimless saunter. Their body language suggested the unthreatening amble of two slow-witted laggards out for a stroll in innocence or ignorance of the 'shoot-at-sight' announcement.

The roar of approaching engines grew louder, deafeningly close, and came right up behind them as they put one slothful foot after the other in lackadaisical step. But, seconds later, the jeeps of the military patrol thundered past, carrying tommies with guns held in position, ready to take aim and shoot at the slightest hint of provocation. To walk fast or to break into a run would have meant a bullet in the back, but the loitering pace probably saved their lives, passing them off as two harmless fellows who posed no risk. My mother too had been taking part in marches and demonstrations, as so many girl students were, but when on 12 August 1942 the police opened fire on a procession led by girls, my recently widowed grandmother ordered her to stop courting arrest and stay home. Thereafter my mother and aunt acted as message-bearers and spies.

Their house stood at the extreme edge of Lawrencegunj, commanding a clear view of the Colonelgunj police station that had jurisdiction over the University areas. Arrested student leaders were brought in vans and led into that thana. As they would walk, handcuffed, across the dusty footpath, on to which the main gate of the old Colonelgunj thana opened, no one would notice them turning to look at a particular old three-storeyed house a little way down the road. Nor would anything be thought of the two young girls ostensibly taking the air on a high terrace of that house. Sometime later, unnoticed, the two girls would walk out of the lane and hasten towards Swaraj Bhavan, situated at the end of the road. Their job was to keep a lookout for, and carry reports on, who had been arrested and when.

Eventually, somebody did notice, and the police came to ask uncomfortable questions. When Hemwati Nandan Bahuguna of the Students' Union's Working Committee was arrested, his close aide, Prafulya Kumar Sharman, escaped and sought shelter in my mother's house, where he was hidden in a coal-and-wood closet. The women of the house helped him get away, dressed in female clothes. Jagat Mehta recalls that

> Shri Hemwati Bahuguna, who was the Secretary of the Union (Mehta was the Vice President) in the same term

launched on his political career in that fateful August of 1942. Several other future Ministers, including Narain Dutt Tewari, Sushilaji Rohatagi, Roshanlala Ji Chaturvedi etc... received their baptism for their political ascendancy in the atmosphere of political activism which pervaded the University.[34]

Meanwhile, telegraph wires were cut, telephone lines disturbed and railway tracks tampered with. A reward of a thousand rupees was announced for anyone bringing information against the perpetrators. I don't know if anyone ever sought that award. Bahuguna, after his release, went underground. My mother and her sisters returned to their studies. It was an animated and stimulating era. Nationalism affected the average Allahabad University student in many interesting ways. H.S. Saxena has recorded one particularly riveting account:

> A naïve undergraduate from a small town used to keep the bathroom in our hostel occupied for a long time. It was the winter of 1944–45. There was no arrangement for hot water. Some students went without a bath for days. Those who wanted a bath had to take a shower early in the morning. It was discovered that this young man was talking to someone in the bathroom. We were curious. One of us peeped in. The tap was on and our friend stood half naked in a corner. He was talking to himself, 'You are afraid of cold water. How can you drive out the British if you are afraid of cold water? Think of the plight of the Indian National Army in Burma...'
>
> After some time he mustered up enough courage and, shouting *Vande Mataram* like a war-cry, jumped right under the running water. We laughed and laughed till our ribs ached. Our friend was a dreamer. We were all dreamers...[35]

The nationalist dream, a mass intoxication, was already advancing towards the awakening of a sober self-awareness. In 1946, Gandhi's suggestion to students and party workers was: to serve the country and its deprived sections, its peasants and labourers, rather than turn to active politics. Dr Rajendra Prasad and Jawaharlal Nehru both urged the cultivation of responsible service. The period of marching around, waving flags and shouting slogans, was over, said Nehru. It was time to create a coherent nation, not lose focus in the wranglings of power struggles. In 1947, when the 'tryst with destiny' actually came to pass, it was a complicated tryst with a sombre destiny, as the country violently split in two amid hysterical, genocide-like conditions. H.S. Saxena recalls the student mind's reactions at this point:

> The curtain finally came down on the British Raj. Power was transferred to India at midnight, August 14 / 15, 1947. We could not listen to Nehru's 'tryst with destiny' speech as we had no access to a radio-set. We were happy—but not very demonstrative, as we were psychologically not prepared for a truncated India—giving expression to our complex feelings in tawdry quotations from our classes. 'Our sincerest laughter with some pain is fraught,' an undergraduate quoted Shelley. A budding student leader retorted, 'No use pining for what is not.' Student leaders in those days delivered their speeches in English.... One of them coined a slogan: 'Let freedom won be freedom preserved.' For Pandit Nehru had declared earlier: 'We shall never allow the torch of freedom to be blown out, however high the wind, or stormy the tempest.'[36]

Saxena remembers quirky details—how political amnesty was granted to prisoners and grace marks to students, in celebration of Independence. A young nation has the luxury of thinking in magnificent abstractions. The convocation addresses of the time sound like ceremonial invocations uttered on a rising note of mantric moralizing. To us citizens of a country that has lost its innocence, the roll of that rhetoric does seem to err on the side of excess, to the point of sounding mildly banal, until we remind ourselves that there really was a millennial mood on, a euphoric charge in the air. And what seems like visionary indulgence in the vocabulary of model values was supported by authentic conviction.

So when, in mid-December 1947, Nehru spoke to the Allahabad University faculty and students—of reason, progress, humanism, the search for truth as the ideals a university must strive for, and when he cautioned against narrow bigotry, petty university politics, communalism and caste prejudice—we detect a ring of sincere faith in the new country's commitment to the principles he preached. (That was the first convocation after the attainment of Independence). Nehru then spoke of Gandhi and the near-sublimity of his compelling example in the recent months, pacifying a nation wracked by sectarian strife. He spoke of the great moral responsibility that universities carried in the creation of a 'strong, free and democratic' India.

A little over a month later, Gandhi was shot dead. The famous Hindi writer, Amarkant, describes the way in which the students of the Hindu Hostel received the news:

> I remember that depressing evening of January 30, 1948. It must have been around six in the evening, suddenly noisy rumours began circulating that someone had shot Mahatma Gandhi. Great agitation and passion spread, and excited students began running helter-skelter to confirm the news. Voices arose from all sides—first, that a Muslim has killed him. One or two boys in the hostel owned a radio-set,

and soon Prime Minister Pandit Nehru's repudiation of this rumour was broadcast, along with the information that the assassin was a young man and a Hindu. The Prime Minister also said that Mahatma Gandhi is no longer with us.

The entire hostel was immersed in grief. Every face fallen, dark with sorrow. Sobs heard here and there. My two room partners could not control themselves. People wanted to know the details—what happened, how, who did it after all, which party did he belong to? etc. Some boys ran to the offices of the *Amrit* [sic] *Bazar Patrika* and *The Leader*. All the hostel messes closed. Not all but most of the students fasted that night. Next morning's paper, beneath broad headlines, contained all the details.

A little while later someone disclosed that one of our hostel boys had, around midnight, bullied the cooks who worked in the mess, into cooking dinner and partaken of it. Then all hell broke loose. From all the blocks of the University's largest hostel, students came pouring in. That particular student could not be identified, but it was later learnt that some ten or twelve students had locked themselves in a room. Then crowds of students gathered outside the door and started hammering on it. Before the door broke, someone carried the news to our elderly warden, Sri Devi Prasad Shukla, who came and stood, trembling before the door and, with folded hands, begged the students not to do anything drastic. The boys locked in agreed, only on condition that the boys who ate the previous night should be expelled from the hostel.[37]

Amarkant has movingly described the day when Gandhi's ashes arrived in Allahabad for immersion in the Sangam, the streets lined with countless people of all religious denominations, castes, classes and political parties. Some stood with folded hands, some wept. He was then a BA student and characteristically, like many students of the time, he quotes a line of English poetry: 'Home they brought the (sic) warrior dead.' But that hushed silence that 'spread across the nation…across villages and towns' when Nehru announced on the radio that 'the light has gone out of our lives', is recalled by Indians with awe, and analysed by writers, academics and artists in numerous category-defying ways.

'Do history books record such a moment? …of one nation, one people falling silent when an announcement is made over the radio?' asked Peter Ronald DeSouza, inaugurating a seminar on the meaning of Gandhi's death. Did that silence leave us wordlessly conscious of being 'morally orphaned'?—is one of the questions he poses.[38] The project of nation building had started, but did it involve things that inherently 'transgressed some fundamental moral principles,'[39] and, that Gandhi might not have allowed to happen, or protested against? And, was his death therefore a green signal for counter-ideologies to begin asserting? The incident on the night of 30 January at the Hindu Hostel, small as it was, provokes questions that were, in the long run, to colour Indian politics, and by default, the fate of the University in the era to come.

5
PICTURE GALLERY

Putting together a picture gallery of campus personalities is a job both problematic and potentially controversial. There are, to begin with, the twin issues of selectivity and subjectivity. It is in the nature of retrospective reporting that visibility fastens on to some personalities, to the exclusion of others, whose trail is blurred or lost for lack of sufficient recorded material, even when claims to merit may be equal or more. There are others who are not merely the stuff of legend but who, perhaps consciously, ensured the perpetuation of their personal story, occupying a position of highlighted visibility that the passage of time has only magnified. Reminiscence and a mosaic of anecdotage being the only sources for our reconstructions of people, the element of subjectivity becomes a qualifying filter.

My choice of personalities in this gallery is dictated to a large extent by availability of material, both written and orally transmitted. If a great many worthy candidates find no mention, the deficiency is not theirs but the lack of detailed documentation by the University—limited to a bunch of selective anecdotes alone, about its staff. History edits and erases more than it preserves.

To do justice to the unsung teacher, a category into which so many fall, I shall start with one lone representative stalwart,

E.A. Wodehouse. For long, his name had clung like a lapsed myth to the Department of English and that too not in his own capacity, but as brother of the famous P.G. Wodehouse. There is no photograph, nor any interesting story about him. All that exists is a faint and mostly forgotten ghost of a rumour that P.G. Wodehouse's brother actually taught in the department. My fondness for that iconic author led me down this untrodden trail, and when my search ended the findings were mind-boggling.

In one of P.G. Wodehouse's popular novels, *My Man Jeeves*, the principal character, Bertie Wooster, describes his valet: 'Jeeves...resembles one of those weird chappies in India who dissolve themselves into the air and nip through the space...I have got a cousin who is what they call a theosophist and he says he has nearly worked the thing himself.'[1] The jocular second line is most definitely a piece of oblique leg-pulling, younger brother kidding older brother, and the 'cousin' referred to is actually his sibling, Ernest Armine Wodehouse, two years older than Pelham Grenville Wodehouse.

EA was born on 11 May 1879, went to school at Croydon and subsequently to Corpus Christi College, Oxford, from where he acquired a first-class degree in the classics. Records indicate that he had two separate stints in India, though the exact dates seem somewhat muddled. One account states that he came to Maharashtra, taught for a brief spell at Elphinstone College in Mumbai, then moved to Deccan College, Pune. His connection with Mumbai is confirmed via a road in Colaba named after him—Wodehouse Road (which has now been renamed the Nathilal Parekh Marg)—one that I have often driven down.

Another account asserts that he arrived as an English teacher to Central Hindu College (now Benaras Hindu University). While in Benaras, Wodehouse came under the influence of Annie Besant and joining the Theosophical Society of India as a member, is said to have held the office of its organizing secretary. Reassuringly, there is some documentation in the society records that affirm his coming to India in 1911. The most conspicuous fact is that he was a tutor of English to Jiddu Krishnamurti, the future messiah, as announced in the society's prophetic literature. Along with his brother Raja, Jiddu was sent to England to prepare for his great function and as their English tutor, E.A. Wodehouse escorted the two brothers there.

Krishnamurti returned to India, but Wodehouse stayed back, looking after the society's journal, *The Herald of the Star*. His writings on the nature of the mind and the individual's inner progress display an extremely insightful understanding—quite at par with, and possibly exceeding, the writings of his famous pupil, Krishnamurti. Interestingly, even after Krishnamurti abdicated his messianic position in 1929, he and EA stayed in touch. When the First World War broke out, EA is said to have enlisted in the Scots Guards. He was wounded in action in May 1918, and returned to editing the journal. It is here that the chronology gets confused, although we know that soon afterwards he returned to India and joined the Indian Educational Service. By some accounts it was then that his Mumbai and Pune stints began.

Regarding Allahabad University—although there is an information gap here, and no records to go by—this phase *did* feature in EA's career. It is vouched for by the fact that the senior-most extant teacher of the Department of English, H.S. Saxena, remembers a photograph of him that once hung in the staffroom. He also recalls a remark by Raghupati Sahai 'Firaq Gorakhpuri' that he, Firaq, had been appointed to the post vacated by E.A. Wodehouse. My immense interest in EA was further sharpened when I read a breathtaking essay by him, 'The Scientific Quest for Ideals', in the very first issue of *The Allahabad University*

Magazine of late 1922. The voice that rose from those pages—calm, lucid, original and so advanced in the understanding of the mind and its fundamental processes—cast a spell on me. Pursuing his trail, I came across a letter from EA to R.D. Ranade. My researches into him were amply rewarded when I came across a few lines in Amaranatha Jha's diary jottings of 1922: *Sept. 5: Met E.A. Wodehouse, the new English Reader. I was familiar with his name, as he had at one time been on the staff of the Central Hindu College. He seems a likeable person.*[2]

And again, five days later: *Sept. 10: I presided over E.A. Wodehouse's lecture on 'The Scientific Quest For Ideals'.*[3]

The following month, another mention: *Oct. 16: Lectured at the Oxford and Cambridge Hostel on 'The New University'. Wodehouse presided.*[4]

Going by oral history, the year of Firaq Sahib's appointment would be 1930. So if 'the new Reader' had joined in 1922 and if he vacated a post to which Firaq Sahib was appointed, that EA served in the Department of English between 1922 and 1930 is therefore proved, even though we do not know anything more about him. All this apart, there is still no recorded proof of his presence amongst the staff of the English department, and the sinister absence on the Allahabad University front remains, which—aside from that essay and an article on poetry—seems to betray its chronic and characteristic amnesia in EA's case.

Tantalizingly, there was an answer to E.A. Wodehouse's theories in Bertrand Russell's records, by way of an academic debate couched in essay form, entitled 'The Conscientious Objector: A Reply To Mr. E.A. Wodehouse'. Presumably this was in response to Wodehouse's messianic theosophical theories expressed in his book, *A World Expectant: The Study of a Great Possibility*. There were also some scraps of information regarding poetry, of a high order, that Wodehouse contributed to *The Times of India* in the early years of the twentieth century, published under the pseudonym 'Senex'. He is said to have tutored the sons of the maharaja of a princely state named Sangli, as well. The final recorded detail is the date of his death on 9 October 1936 at Cheltenham, where he lived after his return to England.

I have taken up this example of E.A. Wodehouse not merely because of my enormous interest in this calm, spiritual instructor who seems to speak directly to our age across almost a century, but also to make a point. EA stands for the brilliant, invisible galaxy of names that served the University and faded away undocumented. Were it possible to include them all, this history might have achieved a higher degree of worth. But in the absence of documentation, I must make do with what is available, and which refers—in reminder—only to the highly visible.

I must also state at the very outset that this picture gallery comprises people who taught at the University; it does not include its alumni, a bare list of whose names is enough to constitute an extensive chapter in itself, and which size constraints for this volume forbid. Finally, there is another particular pitfall to avoid. Some of the competent local reports about prominent university personalities display a heightened tendency towards hagiography and resounding hyperbole, characteristic of that era of personality cults. We must make of them what we can, keeping our instincts of critical scrutiny alert to every scrap of telling information that can give us a rounded and realistic picture.

The first Indian vice chancellor of the Allahabad University was Sir Sunder Lal, who served two terms—1906 to 1908 and 1912 to 1917. He had descended from a long line of Nagar Brahmins who had emigrated from Gujarat in the seventeenth century. The destinies of his family took them to Kashmir in the eighteenth century where they served in the army, then to Jammu and eventually, via Anuppur, to Agra where they settled, more or less

Sir Sunder Lal

stably, while it was the capital of the United Provinces. Sir Sunder Lal's grandfather was a Sanskrit scholar, on visiting terms with the Raja of Benaras, Chait Singh; his father, Pundit Govind Ram Dave, superintendent of the Agra Fort. The family moved to Allahabad when it became the new capital of the North-West Provinces.[5] The extended family of four brothers was one of considerable affluence.

Sunder Lal was born in Jaspur village in Nainital District on 21 May 1857. As a student in Muir Central College, he was a favourite with Prof. Augustus Harrison who predicted a great future for him. Graduating in law, he took his place in 1896 amongst the famous barristers of his time: Sir Walter Colvin, Mr Colin, Mr Hill, Mr Ross and Indian lawyers of the stature of Pundit Ajudhianath, Pundit Vishvambharnath, Munshi Jwalaprasad and Dwarkanath Banerjee. An expert in Hindu, Muslim and company laws, he was knowledgeable in several languages and—though unremarkable for any flights of eloquence or scintillating argument—his thoroughness of preparation and study of finer details more than made up for his underplayed but concentrated court performances.

An active participant in public life, he was also extremely generous with donations, making liberal endowments to the Hindu Boarding House, the Red Cross Society, the City Anglo Vernacular Inter College, Crosthwaite Girls' College and sundry other institutions. His administrative connection with Allahabad

University began in 1894, when he became a member of its Syndicate. His private scholarly interests included reading history and, amazingly, chemistry. He was also a keen cricketer. His garden parties, hosted after convocations, were famous, with the guests sitting in the green quad of Muir College, and students in the long corridor of the physics department. When the Benaras Hindu University was envisaged, his name figured amongst the principal consultants. Amaranatha Jha has provided the most vivid portrayal of Sir Sunder Lal in an essay: 'Some Vice Chancellors I Have Known'. He begins with a ruthless observation:

> Whatever other great qualities he had, brilliance was not one of them. As a student at the Muir College he was by no means distinguished, indeed, he failed once at the B.A. examination. But at the bar his success was phenomenal. He was no orator. He spoke haltingly; he had a trying trick of coughing while he sought for a word or a phrase; he made no endeavour to be bright or witty; he was always serious. But he had remarkable industry and the capacity to take pains. He had thorough mastery over his case. He was never overbearing. As far as I know, he never had any 'breeze' with any judge. He seemed to accept the judge's opinion, even if it went against him; but he came back to his own point of view, repeated it in a score of other ways, until through sheer persistence and conviction in the righteousness of his cause, he won a verdict in favour of his client.
>
> Irreverent youngsters made fun of his speaking. During the Coronation festivities of 1911 he spoke at the Government High School and more than once referred to His Majesty Victoria. But there was no citizen of Allahabad who was held in higher esteem by every section of the community. The government valued his opinion because of

> what Lord Meston described as his 'sweet reasonableness'; the public respected him for it and recognised that no official favours could affect his sturdy patriotism. He was Chairman of the Reception Committee of the Allahabad session of the Congress, which was presided over by Sir William Wedderburn. I remember that we rather made fun of the lines from Wesley with which he ended his Welcome Address but the years have brought greater understanding and we can generally profit by the precept…
>
> He literally killed himself by overwork. The heavy duties involved in bringing the Hindu University into existence, of framing its first statutes, of constituting its first authorities, of planning the campus and erecting the buildings, of collecting funds, brought to a premature end a career of singularly selfless service. Those who knew him remember his simplicity, his goodness, his charitable disposition; those who belong to a later generation can see some aspects of his personality faithfully reproduced in a fine painting by Ganguly which adorns the walls of the Senate House.[6]

Honoured with titles like Rai Bahadur, CIE and a knighthood by the British government, Sir Sunder Lal also received honorary degrees from several universities. For a brief period he was vice chancellor of the Benaras Hindu University as well, when he made endowments worth lakhs of rupees to the institution. He was honorary president at the Congress meet of 1910, and a key figure in the organization of the great UP exhibition of 1911. As vice chancellor, he was known for his patience and conscientious application, as also for his generosity and genial friendliness. He died on 13 February 1918. The enormous *Sir Sunder Lal Hostel* is named after him. It is one of the remaining mysteries of campus history that the hostel was originally called Lady Sunder Lal Hostel. Lady was changed to Sir possibly because there were chances of it being mistaken for a girls' hostel, but this is just my guess.

In chronological order, the next vice chancellor of eminence was Ganganatha Jha. Born in 1871, to a Maithil Brahmin family in Darbhanga, he completed his matriculation and joined Queen's College, Benaras, for his FA (or Intermediate). Passing out in 1888, he scored the highest marks in Sanskrit, won a number of medals and a national scholarship. He joined Muir Central College and although he initially did not feel comfortable there—coming from Queen's, Benaras—he passed his BA examinations with flying colours in 1890, securing both a first division and the first position. An MA in Sanskrit from Allahabad University followed in 1892, once again a first class first.

The exceptional scholarship of the man reveals itself in the fact that for the next two years, instead of finding a conventional job as most successful students did, he withdrew to Benaras and devoted himself to studying the Sanskrit classics. His studies were conducted under the informal tutelage of such scholarly heavyweights as Shivkumar Mishra, Adityaram Bhattacharya, Gangadhar Shastri, Kailash Chandra Shiromani, Jaydev Mishra, Prof. Thibaut, Prof. Venis and numerous Benaras pundits. His Sanskrit scholarship was tempered to a more nuanced sensibility when he 'came under the influence of Dr. Besant. This brought about a change in his outlook, for, although he remained true to Sanskrit tradition, yet he welcomed Western thought and scholarship.'[7] Prof. Sylvan Levi described him as 'an ocean of learning', and for his outstanding expertise in Sanskrit he received government recognition in the form of the honorific 'Mahamahopadhyaya'.

After a rigorous spell of study, he accepted the Maharaja of Darbhanga's offer to join the royal library of the Darbhanga state as head librarian—a position he held till 1902. That year saw his appointment at the Muir Central College as professor of Sanskrit. In 1909, he acquired a DLitt from Allahabad University on a subject related to the Mimamsa school of Indian philosophy. Together with Prof. Thibaut, he helped bring out a journal on philosophy called *Indian Thought*, which appeared regularly between the years 1907 and 1918; there was also a second journal started by him, named *Pundit*. In 1919, he returned to Queen's College, Benaras, this time as principal, and was promoted from the United Provinces Educational Service to the Indian Educational Service.[8] At around the same time, the viceroy also made him a member of the Council of the States of India.

From 1923 till 1932, he served as vice chancellor of Allahabad University—the thirteenth to occupy the chair—for three successive terms. They were disturbed years politically, and Ganganatha Jha handled them with exemplary tact and wisdom, walking the tightrope between respecting the nascent nationalistic stirrings in the student community and the compulsions of toeing the government's line. There is, however, a contrary opinion held by Congress nationalists of the time, chiefly Nehru, who felt that Ganganatha Jha and later, his son Amaranatha Jha, had an unseemly inclination towards the British government's designs and did not go out of their way to lend support to the national movement.

But a university dependent on the government's grace and favour had to tread carefully—the preceding chapters of this book have already referred to Ganganatha Jha's intelligent crisis management during the boycott and civil disobedience demonstrations. Despite dissenting voices, he continued to command respect as a figure of saintly and principled austerity, known for the impetus he gave towards founding departments that gave primacy to the study of Indian culture. Some critics regarded him as generally anti-empirical, alleging that he was suspicious of modern science; others felt he was not progressive enough, especially in the matter of women's education. Many scholars of the time were a trifle discouraging of the idea of women receiving higher education and Ganganatha Jha, with all his erudition, was a conservative Maithil Brahmin in thinking and his habits of life.

For his distinguished services, he was awarded numerous marks of recognition: an LLD from Allahabad University, a DLitt from Benaras Hindu University and a knighthood from the British government. It is a proof of his commitment to learning that even while discharging the problematic duties of a vice chancellor in politically volatile times, he produced an impressive body of work—twenty-seven books, nineteen translated works and twenty-two edited volumes! There is an oft-repeated anecdote about him in which a teacher of the English department, Damri Ojha, advises him not to meet unruly students alone and unguarded, because of the possibility of violence to his person. Ganganatha Jha retorted: 'How long can I preserve myself from Amaranatha?' In other words, as his biographers have inferred, he looked upon every university student with paternal indulgence, making no distinction between his son Amaranatha and any other.[9]

Ganganatha Jha died on 18 November 1941. There is a hostel named after him, as well as a research institute for Sanskrit studies situated in Chandra Shekhar Azad Park.

His immediate successor as vice chancellor of the Allahabad University was Iqbal Narain Gurtu who held office for two terms from 1932 till 1937. Born on 25 September 1878, he passed out of Muir Central College and joined the legal profession in Kanpur. Quitting it soon afterwards, he moved to Benaras and became associated with a number of educational institutions there. He also came in close contact with Annie Besant and Dr Bhagwandas, the philosopher; later, Gurtu was to become the founder of the Annie Besant School and a patron of Ishwar Saran's Harijan Ashram.[10] Among other things, he was chairman of the Benaras Municipality, from which he resigned when appointed vice chancellor of Allahabad University. The University Court elected the post in those days. Known for and true to his inflexible stances on points of principle and his absolute freedom from partisan attitudes, when Gurtu found his name among those proposed for the position, he stubbornly refused either to canvass for himself or to cast a vote in his own favour. It was an obstinacy that perplexed and exasperated his supporters. The same impressive, though stubborn, adherence to issues of moral or technical probity marked his term as vice chancellor. Amongst the various references to this quality it is Dr Baburam Saxena's commentary that stands out. He mentions how, although he hadn't supported Gurtu—either in the election to the vice chancellor's office, or for his seat in the UP Legislative Council—this did not in any way prevent Gurtu from promoting him to the position of Reader.

He goes on to recount how, when once he approached Gurtu with a complaint against a colleague who happened to be one of the latter's staunch supporters, Gurtu did not hesitate to summon the teacher concerned and to reprimand him severely. When his close friend C.Y. Chintamani's son, C.B. Rao (who later joined the ICS), fell short of attendance and

Pundit Iqbal Narain Gurtu

had to be 'detained' for a year (i.e. refused permission to write the examination that year), no pressures or appeals to friendship could coax Gurtu into relaxing the rule. C.B. Rao's mock-tragic essay, 'On Being Detained', published in an issue of *The Allahabad University Magazine*, makes amusing reading. There were other instances of Gurtu utterly refusing to bow down to pressure in the matter of appointments.

In his dealings with teachers and students he maintained an equable friendliness and a reasonable openness to persuasion, through cogent logic rather than by influence. To agitating students he would say: 'Convince me by your arguments and if I am satisfied I shall willingly accede to your demands.' He would invite small groups of teachers to tea parties at his home, to sound out them on university issues in an informal environment. It was during his term as vice chancellor that Allahabad University celebrated its golden jubilee—a grand event planned and conducted by him with great pomp and ceremony.

Iqbal Narain Gurtu's term bridged the official tenures of the two Jhas, Ganganatha and Amaranatha, men of contrasting charismas whose names have become inseparably encoded in the fabric of Allahabad University.

The vast body of information about Amaranatha Jha—memorabilia, legends, writings—make any kind of attempted characterization of the essential man a daunting prospect. Just as his personality appeared to have overwhelmed a generation, so does

Amaranatha Jha

the volume of writings about him inundate and overwhelm the historian by its excess of lush idolatry or wry innuendo—both obstructions in the way of fair appraisal. The only hope for the retrospective raconteur is to put together, quite at random, the abundant scraps of detail that come to mind—after a long and intensive exposure to the Jha legend—in the tentative expectation that an accessible picture of the personality shall form.

For a long period of time Amaranatha Jha and Allahabad University were, as was said, synonymous entities, the association between the two inalienable. Many recollections in several voices acquaint us with a man who filled every conceivable academic and administrative position in the University and numerous positions outside it: lecturer; reader; professor; head librarian; editor, *The Allahabad University Magazine*; warden, Muir Hostel; commanding officer, University Training Corps; dean; registrar; vice chancellor; president, Athletic Association; president, Gymkhana Club; president, All India Lawn Tennis Association; vice chancellor, Benaras Hindu University; pro-chancellor, Rishikul University; president, All India Hindi Sahitya Sammelan; president, UP Hindi Sahitya Sammelan; chairman, Inter-university Board; president, All India Federation of Educational Associations; president, All India Education Association; and president of the All India Adult Education Association.

As though that were not enough, the Allahabad municipality, the Public Library of Allahabad, the Hindustani Academy and the Nagri Pracharini Sabha all enjoyed his membership and, more often than not, his leadership. Further, he was vice chairman, National War Academy Commission; vice chairman, Allahabad Municipal Board; member, Central Advisory Board of Education; president, UP Boy Scouts Association; member, National Cadet Corps; and governor, 90th District of Rotary International.

The list doesn't end yet! Doing justice to S.G. Dunn's fond

description of Jha as 'Mr Everything' are his international associations: fellow, Royal Society of Literature, London; honorary member, Iran Academy; vice president, Poetry Society, London; and member, League of Nations Committee on Education of Youth. In addition, he was a delegate to the International Universities Conference in Oxford, represented India at the Preparatory Commission of UNESCO, London, and represented the World Organization of the Teaching Profession of UNESCO, Paris. His conferrals included a DLitt degree as an honoris causa from the universities of Agra and Patna, the LLD from Allahabad University and the title of Sahitya Vachaspati from the Hindi Sahitya Sammelan. The list of convocation addresses adds to the weighty curriculum vitae. The books authored are not as many as might be expected, but remarkable nonetheless, considering the hectic public life of the man.

It all adds up to constitute a mind-boggling barrage of official information about Amaranatha Jha, born on 25 February 1897. A man of singular focus and uncanny powers of retention, he never forgot a name, conducted the students' roll call from memory and dictated memorized notes. His exceptional mind was stored with anecdotes, quips, quotes and stories that he readily related with wit, sensitivity and always with an acute sense of occasion. He taught as he spoke, first reading the text, then reading out the criticism along with his own observations. Even as vice chancellor he continued conducting BA undergraduate seminar classes, and functioning as warden of Muir Hostel.

There is also the bigger corpus of informal information preserved in the accounts of admiring colleagues, students and associates. Reading them is to conjure up a multidimensional image. The way he walked, talked, held his cigar or his stick; his dress, his voice, his great style, flourish and finesse. Sartorially perfect on all counts, he was seen in a dhoti, kurta, chaddar,

Maithil cap and a tilak to complete the get-up when he went to kavi sammelans; in a shervani and churidar pajamas at mushairas; and a high-collared coat, trousers and high-class pump shoes on other occasions. The rose in his buttonhole was inspired by S.G. Dunn's example, and his wardrobe was expensive and carefully maintained.

Evocative of a campus superstar, his contemporaries were prone to describe him in lavish Shakespearean quotes conveying that idea: a mountain top bathed in sublime sunshine, a man who was all men in one, a maker and moulder of men, a Renaissance man, a great Moghul, a Roman emperor, Pitt the Younger, a combination of Brahmin pundit and Oxford don, a prince among professors, a silver-tongued orator, etc. One comes away with a host of unforgettable pictures of an aristocratic being leading a life of majestic dignity and intellectual and social achievement—'a superior person (who) wanted to have about him everything that was superior. He wore first class clothes; he used first class fountain pens and first class stationery; he had first class articles of furniture. He encouraged first class talent—first class students, first class artists, first class athletes and sportsmen, first class researchers...'[11]

His library was enormous and stocked with the best books in several languages. He himself could speak, read and write in English, Hindi, Urdu, Bengali, Maithili and Sanskrit. There were standing instructions to booksellers to send around the latest books as soon as they were released. He read everything that came to hand—including detective and light fiction. He read fast, finishing two average-sized novels in a single day, and he remembered them all. There is a picture of him embedded in the visual memory of his contemporaries: sitting in that impeccably appointed library, surrounded by books and rare curios, incense burning, soft music playing on the radio, fresh flowers in the vases—an aura of a life of quality, lived in public view on an exalted plane of aesthetic distinction.

As emerges from a survey of the Jha records, his life was an artwork in progress, the artefact being his own personality, so toweringly impressive, so formidably competent that it overwhelmed every space he occupied. His punctuality was on the dot, his hospitality splendid and artistic. At least four times a year there were kavi sammelans and mushairas at his home, followed by sumptuous dinners, to say nothing of parties thrown in honour of any pretext—colleagues and students going abroad, or publishing a new book, or securing a prestigious job. He responded to letters speedily and one house guest even found him replying to a letter in Sanskrit! His voice has come in for much adulation too—his exquisite slow articulation, and the rounded mesmerizing fall of his syllables.

Summers were spent in Mussoorie, where he had either rented or bought a cottage named Lynwood, on Dick Road. It is possible that he did buy it because it was furnished with a library and other appurtenances exactly like his Allahabad bungalow, only on a smaller scale. Here he welcomed visitors for long stays, his house guests enjoying his hospitality for weeks at a stretch. His brand of hospitality meant that they were free to do as they pleased, meeting their host at fixed mealtimes, and in the evenings, when there was a somewhat longer interaction. For Jha Sahib kept to his own schedule, reading or writing in his library, going to Hackman's in his private rickshaw drawn by a uniformed rickshaw puller and returning for an early dinner at home. As Harivansh Rai Bachchan mentions in his autobiography, there was always a solemn hush in the house, no raised voices, no spontaneous rushing about. An imperial reserve pervaded the air, like Jha's own personality.[12]

It is a challenging exercise trying to get under a public

figure's skin, half a century after his death. There are some intriguing paradoxes of personality. Jha Sahib in his social role was charm and dynamism personified, a brilliant raconteur who took the microphone whenever there was an unplanned lull in any programme and regaled the audience with amusing and extempore sallies of witty words. Once he even delivered an extempore convocation address when the governor, Maurice Hallet, refused to attend. Cinema was a great interest and he patronized artists as well, often buying paintings from novices just by way of encouragement.

Jha Sahib lent a sympathetic ear to countless private confidences shared with him in the secrecy of his study, and helped generously in matters of money or employment or counsel. His deep voice would instruct his peon: 'Send him in', and then his typical opening words: 'What brings you here?' His imposing form sitting on a Sunday morning—browsing in his library, clad in his dressing gown with the tasselled cord tied tightly around his ample girth—has been fondly remembered by many recipients of his patronage. For he was patronizing by nature, his afternoon gatherings in which he met friends and students—popularly called 'Jha Sahib's durbar'—after his regal mode of granting audience to those lesser mortals. A man of great likes and dislikes, he was free with his purse with the poorer students, but very selective in the choice of his special circle, disposed favourably towards people of distinguished family or scholarly lineage. His critics ironically called the Friday Club, which was an exclusive affair, open to the chosen elite, the Man Friday Club.

Jha Sahib was fully aware of his own stardom, did nothing to discourage it and may even have consciously contributed to it, leaving a breathless trail of admirers and carping critics busily propagating or debunking the great legend. He provided opportunities enough: when he changed his shabby new tennis racquet for a classy new foreign one; when he chose to remain seated in his chair as the governor arrived at a tennis tournament; when he guffawed and told a callow visitor who had confessed to reading Hindi books, 'Then, sir, on behalf of Hindi I thank you'; when, as a very young lecturer, he interjected 'Not yet', as someone accidentally called him a vice chancellor—all these little details are inscribed in scores of sketches, diaries and records of the time.

In the tomes of information about Jha Sahib, some intriguing paradoxes of personality have inexorably surfaced, as also a few strange discords in an otherwise well-composed life. It would be churlish to mention that in the drumbeat of first-class trappings there are a few unknown second classes—the second division in his Intermediate examination, the fourth position in the BA examination—facts he disarmingly includes in his diary jottings of 15 June 1915.[13] This does not in any way discredit the man, though it does disturb the legend that others created. If anything, it makes him real and approachable to us lesser beings, who inhabit a less effusive age.

Amongst those more unsavoury anecdotes about Jha Sahib is the one in which he carries a bunch of pencils to class, and throws them with perfect aim at students who were underequipped to write, so that they could take down whatever he dictated, from memory. On one occasion a boy sat listening without writing and when asked why, he is said to have answered: 'I know which book you're dictating from and I have it.' In a myth-busting detail, the boy got very poor marks in the examination, which may, of course have been caused entirely by his deficient knowledge, but might also have resulted from, as local belief has it, Jha Sahib's injured amour proper.

There are some references to his solitary nature, his remoteness, lofty aloofness and ascetic discipline, which are interesting to the psychologist. He liked having people around him but did not allow anyone to be really close, maintaining an impersonal mask of reserve. When his voice hit an extra shade of emotion while reading out a poem in class, he quickly disguised it. His diary, which is more a bunch of clipped memoranda than a self-revelation, has no personal details. I find only three amazing entries, two absolutely minimal and one astonishingly emotional. The first two are given below:

22 June 1922: '*I was married at Bettiah at midday to the youngest daughter of the late Harimohan Jha.*'[14] There is no further mention of his wife, her name, her age, her early death, not even a date. Allahabad's octogenarians cite a version that Mrs Amaranatha Jha was uneducated, orthodox and did not even wear a blouse, stitched garments being considered un-Brahmanical in certain communities. Jha himself is silent on the subject of his marriage.

Then again there is a fairly unemotional assertion dated 24 February 1947: '*On this day I complete my fiftieth year. Except for the complete absence of all domestic life, I have got much out of life.*'[15]

Amaranatha Jha might have been a great journalist—C.Y. Chintamani, editor of *The Leader*, frequently asked him to join the paper. He might have been a great politician—his eloquence and charisma qualified him amply in those politically opportune times. But, there are plenty of hints about the animosity that existed between Amaranatha Jha and Jawaharlal Nehru, natural when two stalwarts find the local space too small for their competing legends. Jha was even known to have publicly declared that Nehru wrote bad prose, the press making capital of it. His sufficiency and confidence precluded the acceptance of political appointments, which in those days were offered as largesse to any worthy candidate in Nehru's grace and favour.

Instead, and with organic ease, he was drawn to the portals of the University—what with administration being his forte and the brilliance of his University career winning him the prestigious Queen Empress Jubilee award for topping in both his BA and MA examinations. The University was the richer for his contribution, despite the plentiful counter-narratives which superlative eminence of any kind often generates, and which Jha's detractors did not fail to produce, over tales of authentic grandeur and refined posturing. He founded a Jha school of personality, as it were, for much after his death there were people who copied his style, his pearly handwriting, his style of dress, and his interest in collecting artefacts. His loyal supporters defended him forcefully, arguing that there was no 'pose' to 'expose' when the style was the real man, and if he was a proud being, he had well-justified reasons to be so.

Dr Amaranatha Jha and Dr Sarojini Naidu when she came to address the convocation in 1938

On leaving the Allahabad University, there is an uncharacteristic overflow of quivering emotion, expressed in several diary entries (the third group of entries mentioned earlier)—of desolate leave-taking, overwrought and uncontained, culminating in words like: *'I wrote to Kewal Krishna and Ramji— and wept as I wrote, making over charge of the Muir Hostel to them. No one can realise what these boys have meant to a lonely man...*'[16] Suddenly the essential truth of the person clicks into place—an artist who worked on himself and on what he loved most, the University.

'Self-centred', 'self-contained', 'self-sufficient', 'snob' are words used to describe AJ, as he was called. But for that sufficiency and centrality, the medium was the institution he created lovingly and with complete dedication. It was he who built the image of Allahabad University as an IAS officer-producing centre, calling it the University's 'trade secret', organizing students in study circles and allocating topics for them to write intensively researched essays to be shared and discussed with the rest of the group. He initiated the process of founding several new departments—from military science to music. It is not to be wondered that on his leave-taking, he declared that he knew and loved every brick and stone of the University, for which he reserved his concentrated and controlled love; no other word will do.

Jha left in 1947 after serving three terms. Some said he had grown too large for the position of vice chancellor, which no longer afforded scope for a man of his gifts. Some believed that he grew disenchanted with the decline, already evident, due to state interference and the lack of funding. The simpler explanation seems to be that, being 'Amaranatha Jha' 24/7 was a demanding and exhausting job, and that he was undergoing an inevitable burnout. The hectic whirl no longer pleased him. Those he'd helped often proved ungrateful, as is often the case. Those he could not help bore a grudge against him. The curtain had to be rung down. The maestro who carried two bouquets of flowers in his car to perfume the air and who bought a large quantity of sandalwood for his own funeral pyre, carrying it to Patna, had designed the last act of his life as carefully as he had every scene heretofore.

R.D. Ranade (1886—1957) is another legendary teacher

of philosophy of that age. I was lucky to have come across an intimately recalled account of this extraordinary campus personality penned by a favourite student of his, V.S. Naravane. What a treasure to alight upon! For years I have depended on Naravane's brilliant book on Ananda Coomaraswamy for my MA teaching, a fact I confessed to him when I met him, much after I had been acquainted with his work for years. He expressed surprise and told me that he himself did not have a single copy of the book which had long gone out of print. But I was also an admirer of his long series of articles on Indian mythology which were published in *The Illustrated Weekly of India* in the 1950s, copies of which I had inherited from my father, a keen collector of the *Weekly* in the old days. V.S. Naravane was one of the most articulate and insightful of teachers, but whose term in the philosophy department was relatively brief. He did, though, return from Poona to take up residence at Allahabad, devoting himself to reading and writing on philosophical subjects.

When a writer-philosopher writes about his guru, the satisfaction of reading his account comes to us with compound interest. I will not presume to improve upon his writing with any raw editorial authority. The portrait he paints of one of the greatest teachers of the University must be presented in his own more than competent depiction:

> When Dr. S. Radhakrishnan was President of India, he was once invited to address an international conference of philosophers in Europe. He was introduced as 'the greatest living Indian philosopher'. In his speech Prof. Radhakrishnan said that he did not deserve such praise. 'The greatest philosopher in my country today,' he is reported to have said, 'is a person with whose name some of you may not be familiar. He is a simple, saintly man who lives in

an ashram in a small town in South India. Every year he spends a couple of months at Allahabad, where he taught philosophy for many years. His name is Ranade.'[17]

Naravane's own area being philosophy, he has a more comprehensive perspective on the personality he is describing:

'What is it that we should expect from a true philosopher?' John Cowper Powys, one of my favourite English authors raises this question in his delightful book, *Culture And Philosophy*. 'We should not ask a philosopher,' Powys says, 'why he supports a particular theory. We should rather ask him: What can you reveal to me? What depths and heights can you plunge and lift me to? What inexpressible feeling can you arouse in me of the wordless essence of things?' Professor Ranade was one of those rare teachers who could fulfil these expectations. He could help his students dive into the depths and ascend the heights of thought. He could arouse a feeling for the mystery of existence.[18]

Other contemporaneous renderings refer to Ranade as a sort of seer rather than an academic, a rishi out of an epic age rather than a teacher of philosophy. Naravane too maintains this version:

He was known to his students as a mystic. A mystic is not one who discards reason but one who assimilates, masters and then transcends whatever the rational faculty can offer. (His) thorough grounding in philosophy was enriched by his proficiency in Sanskrit that gave him access to the primary sources of Indian thought…He held high offices in the University of Allahabad as Head of the Philosophy Department, Dean of the Arts Faculty and for a brief period as Vice Chancellor. He discharged his duties while scrupulously avoiding the intrigues and party politics that later vitiated the atmosphere of the University. He never spoke ill of anybody and was admired for his gentleness and tolerance.

His physical appearance was unusually striking. He was extremely frail. He was so delicate that I sometimes thought that he might be blown away by the wind. He had a fair complexion. The features of his face were sharp and finely chiseled. One could not help thinking that he must have been strikingly handsome in his youth. Although he was so slender, he had an inner stream of energy that sparkled in his eyes. Whenever I saw Professor Ranade I was reminded of Houdon's famous bronze head of Voltaire who had the same emaciated face and brilliant eyes.

Everyone in the University had heard of Professor Ranade's lifestyle. Two of these were particularly well known. He felt the need to change his clothes frequently. Even when he came to the University his personal chaprasi, Bhagwan Din, used to carry a suitcase containing two or three sets of kurta and dhoti made of fine cotton fabric, immaculately white. Sometimes even in the middle of a lecture he would leave the class and go to the dressing room to change his clothes. I have never heard any convincing explanation for this habit. Was he merely carrying his obsession with cleanliness to an extreme limit? Did he have the illusory feeling that he was sweating, even in winter? Or was his habit the result of some repressed childhood experience, as a psychoanalyst might suggest? I simply do not know. And I do not attach much importance to it.

But even more astounding was the fact that Professor Ranade did not eat. When I say 'he did not eat' I do not mean that he ate seldom or very little. He simply did not eat. A complete meal, served in a 'thali', was placed before him. He looked at it and blessed the food that was given to the disciples. How could he live without eating? There were two contrary schools of thought on this question. According to one school, he had stopped eating because his body was so small. Others took the opposite view and said that his body was so frail just because he did not eat. Tea with milk was made for him at frequent intervals. But no one ever saw him eating anything solid. There is an interesting story about this aspect of the Professor's life. During a conversation on the campus some friends were trying to remember the year in which an important event had taken place. One of them said: 'It must have been 1931 or perhaps 1932. That was the year when Professor Ranade ate half a banana.'

When I first met Professor Ranade he lived in a rented house on Beli Road in a locality known as New Katra. Later he moved to his own house in…Ashok Nagar… It was a large house with spacious rooms, bare and unadorned. There was a large compound but no garden was maintained. Professor Ranade supported many students. They had to be at his beck and call any time he wanted to dictate something or have something read to him. Even if it was two-thirty in the morning, some student had to be at his disposal if the Professor was in the mood for work. The disciples got free room and board, but their life was spartan indeed…

Visitors were received in a large room devoid of furniture. There was a mat that covered the entire floor. Chairs were brought into the room for foreign visitors or people who could not sit on the floor. Professor Ranade sat in a corner of the room. In the other three corners tea was made. A servant would come with a kerosene stove and put it in one of the corners. It had to be a different corner each time. Then he went back to the kitchen and brought a saucepan containing a mixture of milk, sugar and water. The stove could not be lighted without vigorous pumping preceded by cleaning of the burner with a pin. Professor Ranade watched the operation with childlike fascination. I remember the smile on his face when the tealeaves were put into the boiling mixture of milk, water and sugar, and steam came out from the edges of the lid. Professor Ranade was a very hospitable host...[19]

Rishis are known to be different from the general run of men and Naravane's account does indeed paint him in the light of a transcendental innocent of Blakean sublimity who has access to planes of knowledge exceeding common comprehension. Even at its most hagiographic, Naravane's picture is scrupulously honest:

The first exposure to an outstanding teacher can be disappointing. When I attended the first lecture by Professor Ranade, as a student in the M.A. Previous class in philosophy, I felt a bit let down. Many of my classmates had the same feeling. His reputation had conditioned us to expect something original and brilliant. But we found that he was neither eloquent nor systematic. He made a few general comments on philosophy and after fifteen minutes said: 'You may go.' Later we found that whenever he wanted to terminate a class he said: 'You may go.' There were less than twenty students in the class. But he rarely made eye contact. He let it be known, though indirectly, that he did not like girl students to sit in the front row. Surprisingly the girls did not resent this male chauvinism. 'On the contrary,' one of them confided, 'we prefer the rear benches. There we feel more free to whisper, giggle and gossip.' The Professor was blissfully oblivious to what was happening at the other end of the classroom.

When we gradually became accustomed to his idiosyncrasies and his apparently casual method of exposition, we realised the value of what he was giving us. We saw how insightful and perceptive were his comments and we appreciated the ease with which he clarified the most abstruse philosophical issues in a few well-chosen words. It did not take us more than a couple of weeks to discover that we could get from Professor Ranade in ten minutes what an ordinary scholar, with bookish and superficial knowledge could not have given in an entire week.

I remember an incident that made a deep impression on me. Professor Ranade had encouraged the class to quote from the Upanisads. One of the students got up and quoted the famous lines in praise of the ashvattha tree which has 'roots above and branches below.' The student had barely uttered the first two words *urdhvo mullah* (roots above) when Professor Ranade became excited. He must have quoted or uttered these lines countless times. But on that occasion his imagination was stirred very powerfully. 'Wonderful! Wonderful!' he exclaimed. 'Do you understand? Do you see? Roots above and branches below. Wonderful, wonderful. You may go.' The class had been dismissed. I turned back and looked at him. I found that the philosopher was still contemplating the beauty of the metaphor and the deep meaning condensed in the symbol of the tree. His head was tilted slightly, his eyes were closed, and it seemed as though the ashvattha tree actually stood before him with ascending roots and descending branches.

It is a memorable picture to carry away!

Among the personages who achieved a monumental image in Allahabad University's golden era was Dr Ishwari Prasad, born in 1888 in the rural hinterland of Agra district. Here, he had had an early exposure to the hardships faced by villagers harried by moneylenders and their henchmen and had personally witnessed the lot of peasants beset by crop failures, devastating famines and displacements. He passed his MA from the Agra College in 1914 and began teaching there. It was Prof. Rushbrook Williams who, impressed by Prasad's lecture on Lord Dalhousie at a BA class, invited him to join the staff of the Department of Medieval and Modern History, which Dr Prasad did in February 1919.[20]

It is said that when his major lectures took place, not merely the lecture theatre but the verandahs outside overflowed with listeners—students and teachers from other departments flocking to find a place of vantage. His lectures on the French Revolution remain in the memories of senior alumni of the University. Although the Hindi he spoke carried a heavy Western UP accent, his expression and delivery of the English language were flawless. His life was one of exemplary devotion to scholarship. There is a well-known anecdote of the time when he found himself locked in after closing hours in the University library, and was let out in the middle of the night by a member of the embarrassed library staff. Well versed in English, Hindi, Urdu, Arabic and Persian, he was an expert in reading Mughal firmans, of which he possessed a rich collection. He declined repeated invitations to go on lecture tours abroad and chose to stay on native soil rather than incur the impurity of an overseas journey, in keeping with the rigorous Brahminical rules he subscribed to in an austere lifestyle.

He was awarded the Padma Bhushan, which he initially declined, until the persuasion of devoted students prevailed on him to accept it. He was also honoured by the Allahabad University with the conferral of the degree of Doctor of Law, and the title of Itihas Shiromani by the Royal House of Nepal. Dr Prasad embodied the qualities of the hardcore scholar who made his knowledge accessible to generations through his erudite books, and through which his real worth is to be measured. These included, amongst several others: *Muslim Rule in India, A History of Medieval India, The Mughal Empire, Hindu-Muslim Problems, Humayun and His Times, A History of Europe* and *India in the Eighteenth Century*. He also founded an organization for historical studies in his Bank Road bungalow, initiating its journal with the government grants he had managed to arrange, in addition to his own personal contributions. Sadly the organization faded away after his death.

Dr Ishwari Prasad was frugal to the point of absurd stinginess. The funniest campus anecdote about his adamantine restraint with his purse has to do with the time he bought a car, a Vauxhall that cost him ₹16,000. The prospect of signing away such a colossal sum in one fell swoop was an inhibition he just could not overcome. The payment was made through two consecutive cheques, signed on two consecutive days, which made the parting more bearable! But he was apt to set aside all stint when moved by appeals to his kindness, giving material help to needy persons who approached him. He is also said to have arranged employment for poor candidates, going out of his way to do so. His students were scattered all over the higher echelons of government, and he would happily write out references and requests on behalf of the humblest of candidates to the most influential of people.

Retiring in 1954, he went on to become a member of the UP Legislative Council, occupying the seat for three terms. It was said that his mere presence imposed greater accountability on the other members of the assembly. To the end of his days he kept himself keenly involved in national and local issues, writing articles in the local papers or prompting editors to address particular subjects of concern to Allahabad citizens. The decline in the University's standards was a subject that he was given to discussing with great passion. His two greatest aspirations went unmet—of completing a hundred years of age and of becoming vice chancellor of AU. He fell short of a century by two years, and lost the vice chancellorship by just one vote, a fact that saddened him considerably. He was offered vice chancellorships of other universities but refused them all.

The name of Tara Chand closely follows that of Ishwari Prasad as one of the luminaries of the Department of Medieval and Modern History. His books on the influence of Islam on Indian culture and the history of the Indian National Movement are world-class contributions. It is a lesser-known detail of his life that he was very closely connected with the secret wing of the Indian National Movement, related through marriage to the famous revolutionary Lala Hardayal whose establishment he had joined. His name was included in the list of people kept under close CID surveillance by the British government. There are references to him in the writings of well-known revolutionaries of the period, such as Sachindra Nath Sanyal and Pundit Sunder Lal, to whose journal *Karmayogi* he was a regular contributor.[21]

He served as the principal of the Kayastha Pathshala, as well as the Kayastha Pathshala University College. Rajeshwar Dayal's memoirs recall how Dr Tara Chand had prescribed a dress code for the teachers and students of the KPUC—khaki shorts and white shirts, even for the principal! He remembers the spectacle as comic, to the point of being bizarre.[22]

Dr Tara Chand held the vice chancellor's chair in AU from 1947 till 1949, followed by two terms as member of the Rajya Sabha, and a subsequent ambassadorial assignment to Iran. Proficient in several languages, he was known for his absolute freedom from caste, regional and religious partisanship, a virtue that earned him the appreciation of Mahatma Gandhi. There is a hostel named after him in the Allahabad University.

Dr R.P. Tripathi, of the same faculty, is remembered for his unique style of teaching. Saeed Jaffrey, in his *An Actor's Journey*, describes him as a man who carried his learning lightly and whose lively lectures were hugely enjoyable. He says:

> The bald, paan-chewing and totally delightful Dr. Tripathi… would bring the characters from history totally alive. Talking about Emperor Babur's son, Humayun, he would describe the time when his younger brother had mutinied in this manner, in his dulcet Purabiya (eastern U.P.) tones: 'So Humayun sent a message to his brother Askari and said, "I say, look, you are my younger brother. You are a bit cheeky rebelling against me. But younger brothers are known to make mistakes after a sudden rush of blood. So, being your Bare Bhai Sahab, I shall forgive you. Come home and be a good boy. But Askari was adamant. So Humayun said. "To hell with you," sent his troops to Gujarat, defeated Askari, brought him back to Delhi and threw him into prison.'[23]

R.P. Tripathi was a weighty scholar but his light manner not only belied his considerable stature as a historian but fixed the content of his lectures permanently in the retention of his students.

Although Prof. Meghnad Saha spent only fifteen years in Allahabad, his name belongs firmly to the gallery of illustrious dons who lent lustre to the University. His personal history is an inspiring one. Born on 6 October 1896 in the small hamlet of Shevdatali, in Dacca district in undivided India, he was the son of Jagannath Saha, the village grain and grocery storekeeper. His early education was received in a village school, situated seven miles away at the neighbouring village of Simulia. Brilliant from the start, he topped the list of candidates in the middle school examination of the entire Dacca district, and won a fee waiver and a scholarship.

At that point, the Partition of Bengal took place and students in large numbers boycotted educational institutions. When the governor, Sir Ramfylde Fuller, visited Dacca to find the class rooms deserted, stern punitive measures were taken against the offending students, among them Saha, who lost both his college admission and his scholarship. Not to be defeated, Saha appeared in the entrance examination of another college some months later, and once again topped the list of candidates in the entire province. After a short spell at Dacca College, he moved on to Presidency College, Calcutta, where he completed his BSc and MSc courses. Among his famous batch-mates were the scientist Satyendra Nath Bose; Allahabad University's celebrity academic-to-be, Neel Ratan Dhar; and Sarat Chandra Bose, Subhas Chandra Bose's elder brother.[24]

Early plans to take the Civil Service examinations were abandoned because he was denied permission, presumably on account of his friendship with 'Bagha' Jatin and other revolutionaries, although he was never an active member of their group. He was appointed as a lecturer in Calcutta University's mathematics department, but personal differences with his department head, Prof. Ganesh Prasad, led to his transfer to the Department of Physics. It was around this time that his trademark work in thermal ionization and spectroscopic research began, for which Calcutta University awarded him the DSc degree.

A travel grant from the University afforded him an extensive tour of Europe, in the course of which he made the acquaintance of international scientists like Prof. Ralph H. Fowler and Sir J.J. Thompson. On his return to India, the vice chancellor of Calcutta University, Sir Ashutosh Mukherjee, offered him the position of professor of physics. There were other viable offers too, from the Benaras Hindu University, the Aligarh Muslim University and other institutions, but Dr Saha chose to come to Allahabad University as that, to his view, offered better opportunities for research. He joined as professor of physics on 17 September 1923.

The fifteen years that he spent in the University completely transformed the physics department—its workshop, laboratory, library and research-work—prompting international figures like Arthur H. Compton, Arnold Summerfeld and Sir Arthur Eddington to visit the department. An extremely conscientious teacher, Prof. Saha could make time for his personal researches only during the summer vacations. In that scorching heat, from April till July, he plunged into intensive work, for which he sought sponsors wherever he could—from the governor to the Royal Society in London, as also from private parties, industrial entrepreneurs and affluent patrons.

He was a great organizer, phenomenally focused and hardworking, expecting others to be as painstaking as himself and becoming impatient when his standards were not met. He was, as his contemporaries observed, a free soul, careless of dress or appearance, and fearlessly outspoken. In 1927, he was made a Fellow of the Royal Society. As a scientist he went all out to requisition funds and knowledge resources for his department's research work. Once, when a request for ₹6,000, to develop wireless telegraphy was not fully met, he persuaded a local financier to arrange funds for equipment to create a transmitter, capable of a hundred watts for a year. Another time he sent a research scholar to consult with Prof. Chatterton-Smith at Bangalore on the subject of wireless telegraphy.

He was an energetic teacher, doing brisk blackboard work, even using a lantern to project slides for his class. What made him different from many other men of science was his breadth of vision and range of interests. He believed that a scientist must understand the history and philosophy of science. He also strongly believed that science was for human betterment and not a closed field sufficient unto itself. He once proposed that X-ray facilities, developed in the physics lab, be thrown open to the general public for diagnostic purposes. He helped the Allahabad Municipality's electricity and water supply departments with calculations, detecting errors in functioning, and urging the University not to pay water dues that were miscalculated.

It is not generally known that Meghnad Saha was keenly interested in history, especially the history of Kaushambi, and the script of the Indus Valley Civilization. He published a journal called *Science and Culture,* printed at the Indian Press, which appeared regularly for two years. His dream was to help create a combined museum of the arts and sciences. There were other farsighted and practical proposals that he made: the establishment of a photography department, the management of grain reserves in the state, the reform of the calendar and the proper utilization of energy. In 1931 he cofounded, along with Prof. A.C. Banerjee, the UP Academy of Science, later renamed the National Academy of Science. During a conference on energy resources he came in contact with Jawaharlal Nehru, upon whom he made a great impression. In 1936 he won a Carnegie Fellowship to Europe and the US, again visiting Harvard and Berkeley and forming creative partnerships with leading physicists there.

He left Allahabad University in 1938, by some accounts due to unbridgeable differences with Amaranatha Jha, and returned to Calcutta.

Saha continued his cutting-edge researches in nuclear physics—designing an electron microscope with the help of Prof. Morton of Stanford University and contributing plans for harnessing the Damodar River for irrigation and for generating hydroelectricity. He worked on a simple universal calendar and in 1952 even won an independent seat in the Lok Sabha, where he distinguished himself for the acuteness of his discourses and the practicality of his inputs. In his last days, he wore himself out working for people displaced from northeast Bengal and Assam, visiting refugee camps even in a state of ill-health. He died in 1956 in Delhi, where he had gone to attend the Budget Session of Parliament. His name remains a prized one in the University of Allahabad, and there is a prestigious institute named after him in Kolkata.[25]

Professor Neel Ratan Dhar's contributions to the chemistry department have been touched upon in an earlier chapter. Like Meghnad Saha, Prof. Dhar's origins lay in East Bengal, in the city of Jessore in present-day Bangladesh. There is a major road close to Jessore still named after him. Unlike Saha, he made Allahabad his permanent home. Born on 2 January 1892, he received his early education in Jessore, then moved on to Presidency College in Calcutta where he earned the favour of the principal, H.R. James. After completing his MSc in 1913, he was appointed in the Calcutta University. A year later he went to Europe on a scholarship and completed his course for the DSc degree from London University, coming into fruitful contact with several eminent men of science there. This was followed by the acquisition of a state doctorate from the University of Paris. Thereafter, he qualified in the Indian Educational Service and was appointed professor of chemistry at Muir Central College, Allahabad, a position he joined on 19 July 1919.

Professor Dhar's work in the Allahabad University put the chemistry department on the international radar through its valuable research work. His students recall that his teaching was extremely lucid, clarifying the fundamental principles of the subject in an unforgettable manner and demonstrating a great variety of samples and well-planned experiments with great sophistication before the class. He made chemistry such an interesting subject that passers-by in the corridor would hear gales of laughter emanating from Prof. Dhar's classroom.[26] But this ease of execution was the outcome of very hard work, for the professor spared neither himself nor his students, often declaring that there was no shortcut to success, only intense dedication and diligence. This was something he had learnt from his own teacher, the celebrated P.C. Roy, who is known as the founder of the study of chemistry in India.

His personal life, apart from being tremendously laborious, was amazingly spartan. He economized on the most ordinary comforts, his spare frame clad in the stereotypical Bengali dhoti, kurta and chaddar (often finely darned), though he was also known to be extremely spry and dapper in Western dress on formal occasions. His house was a picture of austerity, his living room furnished with only a wooden bed and a few chairs where, even on Sundays, research scholars were made to sit and take notes. He rose early, and even at a very advanced age was present at the laboratory at 8 in the morning. He never took an afternoon nap, going back to his institute after lunch and staying busy till 4.30 in the afternoon. Evenings were spent taking long walks, covering 10 or 15 kilometres in a day. Lean and erect till the end, he looked the picture of enduring fitness and concentrated devotion to his chosen field.

His work proved of great benefit to farmers in an agricultural economy like India's in the 1950s. An old student of Prof. Dhar's, S.K. Ghosh, clarifies the nature of his work in accessible terms for the lay reader:

> The pioneering researches of Professor Dhar and his devoted band of research scholars of (the) Allahabad School of Soil Science (was) connected with soil fertility, (the) mechanism of atmospheric nitrogen fixation and loss, soil nitrification,

> (the) role of organic matter, reclamation of saline and alkaline soils etc. (and providing) an easy, practical and economic solution in increasing soil fertility and food production for the teeming... millions of our country. These researches coming out from Allahabad University('s) chemical laboratories have established the key role of soil humus and organic matter in increasing soil nitrogen by slow oxidation of all types of organic waste aided by phosphate and lime. This is accelerated by sunlight specially in (the) tropics where most of the developing countries are situated.[27]

Prof. Dhar supervised about 150 quality research projects, and published more than 600 research papers. He was awarded the DSc degree as an honoris causa by the universities of Calcutta, Vishvabharati, Benaras Hindu, Jadavpur, Gorakhpur and Allahabad. He lectured widely in most of the countries of Europe and in the US. For some inexplicable reason he was not awarded the Nobel Prize, although his name was proposed by a Russian and an English scientist; nor was he given an FRS. When the then prime minister, Indira Gandhi, suggested a Padma Bhushan for him, Prof. Dhar's polite refusal quietly demonstrated the dignity of the scientist-teacher's autonomy. He said that his name had found great affection and respect in the hearts of his students and that was honour enough for him.

The same autonomy, hermit-like in its austerity, was demonstrated when he left his very considerable fortune to the cause of science: the Sheila Dhar Institute of Soil Sciences that he founded; the large building and extensive grounds of his home given to the National Academy of Science; his Mussoorie bungalow and massive cash endowments donated to the Ramakrishna Mission and the universities of Calcutta and Vishvabharati. He died at ninety-three, after a brief illness, walking tall till almost the very end, with concentrated devotion in his field of study and the institution he had created.

Among the illustrious Sanskrit pundits of the Allahabad University, the name of Khetresh Chattopadhyaya is in the frontlines. A pious, modest man, his stature as a scholar was acknowledged widely. Born in 1896 in the East Bengal village of Aamta, he belonged to the lineage of the great Bankim Chandra Chattopadhyaya. Early in life he developed an interest in Vedanta philosophy when his mother, Sursundari Devi, read to him and his sisters a Bengali play based on Sankara. As was the frequent practice among good students in East Bengal, he joined Presidency College, Calcutta, from where he passed his Matric examination. Following his Intermediate (or FA) examination, he secured admission in Muir Central College for his BA, to study Sanskrit intensively, which he did under the celebrated Sanskrit pundits, Adityaram Bhattacharya and Ganganatha Jha. Thereafter he did his MA from Queen's College in Benaras under the tutelage of erudite Sanskrit scholars like Pundit Gopinath Kaviraj, Arthur Venis, Pundit Lakshmi Shastri Tailang and Vama Charan Bhattacharya, among others.

A brief teaching stint at Carmichael College in the city of Rangpur, (now in Bangladesh), was succeeded by yet another spell of learning and a second MA in Vedanta from Calcutta University. He was appointed a lecturer in the Sanskrit department of Allahabad University in 1924, from which he retired in 1958. His contribution to the University lay not only in Sanskrit, but also in helping to conceive and establish the ancient history department. By reason of his profound expertise in Indian philosophy, he was associated with the philosophy department as well. Ved, Mimamsa, Sanskrit shastras, Pali and Prakrit literature, Sanskrit poetics and linguistics—all of these were his province. On retirement he became the director of the research unit, and subsequently the vice chancellor of the Government Sanskrit University in Benaras. Three years later when his term ended, he continued to be actively involved with Sanskrit studies, language and literature as consultant to All India Radio, which would regularly broadcast programmes in Sanskrit.

Prof. Chattopadhyaya is remembered for his great affection for his students, which number quite a few famous names like G.C. Pande, Vidyaniwas Mishra, B.B. Lal and G.R. Sharma. He was given to saying that there was no greater pleasure for a teacher than to be outdone in achievement by his students. In his personal life he was devout and ascetic, preferring to carry his own foodgrains and cooking his meals personally on his lecture trips abroad. It was his life's aspiration to be able to find a common thread running through the world's ancient religious beliefs and ceremonies. He would declare that if not in this life, he hoped to find it in some other life to come—because knowledge is a continuing process that exceeds the illusory limitations of life and death. From among his peers, Prof. Chattopadhyaya's great friends included Subhas Chandra Bose, his classmate in Calcutta—who wrote copious letters to him; the poet Suryakant Tripathi Nirala; the historian Ishwari Prasad; and the English don S.C. Deb. The bonding between them was an enviable example of the nature of intellectual fraternity that is still remembered in Allahabad's older circles.

The name of Raghupati Sahai 'Firaq Gorakhpuri' is surely one of the most colourful in Allahabad University's picture gallery: a character of rare and scathing repartee, with enormous potential to shock and awe middle-class morality. There is a whole oeuvre of Firaq stories—some real, a great many apocryphal—still doing the rounds in literary and academic circles, setting off bursts of laughter at the brilliant eccentricity of Firaq Sahib's doings and sayings. He was a maverick, often credited with genius in all its unconventional manifestations. Whether or not he *was* is not the question, since literary genius cannot be measured by intelligence quotients, but he was certainly possessed of a tremendous creative aptitude and power of expression. As in the case of Amaranatha Jha, there is plenty of Firaq memorabilia. The best-known is the biography of his close associate, Ramesh Chandra Dwivedi. It vividly paints the nimbleness of Firaq Sahib's brain, his vast reserves of learning, his fits of wilful provocation, great mood swings with bouts of despair and rage, his profound sensibility and the many personal trials of his disordered and unusual life.

In recounting his quips and witticisms many of us consign to forgetfulness his eventful life prior to his joining the Allahabad University. Born on 28 August 1896, in Gorakhpur, he inherited the gift of Urdu poetry from his father, Munshi Gorakh Prasad 'Ibrat', himself a good poet. His mother was the third of the Munshi's wives, the earlier two having passed away. Firaq was one of eight siblings, five brothers and three sisters, of whom two brothers and a sister died during his lifetime. His early education was acquired in Gorakhpur, his childhood being remarkable as much for his self-proclaimed intelligence as for his great love for wrestling and gymnastics.[28] After passing out of the Gorakhpur Government Jubilee High School in 1913, he joined the Muir Central College, Allahabad, for an FA course.

At around this time, a family friend 'treacherously' got him married (as he himself was given to bemoaning) to a girl he grew to abhor. Her name was Kishori and he continued to berate her all his life; cursing her looks, her behaviour, her wits with all the venom of his plentiful vocabulary, until one feels rather sorry for the poor lady who was, quite literally, driven away for long periods to Gorakhpur. Neighbours remember Mrs Firaq as an extremely simple and sweet-tempered woman, very gifted in home skills like cooking and pickling, which she happily shared with ladies of the locality. She also shared her misery at the abusive behavior of her husband who was, among other things, a wife-batterer. A village woman with her saree-end pulled over her head, she was beneath the poet's standards, and he made her pay for it. Eventually, after the suicide of their son, who laid himself on the railway tracks after failing in his high school examination, she left for the village; whether on her own initiative or her husband's aggressive banishment is not certain.

As a woman writing this history of the University and its personalities, I have avidly sought clues about other wives, mothers and daughters, but am vexed to have found very few. It was Prof. Jennings's great-grandson who revealed that Mrs Jennings was nanny-tutor to Motilal Nehru's children, and there are some local accounts of the illness and tragic death of Sheila Dhar, N.R. Dhar's first wife and erstwhile student. And that is about all. There was a culture of unnatural reticence, broken only by Harivansh Rai Bachchan's refreshingly public domesticity.

After passing his MA examination, Firaq found himself suddenly fatherless and the inheritor of huge debts. He was soon appointed to the post of deputy collector in 1918, barely taking charge when he received the gladdening information that he had qualified in the ICS examination as well. (It may be clarified here that successful graduates from Muir were automatically called for a Civil Services interview without having to clear the examination, as distinct from candidates who had sat for and cleared the ICS examination). Attempting to show himself up in a better light, Firaq Sahib was given to blurring the line between the two, a bit of autobiographical licence, but one which he committed with his characteristic panache. In fact he wrote of his interview with a disarming flourish of self-congratulation:

In the year 1919, I had to appear for interview as an I.C.S.

candidate before a board consisting of the British Director of Public Instruction, the Secretary U.P. Government, and some senior members of the Revenue Board, the cream of British officialdom in the U.P. I was asked whether I would prefer to join the judiciary, or the executive as an I.C.S. I immediately guessed that if I plumbed for executive officership these die-hard bureaucrats would feel touchy, while if I gave my preference for judicial service they might consider me a spineless fellow. I answered, 'I think I can do equally well in either place.' One of the Sahebs thought I was bragging and in the coldest conceivable tone muttered with what seemed like almost withering contempt: 'It means you will do well in neither.' This put me on my mettle and I retorted, 'Sir, some men have more strong points than one.' The others burst into laughter with the exception of the gentleman who had rattled me and who now looked rather small. I was then asked whether I had been to England. I truthfully answered in the negative. One of the examiners said, 'We don't believe you.' To be thus disbelieved and to be accused of telling a lie was one of the most flattering experiences of my life.[29]

Firaq on Firaq can be counted upon to be endlessly garrulous, in a vein of confessional cockiness. After he was selected for the Civil Services (whether mainstream ICS or its provincial arm, it is uncertain—another point he preferred to evade and artfully obfuscate), he went on to do something unexpected, yet characteristic of him. He cleared his father's debts by selling off his ancestral land, resigned from his job (but had he joined at all?) and plunged into the national movement. He was arrested on 6 December 1920, kept in Malaccca Jail and then sentenced to a year and a half's confinement and a fine of ₹100. Subsequently he was removed to Agra Jail and then to Lucknow Jail.

About this interlude Firaq writes:

> I was not destined to be an I.C.S. officer, even though I had been selected. I joined, instead, Mahatma Gandhi's Freedom Movement and instead of sending others to jail, I was myself sent to jail, though in the best company. My interview with the District Magistrate at my trial is memorable at least for me. I was asked what I had to say in my defence. I answered that my offence (boycotting the Prince of Wales's visit) was being committed at that very hour by millions of demonstrators who were too many to be arrested or tried. This made the British Magistrate feel at a loss but he gave me 18 months all the same.[30]

On his release he spent some time in Gorakhpur, following the death (from tuberculosis) of his younger brother. It was then that an old acquaintance came to stay with him—Jawaharlal Nehru, who guessed his unusual host's financial straits and, as was his habit for persons he liked or respected, offered him employment. (For ₹250 a month he made Raghupati Sahai the inter-secretary of the All India Congress Committee.) The offer was accepted; Firaq Sahib moved to Allahabad and plunged into his new duties with might and main. He came to be closely associated with the Nehru family—visiting Anand Bhavan daily, meeting national leaders and impressing upon them the impact of his extraordinary personality. This phase lasted between 1923 and 1928. Firaq Sahib, keenly involved in the national movement, found himself torn between respect for Gandhi's personality and the disapproval of his ideas.

In 1930 he was appointed lecturer in the Allahabad University's English department and continued thus till his retirement in 1958. His was a dramatic and turbulent presence, magnetic in its idiosyncrasies, argumentative, insightful, provocative and hilarious in turns, described by Harivansh Rai Bachchan as the most colourful person in the English department.[31] Admirers swore by his brilliance though critics disagreed and this debate on his stature continues till the present day. (One of Firaq Sahib's many claims was that he had been asked by Vice Chancellor Ganganatha Jha to drop a year in his examination, so as to allow Amaranatha, Firaq's batchmate and rival, to top. Which, by his accounts, he did.)

A career as a university teacher was in reality just for livelihood, not for life, which belonged to Urdu poetry, as Harivansh Rai Bachchan perceptively recounts, yet Firaq was a man of extensive reading and an active mental life, although all these qualities coexisted with a certain quixotic perversity. For all his eccentricities Firaq was deeply engaged with questions of literature, language and contemporary issues and was passionate in thrashing out these subjects in the staffroom, demolishing dissenters and bulldozing over all contrarian viewpoints. He was easily the most talkative presence in the department and he commanded a wide range of theatrics, from rational persuasion to volatile hyper-pitch, acerbic humour or hard-hitting verbal assault. He accompanied these with a plentiful repertoire of facial expressions that might have done credit to an accomplished actor. One might agree with him or one might not, as Bachchan states, but ignoring him was impossible. Getting away was even harder, for Firaq hung around in the staffroom, holding forth so long as a single member of the staff remained to be talked at.

It was equally entertaining to witness Firaq Sahib baiting his colleagues, so long as one was not personally a victim of his barbs! His famous joke on the Anglo-Saxon-looking Bhagwat Dayal who pronounced his name 'B. Dial' and who, in Bachchanji's mischievous words 'mimicked the English better than any other Indian'[32] has found its way into several chronicles. Firaq's leg-pulling became a classic oral legacy of the English department:

'Mr. Dayal, I'm beginning to understand your English again. I think it's time you made another trip to England.' Mr Dayal took the joke with true-blue English sportsmanship and continued speaking his upper-crust Oxbridge even when 'half of the English that emerged from his cigar or pipe-clamping lips was completely beyond us.'[33] Parenthetically, it may be mentioned that such was the impact of the Anglophone Bhagwat Dayal on the students that an awestruck and baffled rustic, on hearing him cough into his immaculate white handkerchief, was heard to remark in his Eastern UP dialect: '*Eee toh angreji mein khokhat hain!* (He even coughs in English)'

When news of a public figure's death arrived, Firaq Sahib rolled his eyes reverently and said with mock-resignation: 'He is an angrez, he can do exactly as he pleases.' When someone in the Coffee House remarked that Prof. G.R. Sharma had overnight turned into an international scholar of archaeology, armed only with a shovel and a basket, Firaq Sahib instantly retorted: 'A basket costs a rupee and a shovel costs three rupees. I shall provide the money. You go and turn yourself into an international figure as well.'[34]

My favourite Firaq tale is the dog anecdote, though it may well be a tall story. A friend of Firaq Sahib's, Anand Narain Mulla, visiting him at his house in 8/4 Bank Road one afternoon, noticed a stray dog asleep on the old sofa. Firaq Sahib admonished the dog in courtly diction: '*Ghar mein mehmaan aye hain aur aap so rahe hain! Jaieeye, andar jaake let jaieeye.*' Which roughly translated, in word and mood, would be: 'A guest has come to the house and look at you, sunk in slothful slumber. Take yourself inside and lie down there.' The guest, impressed by Firaq Sahib's chaste reprimand to the dog, exclaimed: 'You address a dog as "aap", Firaq Sahib?' To which Firaq Sahib woefully lamented: 'What to do, mian? If I address him as "tum", this beast starts barking, and if I should dare to call him "tu" he'll surely bite me.'

Firaq Sahib's witticisms were often language-centric and aimed at Hindi writers and their writings, though he did not spare Englishmen either. His muse of creative invention seems to have been hyperactive at all hours. The irrepressibly hilarious anecdotes he spun out, and claimed as true, were too numerous to have consistently occurred in the life of one man. The answer he gave to his English examiners at his viva at the school-leaving certificate examination in 1913 is Brand Firaq at his creative-autobiographical best: 'There were two examiners, both Englishmen. One of them asked me, "Who wrote Scott's Emulsion?" For a moment I was taken aback. I recovered quickly and answered, "Our family doctor did—in one of his prescriptions." The Sahebs went into peals of laughter at thus being caught at their own game.'[35] There is reason to suppose that this was not an original quip, as it has been attributed to another person, but Firaq might have appropriated it.

When Firaq Sahib sat on the other side of the table at vivas and sizarship[36] interviews, the results were just as witty. At a sizarship-selection interview to choose poor students for financial aid, a candidate was 'asked what the expenses of his family were. The earnest student is said to have replied: "My father has to support six adults and six adulteresses."'[37]

There's no point wondering why such jewels of comedy were cast before Firaq alone. It's obvious they were of his own making, like the supposed answer given by a student at a general knowledge viva, on being asked what he knew about Sarojini Naidu: 'Sir, she is U.P.'s governess.'[38] When he got a chance to take a snipe at Sumitranandan Pant, or indeed any Hindi poet, how could Firaq Sahib let it go? His related joke—'An M.A. student of Hindi, asked at a viva to say something about the poetry of Shri Sumitranandan Pant, born in 1900, said in an ecstasy of criticism and knowledge of literary history: "When Keats read the poems of Shri Pant, the former bowed down his head in shame."[39] Whatever was Firaq Sahib doing at an MA Final Hindi viva? One doesn't ask such banal questions.

His impromptu micro-recitals were a riot and his overawed audience laughed while he probably sat savouring the public response with a diabolical roll of his eyes. The mischief of it clearly exceeds the probability. His cracks and quips are irresistible and bear repeating for their sharp impishness—and there is a treasure house of them for the Firaq-story collector. A student, purportedly asked to explain the meaning of Robert Browning's line 'God's in his heaven, all's right with the world', answered with great earnestness: 'You see, sir, Browning heartily disliked God. So he said that as long as the gentleman remained quarantined in Heaven and did not interfere in the affairs of the world through Christianity and other religions, the world was safe!'[40] In actuality, no student would have had the gumption to say that to Firaq!

Firaq did not exclude Urdu verse either from his raucous caricatures.

> Listen to this super-nonsense. One of the famous Indian poet(s) Ghalib's couplets done into English read: 'Wonder of wonders, the loved one has come to my house, I look incredulously, now at the loved one, now at my house.' A young boy, when asked to explain this couplet, gave the bright answer that the lover was taking all this precaution so that the loved one might not pilfer something from the house. 'Woh aye hamare ghar pe khuda ki kudrat hai, Hum kabhi unhein dekhein, kabhi apne ghar ko' has found a new interpretation, hair-raising enough to make Ghalib turn in his grave, thanks to Firaq Sahib's rakish humour![41]

The merriest one has to do with the politics of his younger days:

> During the non-cooperation movement Sir Harcourt Butler, who was Governor of U.P., wanted to send an urgent message on the phone. The ensuing conversation between the Governor and the telephone operator, in Firaq's version, goes like this: 'Sir Harcourt: "Are you a non-cooperator?" Voice on the phone: "Sir, I am neither a co-operator nor a non-cooperator. I am simply an operator."'[42]

The great fractious brain that generated all that coruscating wit, dictated notes extempore, where others only read or repeated their reading, could—and did—occasionally draw a blank in the all-important business of finding that just-right word. I never personally knew Firaq Gorakhpuri but the descriptions of others have fixed him in the literary memory of my generation. We can easily visualize him pacing the floor with leonine stride, his brow furrowed under the pressure of tortuous thought, seeking those elusive, right-ringing words to sum up Robert Stevenson to his class. Until suddenly the light of truth in the utterness of its simplicity shone in his bulbous eye and he pronounced with immense, cataclysmic relief: 'Stevenson WAS AN ESSAYIST.' From the back row resounded the voice of the most mischievous lad in the class: *'Huzoor, kalam tod diya!'*

Firaq Sahib's bohemian life has come in for much storytelling, as has his off-beat appearance: hair dishevelled, a cigarette in one hand, a stick in the other, an unbuttoned shervani, loose pajamas with long, dangling drawstring, smouldering eyes and wild looks. He was fond of country liquor that he poured out of a spouted vessel. His sexual preference would not have evoked as much comment in our century as it did in his time, giving rise to a whole set of sleazy anecdotes exchanged with knowing whispers and titters, by people torn between awe and scandalized horror. Firaq Sahib was utterly open about his life, and entirely democratic in his choices; he could stop the man come to deliver the gas cylinder with the disarmingly candid proposition: '*Tum mujhse muhobbat karoge?*' (Will you love me?)[43]

Paradoxically, there was a current of aggrieved dissatisfaction, loss and loneliness, which were both real and a classic stance. Regarding Firaq Sahib's public posturing of this tragic aspect, it is easy to assign some responsibility to his quixotic nature, his own accounts being both self-valourizing and creatively memorable. After a noisy evening at the Coffee House, holding forth on a range of subjects, from existential angst to the prissiness of Hindi poetry—his audience speechless—Firaq Sahib went home to a solitary bohemian night. Hiring a rickshaw, he would pick up a clutch of loaves, something to eat from a roadside eatery in Katra that sold mutton and roti, his supply of country liquor, and revert to that plane of which one of his best known verses sings: '*Koi charagh jalao, kuchch raat kate*' (Light a lamp, someone, that some of this night may pass).

He was not indifferent to public opinion, as it would seem. His craving for social approval while constantly debunking it is another of his quixotic ambiguities of character. He would often get fed up with visitors, and once moved to the PCB Hostel, intending to take up permanent residence there. He propagated a woeful story that ever since he became a leading Urdu poet and was given the title of 'Shair-e-Azam' local Muslim poets, aflame with jealousy, had embarked upon a character-assassination campaign. He even bought a car once, driven by one R. Mukherji, a close friend and daily visitor, who worked in the editorial department of the *Amrita Bazaar Patrika*. Rather than withdraw money from a bank, he would send a cheque to the house of a neighbour and publisher, Ram Narayan Lal Agarwal, and collect cash directly from him.

There was no assumed romantic posture—Firaq Sahib was queer in many inexplicable ways, and subject to fits of ungovernable fury. Impetuously giving away his woollen clothes and food to a beggar woman on a railway platform, he could also actually beat up servants, and then melt in tears of penitence, begging their forgiveness with folded hands. According to local oral history, he even gave electric shocks to an old servant for a badly cooked meal when the Vietnam War had put Firaq Sahib in a state of excruciating agony, and badly in need of the consolation of good food! To all his callers Firaq Sahib made the same request—please arrange a servant for me. For whatever his prowess as an original thinker and man of letters, Firaq Sahib was singularly unfortunate in his retention of servants. He was even said to have resorted to bringing servants from the employment exchange. Of them all only one, named Panna, stayed on till the end.

There is an entertaining local story that much after Firaq Sahib's death, a film company decided to make a movie on his life and started shooting in the Senate Hall campus. Predictably the Students' Union objected, declaring that the film company should have first sought permission from them. In particular the president of the union, a particularly loutish individual (who had even once hijacked the vice chancellor's car), demanded that he be given a role in the film. The movie's director told him, most intelligently: 'All roles have been cast, there's only one left. You can have that one if you like.' 'Which role is that?' the neta wanted to know. 'It's the role of Panna, Firaq Sahib's servant,' the director told him. 'So what will I be expected to do?' the neta enquired cautiously. 'Nothing much,' answered the savvy director. 'You just have to submit to lots of beatings and abuses.' Not even the lure of the silver screen could then induce the student neta to accept.

In his personal life, as witnessed by close neighbours, Firaq

Sahib comes across as highly repellent in some respects. He would sit in his lawn, chain-smoking and drinking, with his dhoti pulled up, making a gratuitous display of his private parts and embarrassing the little girls who lived in the next bungalow, their lawn separated by a knee-high hedge. He had the habit of urinating in the garden, anywhere he pleased, with scant regard for the presence of others. Firaq Sahib seldom bathed and expounded personal theories about the body's natural oils which helped him to, in his words, 'smell like a baby', theories which would have put a dermatologist to flight! He was also given to teasing and provoking his neighbour, the historian Ishwari Prasad, who bore his barbs with quiet fortitude. But he had his ardent defenders who felt that his contribution to Urdu literature far outweighed these immaterial idiosyncrasies and placed him outside the pale of conventional rules.

It cannot be refuted that Firaq Gorakhpuri is credited with having created a special identity for himself. 'Poet, critic, fiction writer, translator, conversationalist, [he] is widely regarded as one of the greatest Urdu men of letters. It is generally held that he revolutionalised the Urdu ghazal, added new dimensions to the rubai and wrote perhaps the best creative criticism in Urdu.'[44] His short stories frequently appeared in the 1940s magazine *Karavan*, edited by Syed Aijaz Husain, the Progressive critic and head of the Urdu department of Allahabad University. Firaq Sahib retired in 1958 as lecturer in the Department of English, his words and ways striking terror in the hearts of his more conventional upwardly mobile colleagues who had progressed to becoming reader or professor. In 1961 he was given the Sahitya Akademi Award for his book *Gul-e-nagma*, and he was professor emeritus till 1962. In 1967 he was awarded the Padma Bhushan, in 1968 the Soviet Land Nehru Award and in 1970 the Gyanpeeth Award.

Yet, despite these honours, his waning years were far from financially comfortable. His various moneymaking schemes would be ridiculous and amusing, were they not so unfortunate. Firaq Sahib tried his hand at running a grocery store, co-owning a publishing house, keeping hens in an experimental domestic poultry farm and is even said to have had plans for starting a pig-keeping business! This final element in his fable only serves to do what his entire personality so effectively did all his life—leave his audience at a loss for words.

A tragi-comic, rarely told story comes from an old student of his who was regularly asked by Firaq Sahib to write news reports to say that the great poet Firaq was terminally ill and dying, and to drop them in at the United News of India (UNI) office, to be carried by newspapers in Bihar, particularly in one named *Searchlight*. This mysterious ruse was aimed at Firaq Sahib's Bihari sons-in-law who subscribed to the paper and who might, he hoped, on reading this item of news, send some money for their (perfectly healthy) father-in-law. For Firaq Sahib did actually have two daughters, married into the same family in Bihar. Firaq as a family man is a lesser-known chapter. The lonely wildly bohemian image is more in keeping with the perverse-genius persona he wore.

Firaq Gorakhpuri died on 3 March 1982, in Delhi.[45] A moment worthy both of poetry and of history was struck when the ninety-four-year-old historian Ishwari Prasad, slowly hobbling down with the support of his stick, stood thoughtfully with impassive face, watching his poet-neighbour's finally silent body being laid out in readiness before his funeral procession.

It is customary to speak of Firaq Sahib and Harivansh Rai Bachchan in the same breath when speaking of the personalities of the English department. But other than their coincidental presence on the staff and the fact that they wrote in the Indian languages, there is little to place the two men in the same bracket. A journey through Bachchan's autobiography acquaints us with a highly emotional being, quite a stubborn dissenter in matters of religion and social custom, extremely laborious and persistent. Born in 1907, his life—before settling down to the relatively stable profession of the university teacher—was an emotional whirlwind of deep and soul-disturbing relationships, intense friendships and responsibilities. He also experienced considerable economic hardship, relieved by the satisfaction of producing a steady stream of successful volumes of verse, which won him a large and admiring audience.

It is not generally known that Bachchan's books of poetry were, for many years, self-published at a small family-owned publishing house named Sushma Nikunj. His father, who had retired as head clerk of the Pioneer Press, ran it, and was helped by his brother and nephew in matters of accounting, distribution and marketing. Ten rubais had been published in *Saraswati* and Bachchan's recitations in tarannum created a ready and willing market for the volumes of verse that Sushma Nikunj churned out: the celebrated *Madhushala, Madhubala, Madhu-kalash, Ekant Geet* and *Nisha Nimantran*. The proceeds from sales were scarcely enough to support a family; in fact, serious debts were incurred to cover paper and printing costs.

It also comes as a surprise that Bachchan was really very young when he wrote his 'bestseller', living a difficult life trying to make ends meet by tutoring students, a practice ever-so-common among indigent university pupils then. It is also a touching fact that he served in various capacities in a number of low-paid jobs—at the Abhyudaya Press, the Pioneer Press and as Hindi teacher at the Prayag Mahila Vidyapeeth. He even did a teachers' training course at the training wing of Government Inter College (later called Central Pedagogical Institute), before picking up on his studies again. It speaks much for his perseverance that these were years of great privation, the chronic illness and death of his first wife, Shyama—his first and most admiring reader who would 'break into a dance'[46] whenever a new book of verse appeared—and some concurrent and equally harrowing emotional experiences.

The reasons for *Madhushala*'s great popularity have been analysed by H.S. Saxena:

> In any kavi sammelan, Bachchanji used to attract large crowds and the audience was restless until (he) recited some stanzas from *Madhushala*. There are about 135 stanzas (rubais) in *Madhushala* and the poet has used the wine symbol as Sufis have used it. He makes fun of the Pundit and the Maulvi, both, and prefers the alehouse to both mandir and masjid: '*Larwate hain mandir, masjid, Mel karati madhushala.*' (The alehouse unites people while the temple and mosque cause dissension).[47]

Wine is also a symbol of the richness and intensity of life, and provides an escape from the worries and frustrations of everyday life. It symbolizes the poet's longing for beauty. Some stanzas reflect the mood of the '30s and refer to the problems of untouchability, Hindu-Muslim unity and the freedom struggle. These stanzas were very popular because of their topical references. Bachchan, who did not drink at all, was descended from a family in which there was an inherited stricture that anyone who touched a drop would fall victim to a family curse and would contract leprosy. His vexing encounters with prospective employers were diverting though they couldn't have been amusing for him. Questions like: 'Have you given up drinking now?' etc. were frequent. The alehouse symbol, which brought in audiences avid for more, certainly proved to be a professional obstruction when he went looking for jobs in various schools and colleges. Whoever wanted a winebibber as a teacher?—was the insinuation he had to constantly repudiate.

His connection with the Allahabad University dates from July 1927, when he joined as a BA student. For one of his struggling social class, even the decision to join a BA course was a big deal. A job, however poorly paid, was much to be preferred. His wife Shyama, away nursing her tuberculosis-stricken mother (she was to catch the disease herself, and die of it after a long illness) sent him a hundred-rupee note to pay for his initial course fees, books and other expenses. Bachchan's first impressions of Muir College are interesting.[48]

Bachchan's subjects were English literature, Hindi literature and philosophy, and his memories of those undergraduate years contain amusing pen-portraits of teachers in all three departments. Such as Mr Dustoor of the English department, 'a thin man of small stature, always very properly and immaculately turned out, suited and booted,'[49] who took a close, personal interest in Bachchan's progress, lending him books from his own very considerable library. Dr Dhirendra Verma, founder-head of the Hindi department, 'in his tight-collared coat and narrow trousers, the tall Vermaji was a perfect geometrical perpendicular … we boys called him Bhindi—"Beanpole".'[50] And the illustrious A.C. Mukherjee, teacher of metaphysics, who

> […] would launch into a seamlessly fluent delivery which would go right above our heads… Nobody dared stand up and ask anything, and when from time to time he himself asked a question, nobody could answer it… Flustered, he would ask, 'What class is this?' 'Sir, B.A. first year.' 'My God, I thought it was M.A. final!' exclaimed the philosopher before presumably rushing out of one class and into another![51]

The undergraduate years were purposive and even enjoyable, Bachchan financing his studies by taking up several tuitions, sleeping just four hours a night and acquiring the habit of reading as he walked the four kilometres to and from University and home. Having scored a first division in his BA, the run-of-the-mill option would have been to appear in the Civil Services examinations. But his family had strong nationalist leanings, and his father suggested that he take up an MA degree and opt for teaching in a college or university. He accordingly enrolled for an MA in English, and even sat for the MA (Previous) examinations, but did not go back to the University thereafter.

Gandhi's salt-satyagraha and the popularization of homespun khadi took up his time. He recounts how, along with a couple of friends, he turned himself into a wandering salesman, one of them carrying a massive bolt of khadi, another managing the accounts and himself measuring it out for customers—an enterprise that earned them the appreciation of Jawaharlal Nehru when he learnt of it.

Those were interesting and impassioned times. Bachchan's photographs show him sporting a fulsome head of lavish locks, in imitation of Sumitranandan Pant, by his own admission, though many people had stopped cutting their hair, having vowed to do so only when Independence was attained!

This was also the time when he wandered from job to job, nursed his ailing wife through a terminal illness, supported certain thankless friends in whom he reposed great faith and lost the battle to save his wife's life. He then reverted to being a lost soul, sustained by poetry and the positive ego-force generated by the continuity of literary creation and the satisfaction of finding kindred souls who responded to his work. A renewed acquaintance with Amaranatha Jha, who—'had been angry when I left university, but my poetry had won me back his favour,'[52]—

motivated him to return to his unfinished MA course after a gap of seven years. He passed his MA in the second division.

Sometime later, after time spent in hectic production and equally hectic performance across the length and breadth of undivided North India, he received an offer to fill a temporary vacancy in the Department of English at Allahabad University at a salary of ₹125 a month.[53] Amaranatha Jha's acerbic advice to Bachchan was that, although he had carved an identity as a popular student cult figure, he should conduct himself as an English teacher now, and keep the Hindi poet's persona in abeyance. Bachchan took this advice very seriously and honoured it throughout his teaching days.

Hair reasonably trimmed (though still a trifle flamboyant), bespectacled, suited and booted, he morphed into a different being. When the duration of the temporary post expired, Amaranatha Jha managed a research scholarship for Bachchan under his own supervision, and Bachchan's association with the poetry of W.B. Yeats began. Jha Sahib's patronage finds its most cited example in the anecdote of the sapphire that he gifted to Bachchan and which is supposed to have transformed the latter's fortunes. Bachchan's permanent appointment in the English department in 1941 was also through Jha Sahib's active interest, at the cost of much whispering and jibing. The pucca-Brit English department regarded a Hindi poet on its staff as an oddity and somewhat beneath its cultural standards. Bachchan's marriage to Teji, or Miss Suri, as she is primly called in his early references to her, followed in 1942, the reception held in the Senate Hall's front lawns.[54]

As a teacher Bachchanji was, in H.S. Saxena's words,

> [...] a strict disciplinarian and his students were a little afraid of him. He did not allow any latecomer to enter his classroom and resented it if anyone addressed him

by his pen name 'Bachchan'. He was Mr. H. Rai in the university campus. He was quiet in the staff-room and was a complete contrast to Firaq Sahib who was very vocal, carelessly dressed and looked every inch a poet. Bachchanji was known as a very hard-working and efficient teacher who never referred to his own poems in the class. He delivered his lectures in Room number 4 which had…some elegant, built-in almirahs with glass panes. Bachchanji collected two rupees each from his students at the beginning of each session and purchased relevant books for them. In this way he built up an enviable library. At the end of the class he issued books to his students and took only five minutes to do so. These books have gone to the Post-graduate English Library.[55]

Bachchan spent two years, between 1952 and 1954, working on a PhD on Yeats in Cambridge. The story of his study grant—refused by every authority, even Maulana Azad, but eventually granted by Nehru—confirms the image we carry about him as a man of enormous tenacity. Unfortunately, the Cambridge chapter created more enemies in Allahabad University than friends, generating great bitterness for him, a bitterness that the subsequent decades did nothing to erase or temper. Our university departments are no strangers to professional jealousy, factionalism and backstairs manoeuvrings that prioritize considerations other than merit. If Bachchan found himself at the receiving end, it is scarcely to be wondered at. What is to be wondered at is that his distaste for Allahabad University reached such a pitch that he resigned in 1955. He joined the Allahabad office of the All India Radio as a Hindi producer on a one-year contract, and subsequently he worked with the Ministry of External Affairs.

The University's rhythm, so well described by Bachchan in his autobiography: 'Student elections… posters… slogans, and finally the Dashera holidays... the campus would be deserted and quiet once more, disturbed on the quarter-hour by the clock in the university tower, ding-dong, ding-dong, dong...dong...dong'[56] was something that Bachchan was never to return to and if he looked back, it was with great anger. In particular, his ire was directed at S.C. Deb, and his autobiography contains information that, if authentic, certainly surprises the reader. 'The irony was that at precisely the time when I had become more fully competent in academia, fate was throwing me far from this area where I belonged,'[57] he was to write. 'I forget the exact date when I began work at the radio station, but I well remember that on that first day I found myself driving inadvertently towards the university; I was to repeat the mistake many times, as though my subconscious were reluctant to accept the decision I had made.'[58]

It must have been a time of great injury and inner turmoil for him; bitterness boils in his voice as he writes. But if anyone was the poorer for it, it was the university: 'The university which made me and broke me...but whose disdain I now ignore.'[59] His own fate continued to be an extraordinary one. After serving as a Rajya Sabha member for six years, the last chapter of his life was spent in Mumbai, living on the summit of worldly achievement and enjoying the phenomenal stardom of his actor son, Amitabh Bachchan. The university clock stopped chiming much before Harivansh Rai Bachchan's did—a karmic loss for the institution, one might be tempted to say.

Perhaps this is the place to introspect on an intriguing feature of university history—the number of stalwarts who left in anger: Meghnad Saha, P.E. Dustoor, Harivansh Rai Bachchan and many more in our own time. It may be fitting to quote Yeats with a local tweak to his lines, especially as we're discussing Bachchan. The university all too often made the best lose all conviction, and allowed the worst to promote themselves and their ilk with passionate intensity, becoming one cause, among others, for its qualitative disintegration. Bachchan's example kindles anger in those who have undergone similar discrimination, long after his association with the Allahabad University ended.

It is perhaps well that I personally knew none of these larger-than-life campus icons. The hesitations and inhibitions of the reverential disciple do not come into play, nor does the obligatory commitment to panegyric that creeps into many portrayals of public figures. It is as a real person that I acquaint myself with the voluble Satish Chandra Deb, distinguished as much by the scale of his corpulent physique as by the volume of his unstoppable utterance. Our very own Dr Samuel Johnson—if a Brit-Lit precedent is sought—in keeping with the character of the department; the man who held forth for half an hour to convey that he just could not spare five minutes for you! Among the stories my generation of teachers grew up hearing, this was one of the first scraps of campus lore. Like Firaq's, Deb's personality seemed to generate anecdotage. There was such a quirky skein of oddity and comedy running through the formidable gravitas of his high learning that it makes for an engaging and amusing composition.

Born on 10 September 1899, Prof. Deb's ancestry went back to the house of Chitpur in Bengal, although the connection seems to be a tenuous one. His forefathers had moved to Fatehgarh, contiguous to Farrukhabad[60], by some accounts, following political dissent with the government. Since his father, Girish Chandra Deb, was a teacher at government high schools and transferred from city to city across the United Provinces, Deb Sahib's early education was received in various places. In 1921 he completed his MA from Allahabad University while an inmate of Holland Hall Hostel, and caught the eye of S.G. Dunn, who regarded him as a promising pupil.

Immediately afterwards, he cleared the Provincial Educational Service examination and for a while taught English at the Government School, Almora. The outbreak of the non-cooperation movement prompted him to put in his papers, since resignation from government service was one of the calls of the movement. His British principal, J.C. Powell-Pryce, however, gave him a glowing testimonial and advised him to meet Prof. S.G. Dunn in Allahabad. In 1922 he was appointed lecturer in the Department of English, Allahabad University, and was to serve till 1959, occupying the head's chair for sixteen years, following S.G. Dunn, Amaranatha Jha and Shiva Adhar Pande. He also acted as proctor, an exceptionally mild and lenient one.

It is his comprehensive range and depth of learning that is best remembered as a university legend, although his interesting appearance and mannerisms were no less striking. 'Encyclopaedic' is a word too often used in our provincial universities. It was, and still is, used to describe Prof. Deb, although there was a tongue-in-cheek aberration of the word coined by the witty P.E. Dustoor, who referred to him as an 'encyclopedestrian'. Dustoor Sahib had reasons to dislike Prof. Deb, as did Bachchan (or, as he was called, Mr Rai), and no history of the university can afford to push these differences under the carpet—but more of that later. Despite the animus between them, it is Harivansh Rai Bachchan's description of S.C. Deb that most vividly establishes his appearance in the mind's eye, and if we can surgically detach ourselves from the personal element of disaffection, it is a brilliant one. We can just see Deb climbing into his tonga 'whose front would tip up as he sat heavily on the back seat'. A man of medium height and dark complexion, a massive head atop a massive body and a flat, shapeless nose and short black hair shiny with oil, one hand gripping a cane, the other awkwardly balancing an unmanageable pile of books, and most individual of all, the moustaches stiff with pomade curving up 'into the erect shape of a scorpion's stings'. His dress was as just as typical—a high-collared coat with a red handkerchief tucked into one sleeve, the few buttons fixed over a Pickwickian trunk, and the exposed triangle of white shirt with a silver watch-chain fastened to one button. He usually taught standing, a downpour of words in torrential descent, emanating from his lips. He was given to emphasizing every fourth or fifth word and embellishing his discourse with lines of French altogether mystifying to the class. More remarkably, he would cite texts entirely sourced to author, publisher, date, edition, chapter, page and line, all emerging from his powerful memory. Bachchan compares him to a veritable Niagara Falls of vocal delivery.[61]

So far, so good. But even Bachchan's retrospective distaste and the mischief of his pen contributes to the sketch: 'I must attribute to my own shortcomings the fact that I could see little logical sequence in what he said: when speaking on a given subject, he would stray into two, three or four others, which had no apparent relevance to the first. He rarely used the word "I", referring to himself as "your humble servant".'[62] It was in keeping with this ceremony of elaborate humility that Deb Sahib, whenever he offered tea and biscuits to a visitor, apologized profusely, saying that in the home of a poor teacher what else could be served?[63] Many years later, in 1941, when Bachchan joined the English department as a lecturer, he writes: 'Deb Sahib was still the same in every respect, though the scorpion-sting moustaches were somewhat in decline.'[64] It was perhaps a little prank of fate that right from the beginning Bachchan was driven to write comic descriptions of S.C. Deb—even before the bad blood started—as the limerick he wrote while still a student, (quoted by H.S. Saxena), reveals:

> Professor Deb was the same in length and breadth
> And a man of encyclopaedic depth
> He was humble to a fault
> And humbler to a somersault
> He could talk of Hafiz, Honolulu and halwa in the same breath.[65]

But Bachchan is not the only one to leave us with images of S.C. Deb. There are a few others, more positive, sometimes even affectionate. Amar Singh, one of Deb Sahib's favourite pupils, has shared his memories of his dress and behaviour: the Parsee double-collared coat, the waistcoat, the black cap which he took off on entering a classroom and put on as soon as he left it, the two handkerchiefs he carried—one in his waistcoat pocket for his face and the other in his left sleeve to wipe the chalk-dust off his stubby fingers after writing on the blackboard.[66] Another account by Govind Mishra[67] fondly recalls the heavy preponderance of black in Deb Sahib's get-up. Dark-skinned, his thick moustache was black, his hair was black, his car was black, his stick was black and his clothes were usually of that colour too. Black is the colour of gravity, he was given to declaring, adding that it was impossible to be a scholar without gravity. As an illustration, he referred to the stately gravity on the face of Queen Empress Victoria, his ideal in many respects.

A sympathetic English commissioner enabled Prof. Deb to buy the building of the Weather Office, Hawa Ghar as it was locally known, and Deb Sahib moved to take up residence there. By now he had given up the tonga for a car, and Govind Mishra has amusingly described his manner of alighting from the car and ascending the steps to his room:

> Professor Deb had great, majestic authority. He was said to be suffering from high blood pressure. His manner of

descending from his car and climbing the three or four steps to his chamber was grand and dramatic—one hand on his stick, the other on his driver's shoulder, who placed a hand in his arm-pit and bodily lifted the side nearest him. Yet his physical ailment did not prevent him from lecturing continuously for three hours...[68]

Conversations with Prof. Deb were edifying, even if one listened for 95 per cent of the time and was allowed to speak for only the balance five. He carried a suitcase full of books in his car and read for nine or ten hours a day, seeming to know everything on everything, barring the pure sciences. Religion, philosophy, history, aesthetics, architecture, sculpture, painting, music, dance, archaeology, economics, political thought, sociology, law, psychology—all knowledge was his province. In the classroom he was comprehensive in quotation and familiar with every area of the course. He eagerly met the classes of absent or unavailable teachers; as an examiner he was extremely bountiful with marks.

The world was his classroom. H.S. Saxena writes of a train journey with Prof. Deb that turned into a lesson in culture studies. When the Saharanpur Passenger stopped at Phaphamau station, the attention of all the travellers (including about ten AU teachers bound for a meeting with Pundit Govind Ballabh Pant, chief minister, at Lucknow) was drawn to a crowd of 'scantily clad', ethnically bejewelled tribal women. They were 'tall and statuesque (whose) healthy skin shone like bronze in the light of the setting sun', and who were cooking their meal, and scouring their pots and pans on the platform, 'laughing with wild excitement'.[69] The sight was enough to invite the gaze of some of the younger men (not AU teachers, one gathers!) who got off the train to ogle them.

For the decorous AU teachers, bashful and blushing (one infers) from the 'impropriety' of the sight beheld in the puritanical presence of the censorious S.C. Deb, the awkwardness of this direct encounter with the earthier attractions of life was smoothly salvaged by the professor.

> [He] started a very learned and interesting discourse on the costume and jewellery worn by Indian women through the ages. We were spellbound. The train had started moving. A ticket checker had also entered the compartment at some wayside station and was quietly listening to the Professor. The train was rushing towards Rae Bareli but we felt that we were travelling from the Vedic age to modern times. When the train stopped at Rae Bareli, Professor Deb was discussing the dress and jewellery worn by women in Ajanta frescoes.[70]

It is no mean feat to lure away the attention of the average man from what is flippantly referred to as eye candy by a learned discourse! If Prof. Deb achieved it that day it only goes to confirm his reputation as a mobile encyclopaedia, and an irresistible one at that.

He had his detractors—who doesn't?—but there can be no question about the extent and genuineness of his scholarship. His wrath was equally voluble. Govind Mishra recalls a day when the students were on strike, going from room to room interrupting classes, shouting at and threatening those who wished to attend class—a very common occurrence in our times. It was Prof. Deb's habit to close the doors of his room and keep all the lights switched on. The windows were covered with chiks so no daylight penetrated into the room. In the reflected light of a table lamp Deb Sahib's bushy moustaches shone with greater brilliance as he produced his handkerchief, gave them a quick swipe, put the tips of his fingers together and launched into his lecture.

On that particular day, the agitating students gathered outside

Deb Sahib's room, hollering out slogans and challenging the students to come out. Deb Sahib sat, sphynx-like, in stolid silence, not reacting to the racket outside. The students in the class sat timid as mice. The crowd outside grew bolder. One intrepid soul climbed and let down the chiks on the two windows. Daylight flooded the room. Still Deb Sahib sat in dangerous stillness, expressionless. Drawing courage from his passivity, a couple of boys pushed open the door. They had barely set foot in the room when all hell broke loose. The professor rose, quivering, his massive bulk drew itself up and, stick in hand, he raced nimbly towards the intruders, roaring: 'How dare you… violate the sanctity of this room…this room of mine?' The intruders fled, not merely the two venturesome ones but the entire crowd, absolutely unstrung by the spectacle of a portly professor sprinting forward in fierce battle mode!⁷¹

On another occasion, when a group of agitating students lay down on the pathway to stop his car, Deb Sahib alighted, went up to them and sat down in their midst. On still another occasion he swore he would join a fasting student and go hungry too. Those strategies worked in the 1950s. They wouldn't now. A pervasive conception of moral authority enforced compliance. It no longer does. H.S. Saxena has recounted the most comic example of Deb Sahib's censorious contempt on finding striped underwear on the grounds of the university: 'Professor Deb had a sturdy walking stick and he was pushing a dirty, striped underwear with it. "Someone has bequeathed this to the university. Let us take this treasure out of the campus." He kept on pushing the offensive garment and left it outside the University gate.' Saxena, in an impish aside, remarks: 'Had he been alive today, he would have resented the use of the word "underwear" in this paragraph.'⁷² I do wonder which words would have been seemly enough in Professor Deb's fastidious vocabulary to describe a ragged, striped underwear: a 'tattered, striated, nether sous-accoutrement maybe'?

Deb Sahib's highest level of irritation was reserved for girl students who dressed in bright colours and sat on the front benches. He would spit brimstone and fire at them: 'If I had my way, I would chase them out of the university to the gates of hell and, if necessary, stone them too. They have nothing to do with studies.'[73] This great gender disapproval that prevailed among some of AU's most respected dons does indeed invite bemused analysis. How would I have reacted if Prof. Deb had turned to glare balefully at me, as he did at a girl in the 1950s, and proceeded to deliver the withering apostrophe: '…and you, young lady in the red bodice?' The use of the word 'bodice' is an outright hilarious example of punctilious Anglophone exactitude and authentic Victorian archaism; I would have been in splits. But in the 1950s the girls sat with bowed heads and very straight faces, submitting to his tirade. It must have been tough, keeping a straight face.

Not students alone but vice chancellors and chief ministers too felt the whiplash of his irascible disgust. Once, at a university event, the vice chancellor was holding forth on the eminence of an institution that had produced so many generations of civil servants. As Govind Mishra describes it in his account: 'Professor Deb pounced on the statement, declaring that a vice chancellor who applauded a university for being a civil-servant-producing factory ought to resign. He went on to expound on the meaning of the word 'university' and the inherent connotation of generating citizens of the world.'[74] When Mishra himself approached him with a request to guide his PhD project, the professor glowered at him through his thick lenses and said wryly: 'Young man, if you are also after those bloody services, I have no time for you.'[75]

Even Govind Ballabh Pant, when he spoke of a teacher's accountability in a country where the head of state could also be called to account, gave great umbrage to Prof. Deb. He protested, most wrathfully, that a teacher and an elected representative could never be compared, and that a teacher was accountable only to his own conscience and to no one else. We've moved on since then; if words like 'conscience' carried more conviction then than now (this alone is an open question), it certainly figured more prominently in public discourse.

Prof. Deb died on 20 December 1970. He wrote no books—just a few scattered essays—but is generally credited with having suggested corrections in the *Oxford Companion to English Literature*, which were acknowledged in the preface to its fourth edition. It is said that he had sent eighty typewritten pages of corrections, a fact that had impelled the editors to make special mention of him among the many others to whom they had excused themselves from mentioning because of their large number. It is even said that he was in the process of compiling another such list of corrections, but death interrupted his ambitious project. He left no other written testimonies of his learning, but the trail of stories he has left behind could fill 'a goodly volume'.

But, the play of personalities could turn edgy, and although unpleasantness was couched in a fine veneer of literary humour—at least in the legendary English department—the animosity showed up in novel ways. Dr P.E. Dustoor, highly dedicated, earnest and witty, did not lack an admiring coterie of his own. He was extremely active and S.C. Deb's superior in terms of actual qualifications. There are different versions of a popular story in which the vice chancellor, B.N. Jha, slid in, undetected, to the backbenches during Dr Dustoor's lecture class. (In some accounts it was S.C. Deb who came up stealthily and sat lurking at the rear of the class—a highly unlikely alternative, simply because Deb Sahib's massive bulk was incapable of doing any lurking anywhere.) Dr Dustoor is said to have spotted the guest and pronounced wryly: 'There is an intruder here. Please take admission before attending my classes' and walked out.

But the most memorable incident involves Dr Dustoor's formal speech when the University administration, struck by bureaucratic compunction, promoted him to the rank of assistant professor (as distinct from the present meaning of the term, and implying a professor of the second place). Although he was better qualified than S.C. Deb, the latter had more years of service, and so was made professor and head. The speech as quoted by Bachchanji:

> It is natural in this busy day and age that 'assistant professor' should be abbreviated to 'Ass. Professor', and if anybody should appear to be ridiculed by such a designation I would blame the English language and not the user of the expression. I am very grateful that the administration has considered me worthy of the title of 'ass professor', but should like to point out that the real 'ass professor' is Mr. S.C. Deb, for it is he who will do the donkey work of the department. He will be an ass professor in deed, and I will be an Ass. Professor indeed...[76]

But Dustoor Sahib, like Bachchan himself, did not accept the situation, and left Allahabad University as soon as he could.

At the beginning of this chapter I had expressed my regret that only a few personalities could be covered, although many more richly deserve to find a place in the history of the University. While writing a chapter on the Allahabad University for a volume on the city of Allahabad that I also edited, Prof. Manas Mukul Das had found his own way to create a large, inclusive fraternal ambience by citing no names at all. What emerged was the sense of an organic institutional personality in which every teacher formed a lively unit in the collective. It played out on the pages like a personality quiz, a refreshing take for old Allahabad University hands. 'An elderly person with a walking stick in one hand and smoking a pipe with the other,'[77] who, noticing a young undergraduate admiring a kachnar tree in bloom, takes him around the beautiful campus. He tells him about the different trees in it and the sound of the wind through different kinds of leaves at different times of the day. An English teacher, also a painter—who once faced a mob of slogan-shouting students who had set fire to a curtain—but who coolly removed his coat and beat down the flames with it. His paintings hang in the National Gallery of Modern Art. Now that's R.N. Deb, of course, who took me, a small girl of ten or eleven, around his house, patiently explaining his paintings to me.

Then there's the 'professor who haggled over the price of potatoes and saved every paisa he could, to gift it all away to science'.[78] A student counted sixty-three patches on his coat; that's N.R. Dhar for sure. There's another professor who 'every winter, would put a stack of blankets on the back seat of his car and drive around on bitterly cold nights, to wrap them round homeless beggars'. This one I could not place and had to phone the author. The answer was Julien Mitter. 'Three professors from the departments of English, Sanskrit and physics, dialoguing over their afternoon tea, identified the location of what later would become the excavation site of the millennia-old buried township of Kausambi.' That's got to be Khetresh Chattopadhyaya, Meghnad Saha and...who? Another phone call to be made. 'A professor of chemistry, after retirement, became a recluse, and worked day and night to complete eight books on occult wisdom.' Might that be Prof. Taimni, who donated liberally to buy and build the Allahabad building of the Theosophical Society? I'll have to phone again.

'An English professor, nearing eighty, travelled back all the way from England because a former servant needed help.' That was S.G. Dunn, I'm told. Here is oral history obfuscating and deleting the names though it hangs on to the tales. 'When a rushing undergraduate inadvertently bumped into the portly figure of a renowned professor at a bend, and began blushing and apologizing profusely, the don reassured him, "Not at all, Sir. It is entirely my pleasure, Sir. Do it again, Sir."' S.C. Deb absolutely.

> When another undergraduate, not quite sure where to use the article in English, asked a professor: 'Please, sir, what is time?' the professor, delighted with the profundity of the question, sat him down beside him, launched into a long soliloquy on time and space, and concluded by offering him tea, standing up to shake his hand, and saying, 'I am so glad, so very, very glad that the two of us could discuss such an abstruse topic for over two hours.'

That has to be S.C. Deb again. But the future can't make phone calls to the past to check out identities and I'm glad that Prof. Das's essay takes to citing certain names too:

> The story of the human presence in the University is a gestalt of many stories. It certainly would include the stories of her distinguished teachers who were great scientists like Megh Nad Saha, Nil Ratan Dhar and K.S. Krishnan; creative writers like Firaq, Bachchan, Dharamvir Bharati and Ram Kumar Verma; historians like Rushbrook Williams, Shafaat Ahmad Khan, R.P. Tripathi, and Tarachand; Indologists like Ganganatha Jha, Khetresh Chattopadhyaya and Govind Chand Pande; mathematicians like Homersham Cox, A.C. Banerjee and Gorakh Prasad; enclyclopaedic

minds like Thibaut, S.C. Deb and Beni Prasad; institution builders like Amaranatha Jha, Durganand Sinha and G.R. Sharma; and perhaps above all else, gentle, incorruptible, authentic, low-profile, caring human beings like Adityaram Bhattacharya, R.D. Ranade, P.S.V. Naidu, Julien Mitter, J.K. Mehta, I.K. Taimni, K.K. Mehrotra, R.N. Deb, A.B. Lal and Mohan Lal. The gestalt could not ignore the doings of distinguished alumni who became great scientists, writers, thinkers, teachers, scholars, judges, lawyers, politicians, administrators, journalists, and even the President, Prime Minister, or Chief Justice of India.[79]

I wish it were possible to put together all the anecdotes and pen portraits of the people who make up this larger gestalt. This book is an attempt to meet part of that challenge. My own student years in Allahabad University lasted from 1973 till 1977, and my teaching career as a permanent member of the English department started within a month of my MA results in September 1977. So I can create a personality quiz of my own for my peers. Many of the characters are still around; a few have passed on, and if I do not name them that shall only lend piquancy to the game.

There were my two philosophy teachers: the shaggy-haired philosopher with the rumbling voice of command, who plunged into his lecture with a sort of fierce frenzy, and who once put me down severely for daring to mention Bergson in a Buddhism lecture. My other philosophy teacher, with his playful manner of addressing complicated axiological issues, a whimsical smile hovering about his lips, as though he was much amused by what he taught. He once walked into the lecture class barefooted, having absent-mindedly removed his sandals in the staffroom, and noticing it well into his lecture only when puzzled over the front-row students staring at his feet. My two history teachers, so old in scholarship they seemed to us that we quite forgot to notice how young they actually were. There was always a floating population of young teachers who taught by day, and pegged away at their preparations for the Civil Services exam by night. They usually cleared the exam and left.

I remember the teacher who delicately rolled back the sleeve on his right arm before marking our attendance, as though he was about to do something unbearably messy. And another, whose eyebrows climbed higher and higher on his forehead as his voice rose in emphasis. My third and enduring subject was English literature, and the pretty lady teachers of the English department left a deep impression on my friends and me. So elegant were they, so well turned out, so pleasing and stylish in the classroom that they might have become the poster-girls of our adolescent imaginations, were they not so compellingly superior and aloof. And there was the grande dame of our department, stately and satiric, irresistibly witty in her speech and utterly damning in her omniscient stare. A stare that made it clear that none of our wiles and guiles could deceive her, that she knew how irremediably wicked we were, and would deal with us with the severity we deserved. But, when she taught Romantic poetry, her eyes closed in rapture and she seemed to float away on the wings of poesy, lost to the world of the women's college and the tittering, whispering girls before her.

There were others, kindly, popular and individual, whose quirky, humorous outlook on life enlivened and enriched the most ordinary of our experiences, teachers who became friends for life. One, who whispered his lectures in a confidential, counselling voice, which, amazingly, stayed perfectly audible even till the last row. I recall that once he was apparently carrying a small torch in his trouser pocket, and every time he established a point, his pocket involuntarily lit up, to the great glee of the students! There was our generation's own walking encyclopaedia, the utter simplicity of whose sitting room was complemented by the rich furnishings of his mind. He was the disciple of an earlier walking encyclopaedia, and he carried forward the legacy ably and abundantly, never forgetting his debt to his mentor, for his first action on entering the staffroom was to fold his hands in a namaskar before an empty mantelpiece. When I asked him why, he told me with disarming earnestness that the mantelpiece had once carried a portrait of S.C. Deb, his guru, and now though the portrait was no longer there, the place was symbolic and sacred to him, and so he saluted it every morning when he arrived.

A member of an affluent family of taluqdars, his artlessness in dress was his signature brand—sometimes a dhoti and kurta with a frayed collar, sometimes a very British-looking tweed coat and impeccable trousers. Much after he had retired from service, I would alight on him as I drove my old Fiat into the lane where his residence was located. I would stop and greet him, and he'd step into the car and tell me his stories. Parked alongside the quiet lane for over an hour, with each talk more fascinating than the last until I remembered the time and asked: 'But weren't you going to the bank, sir?' 'Tomorrow,' he'd reassure me. One of his jolliest adventures, narrated with wry, deadpan humour, tells about how he was once heading home from the university, sitting in a cycle rickshaw racing down the notorious slope close to where the Sage Bharadwaja ran his academy some time back. The gradient is such that rickshaws go down the incline at full tilt, and a sudden application of brakes can tip them over—which is what happened—and he found himself in the deep drain that runs alongside the road. The scholar rose, waist-deep in mire and—philosopher that he was—stood contemplating the situation existentially.

One of the incidental pleasures of the teaching life is that the world seems to be full of old students. Presently, two such students went past on a scooter and stopped short, appalled to see their old teacher standing thoughtfully in the gutter. They hurried up and helped him out. He thanked them profusely, blessed them graciously, but concealing from them the worrying thought in his mind that his precious chappals had been left behind in the drain. When the students left, he seriously contemplated going back into the drain. 'Consider it this way,' he explained the dilemma to me, 'if I were to descend into that gutter again and if perchance those lads were to come past again, whatever would they make of me? Their teacher, whom they gallantly assisted out of the drain, who thanked them most gracefully, why ever should he have descended into the drain again, and of his own volition?' It was this thought that made him give up the idea. But not all his stories were exercises in comedy. Most were erudite, and nuggets of a certain kind of knowledge, of which minds steeped in the realm of Humanities at a certain period of history, were rich repositories.

Then there was our department's Oxford representative, popular equally for the whiff of cosmopolitan language and information he brought into our shrinking, provincial horizons—as for the energetic choreography of his lectures. For he swirled around, paced about, froze upon a word, suddenly taking an athletic spring and landing atop the teacher's table, and then sitting there swinging his legs, delivering the clinching point. There was our resident poet, lanky and loose-jointed, who sped into the campus on his racing bicycle, and who made poetry a fashion statement with its counter-culture costumery. So struck were we by this descendent of Ginsberg and Pound that we recall nothing of what he taught in class! Such classes as the capricious muse spared him to teach.

To be 'counter-culture' was ideologically chic and bona fide avant-garde, and that involved being, on principle, a spirited enemy of the establishment—any and every establishment on earth. Some years before I joined the department, the story goes, the university was in the throes of student unrest, and lathi-charging policemen came chasing after hordes of rampaging boys tearing about the department corridors. Our poet, who might quite easily have been taken for a student himself, apparently well pleased with their vigorous defiance of the forces of state oppression, loudly cheered encouragement in local patois, to an animated stone-pelter who was hurling missiles at the Indian police. But the constable, mistaking him for a student, abandoned the stone-pelter and took to chasing the poet instead, who came galloping into the staffroom with the constable in hot pursuit. It gets murkier; for the lathi fell, not on the object of the chase, but on one of the department's senior teachers who ended up with a fractured wrist and a smashed wristwatch.

There is a wealth of creative in-house oral history and naughty lore, retold by successive generations of senior teachers to junior recruits, carrying on the humorous tradition. I remember the senior critic, very well-known, whose dhoti sat strangely with his puffing pipe—how one side of his tightly clamped mouth kept the pipe firmly in place while scathing words issued forth from the other. There was the Brahmanically purist don, very mindful of the contemptible pollutions of the Western world, considering it a vain pretender to civilization—but who desired the best quality paper for his PhD dissertation to be typed on and asked for guidance on this point. A wicked junior colleague advised him that the best paper for the purpose would indubitably be toilet paper. The rest of the story—that the stationer, on being requested for a few reams of toilet paper, explained to the don that it was available in rolls, not in reams—is plainly fictitious, but remains one of the evergreen stories of the campus.

Many stories have been generated and passed down the years among teachers and students. Who knows how many stories are being spontaneously generated now? They must surely be. It is in the nature of miniature societies to spin their own creative histories, and what is a university but a contingent miniature society to its students? I realized this when an old student sent me a card addressed 'To the lady who carried one umbrella and two bags'!

6

AUTUMN AFTERGLOW

If time could be spatially represented, then the 1960s and '70s might lend themselves to the impression of a gentle decline sloping away from the high eminence of the earlier decades. The gradient of descent is so gradual as to be barely discernable at first, then startlingly obvious, then dizzyingly steep, with the Emergency as a somewhat hairpin bend before the great plunge. Because, as unearthed details show, beneath the stability of this solid bastion of academic distinction, there were—even in the 1940s and '50s—seismic shifts that would, in course of time, implode and crack the edifice.

On the surface, the cumulative energy of the previous decades seemed to keep the institutional engines running. Even those who were not products of the so-called 'golden era'—students who passed out of the Allahabad University in the 1960s and '70s—continued to make it to positions of prestige in the bureaucracy, the bench and bar, politics, the media, the sciences and the world of letters. The names of some of our best-known administrators, jurists, journalists, writers and academics belong to this time, and their accounts recall the University as a place of animated intellectual life, focused, but not without its freshness, relaxing, but equally rewarding. The portraits of the time are peppered with names and nicknames, like a *Who's Who* of the 1960s, making up a large segment of today's educated elite of North India's senior citizenry; for the AU network was spread over a wide area of public life, as it still is.

My professional anchorage in the English department has given me a handy axis around which to locate this freewheeling slideshow of images that catch the pulse of academic life in the early 1960s. Also, my bias in assigning a certain (and maybe to some, questionable) centrality to the Department of English language and literature is more than circumstantial; it is viscerally connected with the very character of the University. This is because the imparting of the English language and its literature, to Indian minds, was part of its founding vision. As with most cases, the university's history has a master narrative, dominating several parallel counter-narratives that somewhat queer the pitch.

But first, the master narrative. The 1960s were still dyed-in-the-wool Brit, at least in the English department. In the earlier part of the decade, Prof. K.K. Mehrotra was the head of the department, a gentle, genial scholar, confined to his wheelchair, which was diligently manoeuvred by his white saree-clad English wife, Phyllis. Saeed Jaffrey, in his biography, *An Actor's Journey*, remembers Prof. 'Kelly' (short for Kewal Krishna or KK) Mehrotra as 'a gentle-voiced bespectacled gentleman with sharp features' whose Oxbridge intonation he reproduces with exact actorly mimicry: 'We seek him heah, we seek him theah, is he in heaven or is he in hell, that demmed elusive Pim-per-nel?'[1] One ardent Hindiphone student of his has recalled how, when Prof. Mehrotra spoke, '*Phool baraste the*', which, roughly translated, would mean 'a rain of flowers would descend'.

Multiple sclerosis had resulted in loss of mobility and severe disablement for twenty years but as his nephew Arvind Krishna Mehrotra records:

> During this period Aunt Phyllis (more devoted to her husband than [any] Indian woman) functioned as an extension of his limbs...she bathed, dressed, and fed Uncle Kelly, drove him to the university and pushed his wheelchair, chased away the mosquitoes that settled on his arm, and turned the pages of the book he was reading... It was Aunt Phyllis alone who got up two or three times each night, and seeing that he was lying in one stiff position, gently turned him on the other side.[2]

K.K. Mehrotra's graceful leadership lent a refined coherence of purpose to the corporate life of the department; a Camelot in which the king sat in his wheelchair and the knights demonstrated an ideal code of academic honour. Or so one would believe. The legendary academics Firaq, Deb and Dustoor had retired or left, yet there were scholars of powerful insight and eloquence like Y. Sahai, and mentors who combined an old-fashioned sensibility with a noble vision of teacherly nurturance, like R.N. Deb. Then there was a whole crop of handpicked third generation teachers who strove to teach as they had been taught, keeping alive both the culture as well as the elegant ambience of old AU's English department.

What distinguished the department was its relaxed colonial country club atmosphere. Unlike the others, there were no separate cabins or chambers for teachers. A large high-ceilinged staffroom with comfortable, low rattan-knit armchairs arranged around circular tables gave it a leisurely coffee house atmosphere. It was a place for what P.G. Wodehouse would have called 'feasts of reason and flows of soul'. The currency of conversational exchange in terms of wit, humour and intellectual dialogue in the department might have transported a visitor into the very interior of the Brit Lit that was taught. 'A penny for your thoughts, sir', a junior teacher might urge a senior professor, and when the senior

The English department

smiled mysteriously and said nothing, another teacher might butt in and say: 'All right then, two pennies.' (And talking of currency, did we actually think in the idiom of pennies for thoughts, pounds of flesh and brass farthings to rub in our pockets?)

'What is the colour of your mind?' a junior might tease a senior who'd exhibited a marked partiality for a particular colour most days of the term, and someone would pipe up: 'Pink.' When a senior teacher was gifted a box of cigars from the USSR, he went through the pantomime of sniffing at it and asking the giver: 'Are you sure I won't go up in smoke if I light one of these?' Clearly, vicarious Kiplingesque memories of the Great Game informed this sally. Or a famous punster might joke with a stammering girl student as she awaited her turn for a viva, clutching a slip of paper thrust into her hand by a boy bustling past: 'He gave you the slip. Why didn't you give him the slip?'

The laughter and leg-pulling, the shafts of wit, the jewels of occasional parley might have decorated the pages of a writer's notebook. The sparkle and zest were fostered by a combination of leisure and the literary life rendered by the department's singular identity as a preserve of colonial privilege, in a provincial university caught in its time warp, but creatively indulging and enjoying it nonetheless. Certainly, the memorabilia of teachers who were young recruits then, create a picture of a rare literary fellowship that the English department enabled.

> We sat in the Staff Room several hours every day and in between classes, joked, laughed, talked, argued, socialised, discussed activities of the English Association, the Postgraduate English Association, the Undergraduate English Association, the Friday Club, the Debating Rostrum, etc… Never a week passed without at least two or three functions in the form of lectures, readings from poetry and drama, play productions, symposia and group discussions, mock sessions of the U.N., debates, quiz contests, essay contests, Western classical orchestra or get-togethers over dinner, lunch or tea. And ever[y] so often, totally impromptu, a group of teachers who happened to be in the Staff Room together, would decide to have snacks from Netram or go off to see a film after class…[3]

Amazing how much teaching got done too! …and boring office chores assigned to teachers.

> Routine work also had to be attended to—enrollment, making the timetable, seminar allotments. But nobody got irritated over the time he had to give to such work. All such work was turned to more fun. While one or two would sit down to slog, five or six would sit around them to fool. After several hours at a stretch of work and tomfoolery, with the tomfools intermittently taking over from the sloggers, the senior-most present would send for kachauris from Netram and the workers and banterers would all join in the banquet with equal appetite.[4]

The big occasions were the Jafa Memorial Debate, the Seshadri Essay Contest, possibly a departmental production of a play in the Dramatic Hall and annual functions of the postgraduate and undergraduate English Associations. The last was organized on such a scale that it was popularly called the 'chhota convocation' in university circles. The vivid recollections of these ceremonies by retired teachers, recreate the fanfare and flourish with which they were held in the front lawns of the Senate Hall campus. About 1,200 students—the full strength of the English department—and invited guests, assembled for an iconic colonial garden tea party, with waiters in cummerbunds and starched white turbans, bustling around tables with three-tiered snack stands.

The catering had been Jagati's monopoly for years—he had serviced the University events since the time of Amaranatha Jha. About him there is an interesting anecdote too. After a particular event, very formal and dressy, Jagati went up to Jha and asked: 'Was it all right, sir?' Jha remained silent but his eyes travelled down Jagati's otherwise well-dressed form and came to rest on his inappropriate white canvas shoes! But Jagati's catering was approved, if not his sartorial lapse, because he continued with it till well into the 1960s, and the style of event I am describing was a generation removed from Amaranatha Jha's time.

There was a quiet civility and protocol about the proceedings. The chief guest, an eminent retired teacher or public figure like V.K. Krishna Menon or someone from the High Court such as Justice Broome or Justice B.D. Mukherjee, would address the gathering. Then the prize distribution would take place, accompanied by the jocular pleasantries of the compere, the cheering and clapping, as close to a hundred students received their prizes.

> The English department had an atmosphere of culture, gentility, brilliant conversation, wit, graciousness, cordiality

and affection binding together its teachers, students and non-teaching staff in its ceremonies of innocence. Students basking in the warmth of that human atmosphere engaged fearlessly in numerous activities. They brought out the Varsity Journal, The Critic and Prospice. (Later they were to found Campus Theatre and Campus Poetry, cyclostyled copies of which were widely circulated.) They wrote essays on the most academic to the most outlandish of topics. With great gusto they debated every week, not for prizes but for fun: 'This House believes in Ghosts.' 'Vice Chancellors should live underground'... 'All is cigarette ash and smoke,' 'We believe in not believing.'[5]

When someone located an inaccessible book for someone else's research 'it was cause for friends to get together and celebrate at the Gymkhana Club and Kwality'.[6] Teachers wrote articles and theses, not, as my senior colleague insists, 'because the UGC dangled carrots before our noses, but because academic work was enjoyable in itself'. They paid close attention and plenty of time to the essays and literary productions of students, some of which saw print in the English version of *The Allahabad University Magazine*, which the department oversaw for more than half a century.

Allowing for the descriptive license of a nostalgic and romanticizing memory, there is much in this idyll that was palpably experienced by me, as late as 1977, when I joined the department as a green-about-the-ears young teacher. And that was well into the Age of Rancour and Litigation, which overtook the University. The close intermesh of university and High Court that existed in the old days had reinvented itself in an unpleasant way by the time of the 'sober' '70s.

But a decade previous to that was globally known as the 'swinging' '60s, which, after a lag time of about five years, had percolated from the West into the consciousness of the Indian students, in the late 1960s and early '70s. The psychological sectioning-off of the English-medium student from the Hindi was never more evidenced than through this influence. The former mentally inhabited the cosmopolitan ambience of the '60s, the time of Rock and Roll and the Beatles, the counter-culture hippiedom, did drugs (but very cautiously), grew their hair, donned psychedelic prints and beads and zodiac signs and joined up with transcendental meditation and ISKCON. Combined with a fashionable socialism in the times of great student movements, anti-Vietnam War demonstrations, and Watergate, they went around spouting Sartre-Camus-Kafka-Ionesco-Neruda. All this while simultaneously slogging over their books for the university or Civil Services exams! The Hindi-medium student remained unaffected by all of this and inhabited a parallel universe.

Some of this classy irreverence in all its fizz and ferment found a local lilt in the writings of the mid to late '60s. The two-and-a-quarter fragments of poetry that I have chosen to reproduce, out of a more or less typical issue of *The Allahabad University Magazine* of 1967, charmingly preserve this mood of inbred, allusive lightness. I may mention here that both student authors are now literary figures of weight and substance.

> A feisty quartet of lines these, a cry of the soul.
> I love you so, Dame!
> But I am flabbergasted
> To see how many blasted
> Other chaps do the same.[7]

This might have prepared the reader for the second and longer piece of ingenious parody by the same author, a brilliant take on Robert Frost's poem 'Stopping by Woods on a Snowy Evening.' It's titled: 'Picking up Some Books on a Lucky Afternoon.'

Whose books these are of course I know
I just watched her drop them—and go!
And now that she is nowhere near
These books I'll walk away with—ho!

The Peon there must think it queer
That I picked up what I dropped ne'er
These are—Poor chap! He little doth know
The prized gains I made this year

He gives his dam' ol' head a shake
And suspects there is some mistake
I look right nonchalant, to keep
Him cool—lest his doubts further awake

The books are lovely, and not cheap
And I have picked 'em up to keep
And reading them I'll fall asleep
And reading them I'll fall asleep.[8]

Harish Trivedi, postcolonial critic of eminence and the author of these irresistible pieces, was quite possibly experiencing intimations of the impulse to make alternative readings of texts, even in his student days.

The other poem I find, on the very next page of this issue of the AU magazine that I randomly picked up, is by 'vinoo' (in lower case) and is titled 'to whomsoever it may concern'.

It reads like this:

this is to inform he who opens this
that
when I have been simplified
to a pair of unbreathing nostrils
and my laugh been eaten

> by beasts of the air, in short,
> after my death
> my throat should be zipped open
> with my wife's claws
> and poems pasted there
> like cinema posters
> be scraped out and sold
> as waste paper
> to cover costs incurred in the
> last rites'
> further,
> my tongue should be thoroughly
> cleaned
> before it is burnt. The few
> punctuation-marks still
> sticking to its pores
> be picked out with tweezers
> by a qualified zoologist.[9]

This meticulous last will and testament for the disposal of stubborn non-biodegradable poetry was published forty-four years ago. Arvind Krishna Mehrotra has been both the English department's enfant terrible and its international footprint, even if he has vehemently shaken the dust of the department off his feet with public disclaimers of belonging. He is not the first recognized Indian writer in English who taught at the department. Ahmed Ali, the well-known Urdu writer, whose English novel *Twilight In Delhi* is a classic, was a member of the staff for a short while in the 1930s. In the fullness of time, others have followed.

But this particular issue of the magazine proves what a tiny world it is. There's that old cliché: you can take a man out of Allahabad but you can't take Allahabad out of him.

Up to the 1970s at least, this was true. On page 35 there's a sparkling piece on Edward Lear, written by none other than A.K. Bhattacharya—the same Arun Kumar Bhattacharya with whose story Mehrotra begins his well-known volume *The Last Bungalow: Writings on Allahabad*. He lived in the last bungalow down the road from Mehrotra's own housing colony, and who was mysteriously murdered, some say by goons of the land mafia. Mehrotra describes Bhattacharya as 'a short, compact, neat-looking man' with a 'bald head' and 'a round, pleasant face', with a 'droll sense of humour' that coexisted with 'something prickly' in his nature'.[10]

In the piece on Lear's limericks that I've chosen, as representative of a flamboyant residual colonial mood, Bhattacharya explains the origin of the word 'limerick', which derives 'from a custom at convivial parties, according to which each member sang an extemporized 'nonsense verse', which was followed by a chorus containing the words: 'Will you come up to Limerick?'[11] Bhattacharya was the essential pucca-Brit, although there were a few other impressive specimens as well. He sprinkles his essay with lively Brit waggeries, of which I present a couple.

On the theory of relativity he quotes this uproarious piece:

There was a young lady named Bright
Who would travel faster than light
She started one day
In the relative way
And returned the previous night.[12]

Bhattacharya speaks of Edward Lear's visit to India, sometime in April 1873, citing what I regard as the most riotous Lear anecdote, which, the author of the piece tells us, is titled 'German Pessimist'. (Two decades after the end of the Second World War, the comic stereotype of the phlegmatic German was a bit of wicked British vengeance.) It proceeds in the form of a dialogue on board an ocean liner bound for India:

> German Pessimist: You wear spegtacles always?
> Lear: Yes.
> GP: They will grack in India; von pair no use.
> Lear: But I have many pairs.
> GP: How many?
> Lear: Twenty or thirty.
> GP: No good. They vill all grack. You should have got of silver.
> Lear: But I have several of silver.
> GP: Dat is no use. They vill rust; you might (haf) got gold.
> Lear: But I have some of gold.
> GP: Dat is more vorse; gold is always stealing.[13]

In class, sometime in the mid-1970s, I have sat through Bhattacharya's classes in which conversations out of Bradley and G. Wilson Knight on *King Lear* or *Henry IV* were punctuated by gems such as these. As Mehrotra recounts in his book, Bhattacharya, that combative optimist, that standoffish and classily crusty raconteur, was killed, reported strangled with the cord of a video cassette player. He was not one of the big names but his personality somehow conveys the style and shrugging banter of the English department in that period.

It must not be imagined that the department was only a place for jokes, all British humour and scintillating witticisms. That same issue of *The Allahabad University Magazine* contains essays of imposing gravitas, entitled: 'Peace Is Attainable', 'Agyeya: Beyond the Outsider', 'The Development of Thumri in Indian Classical Music', and 'Some Trends in Contemporary Fiction.' Some landmark events are reported too: a Tagore centenary celebrated with elegance and spirit, and four hundred years of William Shakespeare.

Rear view of the English department

Outside the rarefied air of the English department, as also perhaps the world of the sure-shot IAS aspirants of Muir, the University had been going about its business in cynical disdain of this angrezi island in Arcadia, peopled by elite, adolescent visionaries. Imperiously fantasizing about unleashing dire discipline, rigorous order and an intensive cleansing of 'the system' which—it was blindingly obvious—was only awaiting their improving crusade. I include here a diverting account of a Students' Union Election, contested by one such aspiring reformer, in the mid-1960s, which, aside from its shattering if facetious discovery of realpolitik in mofussil India, reveals the change in academic climate around this time.

> Of all the hugely enjoyable things I did during my student years in AU from 1963 to 1967, the oddest was to stand for election as an office-bearer of the Students' Union in August 1965. Of course any number of students stood for, or 'fought', the Union elections every year; it was just this that they weren't people like me or 'us'. To specify, none of

them was doing an MA in English (for they were nearly all in the 'Laa' Faculty), none was a student-editor of *The Allahabad University Magazine* and none was a member of those fancy Anglophone clubs, the fresh and youthful Debating Rostrum and the crusty, snooty but deliciously well-catered Friday Club. And certainly, none of them had 'topped' the BA examinations.

But it wasn't individual madness that made me do it; it was all part of a plan. With our idealism or naiveté, some of us (of the above type) decided one evening, while walking out of the campus after debating hotly some topical political issue at the Debating Rostrum, that we should not only talk about everything but actually do something! We decided to begin at home by trying to reform the rowdy and lumpen Students' Union, which we regarded as a bane and a blight, for it seemed to do little else but call for a protracted and violent strike every year, which culminated in a police lathi-charge, with the University then closing down sine die for several weeks.

I had witnessed this process first-hand when one morning in September 1963, just a month or two after admission to the University, I excitedly joined a procession of protesters which marched from the Union Hall under the leadership of Shyam Krishna Pandey, president of the union, to the house of the vice chancellor, Professor Balbhadra Prasad, in George Town. But as soon as the police arrived, I ran like mad, which didn't prevent my earning a big throbbing bruise on my left leg from contact with a police danda and, minutes later, my trousers getting ripped when I negotiated a high hostel wall to seek a place to hide in a friend's room. By that evening, all the student leaders had been arrested, except Pandey, who had gone 'underground' and the University had been closed sine die.

So, my friends and I now decided to stand for the [students'] union elections ourselves and do our best to win them; and then work to restore the academic calendar, and credibility of our University, of which we were intensely proud. But on the day of filing nominations, only I reached the official venue and, to name names: Alok Rai (one year my senior), Rajeev Dhavan and Markandey Katju (both my classmates) were nowhere to be found. With some trepidation, I filed my papers anyhow. My Rostrum / Friday Club friends sheepishly contributed some money towards my campaign fund, which had an official cap of ₹100 except that the total I finally collected was ₹95. As I recall, the largest single contribution, of ₹10, came from Mrinal Pande; she must have had to go without teas and samosas for many days.

But those who actually campaigned for me and did the legwork day in and day out were from another circle altogether: my sturdier Hindi-medium schoolfriends from GIC Allahabad, who had more common sense, and their ears closer to the ground. They included, most notably, my old classmates—Khem Chand Agrawal (a happy and hearty fellow, now prematurely deceased, whose father owned a grocery shop in Katra), Dinesh Shrivastava (a neighbour who in our 'joint study' in BA taught me all the economics I ever knew, while I helped him a little with *Macbeth*), Prabhat Kumar (gentle and genial son of the Hindi writer Gopi Krishna 'Gopesh', who got my 4,000 name cards for the election printed at a 'concession' from a little shop near the Ghantaghar in Chowk, with just one misprint in the whole card), and about a dozen others.

Campaigning involved mainly two kinds of activity.

During the day, one had to go round and round the campus standing in a rickshaw in the hot sun with hands folded, while a cluster of one's supporters walked alongside shouting slogans such as '*Harish hamara bhai hai / Harish ka tempo high hai*'. It was only much later that I wondered how the widely inappropriate musical term 'tempo' (especially as used with the adjective 'high' rather than, say, 'fast') had become a key term in this template slogan, for all candidates alike used it with just a change of name.

But I was told that what actually won me lots of votes and became my USP was our other slogan, '*Hamara bhai Harish Trivedi! BA ka topper Harish Trivedi!!*', or a variation on it: '*Topper hamara bhai hai / Topper ka tempo high hai*'. What innocent times were those when being a topper in an examination could win one votes in an election. But in Allahabad University, a kind of glamour and mystique surrounded the 'topper', for each year his / her name and fame resounded in all the streets and chowrahas around the campus and in all the hostels and teashops. Merit lists were published prominently by *Northern India Patrika* and *The Leader*, and toppers were even bigger celebrities in AU than cricketers (with the one exception in my time of Anand Shukla, who later came close to playing for India).

So the daily rickshaw rounds got a candidate name, recognition and, literally, visibility. But the other even more important part of the campaign was to work what may now be called the vote banks. These were the hostels and the 'lodges' (i.e. smaller private hostels rented and run by the students themselves). It was universally believed that in each hostel and each lodge, all the students held a meeting a day or two before the elections and decided which candidates to vote for en bloc. So, each evening, one went round with one's supporters, now everyone riding their bicycles, from hostel to hostel and lodge to lodge, to catch their residents around dinnertime.

While on these rounds, I had a couple of experiences that I then found truly shocking. One evening we went to a big lodge in Colonelganj, and a hefty man who was obviously the chief there took me aside, and smiled and asked if I had only Agrawals and Shrivastavas among my supporters. He then said, '*Trivedi-ji, aap chinta na karen. Yahan sab Brahmin-hi-Brahmin hain is lodge men aur poora vote aap-hi ko jayega. Aap ko hi kya, sabhi padon ke liye aise hi vote padega yahan se.*' I said, '*Aapko aur kuchh nahin sochna hai?*' He said, smiling again, '*To aur hota kya hai?*' I said, '*To apna vote apne hi paas rakhiye*'—yes, being a 'topper', I did feel very insulted and I did say just that—and walked off.

At age eighteen, this was my first encounter with caste as the bottom-line of our democracy. I found it shocking and upsetting because the Nehruvian glow of secular idealism still blinded us to the ground reality. Nehru had died only the year before, and the procession with his asthi-kalash had passed right in front of the house where I then lived, at 47 Mahatma Gandhi Marg. It now seems ages ago, but elections had not yet become so brazenly and cynically casteist as they did very shortly afterwards, beginning with the General Elections in 1967. I think even Hari Shankar Parsai was yet to write that masterpiece of satire, *Ham Bihar se Chunav Lad Rahe Hain*, in which an utterly devout temple priest refuses to vote for Lord Krishna, because he is a Brahmin and *He* is a Yadav.

My callow and naïve ignorance of these matters soon attracted poetic justice. On Election Day, I virtuously attended all my classes, for campaigning had come to an end the previous evening, and there wasn't anything else for me to do. I recall Dr J.P. Kulshreshtha looking up from the attendance register after I had responded to my name, and giving me an incredulous look, followed by that barest hint of an amused smile that he had perfected. When I reached the Padmadhar Hall in the afternoon I saw my ever-cheerful lieutenant Khem Chand utterly downcast and distraught. He'd just found out that all of KPUC was voting against me, after having promised until late the previous evening that they were all for me. '*Raat-o-raat palat gaye saale, Kayasth kahin ke!*' lamented dear Khem. He was particularly cut up as some of our best friends lived in that hostel. Khem had actually plied my rickshaw himself day after day during my campaign, as a sign of complete solidarity with me as my saarathi, and he was somewhat appeased only when he later discovered that a student who had worked very hard to swing the Women's Hostel for me was named Archana Varma.

Well, I did win by a small margin of about 300 votes in a ten-cornered contest and a Kayasth boy came second. In the ceremony at which we took office, I cracked a terrible joke in my speech; it was so awful and painful that even R.K. Nehru, vice-chancellor, who was famous for always looking down at his shoes so as to avoid all eye contact, looked up at me and grimaced.

The main obligation of the office-bearers and the executive committee, it turned out, was to meet at the Union office once a week, and the main item on the agenda seemed to be to demolish two or three rounds of dosa which came with some very watery white chutney. Dosa must have been a bit of a novelty in Allahabad at that time and a favoured exotic food of the young, for burgers and pizzas were of course far in the future.

So, I was eventually the only one there of our Gang of Four who had conspired to capture the Union, and I soon found myself elaborately ignored and marginalized. I soon stopped going even for the dosas; I'd now go only to executive meetings, which had a substantial agenda. I was anyhow the fourth of the hierarchy of five office-bearers, who were president, vice president, secretary, publications secretary and assistant secretary. My designation in Hindi was prakashan mantri but there was also a delightful informal version, chhaapaa mantri, and my only specific task anyhow was to publish the union magazine, called *Sadhana*, at the end of the academic year.

But when I had collected many good contributions in both Hindi and English and was ready to go to press, the treasurer, who was a senior teacher, told me that the sum of ₹800 that was allocated for the magazine had been spent already by the secretary, who had for several weeks camped in Bombay ostensibly to persuade some film actress or the other to come to perform in a 'cultural show' at AU. (The ostensible noble reason for this absurd plan was to raise money for the National Defence Fund, following the Indo-Pak war which had taken place in August–September 1965.) When I protested, the treasurer shouted at me: 'What a fool you are! Don't you know anything? If you wanted your share of money, you should have come to me as soon as you got elected.' So I ended my term without being able to do the one thing that I was supposed to do: publish that blessed magazine. I felt utterly frustrated and humiliated; indeed I felt robbed of both my role and my honour. I had been taken for a comprehensive ride, and there was nothing I could do about it.

There was a strike in my year too, but not a big one. The day before the strike, as a dress rehearsal about fifteen of us made speeches from the jagat or platform of what was beginning to be called the 'Hindi Kuan' to generally rouse the rabble. On the day itself, we got in early at about 7 a.m. and locked all the gates of the campus from the inside. We also barricaded the Padmadhar gate, by pushing a couple of big takhats against the gate from the inside. I lent no hand in all this nor did the other 'leaders'; a seasoned shamiana wala from Katra who supplied the loudspeakers knew the whole routine from long association. The takhats served a double purpose, for when the crowd had gathered we all stood on top of the takhats and took our turn at making speeches. Our only commonly agreed strategy was to speak as rhetorically and rousingly as we could, in a phadkati hui idiom—to think of and to 'cover' all kinds of topics big and small which could even remotely be regarded as a cause of discontentment—and to speak for as long as we possibly could, because we had to keep the show going until 4 p.m. at least.

I remember speaking for about half an hour. I now haven't the foggiest recollection of what we were complaining about or demanding in our rousing speeches. We were, with some self-important heroism, going through the motions of staging a strike as an annual ritual; had we not done it, the whole Union would have been thoroughly disgraced. But our strike never caught fire, and the two trucks of the PAC that were parked just out of sight near the AN Jha Hostel gate, as in previous years, were not called upon to roll in.

Probably my biggest highlight and gain as a Union office-bearer was that I got to meet and sit on the podium with Ram Manohar Lohia no fewer than seven times, which was how often he came and addressed us at the AU Union that year. With his bushy eyebrows and bristly hair, his sharp political insights expressed in his idiomatic subaltern Hindi, and his acerbic and cutting obiter dicta on all kinds of topics in the world but especially against the Nehru family, he was the one who weaned us away from Nehru and his pervasive influence.

As the leader of the Sanyukta Socialist Party (SSP) in Parliament who had a homespun charisma of his own, he ensured with these frequent visits, that there would follow a virtual monopoly of the Samajwadi Yuvajan Sabha (SYS) over the AU Students' Union for years to come. When he suddenly died in 1967 at the age of fifty-seven, I wrote a heartfelt obituary in a periodical I then edited, *The Varsity Journal*, which the liberal Mr Rajamani among my teachers endorsed warmly but which the committed socialist and Lohia-ite Mr V.D.N. Sahi had some reservations about, partly because I had titled it *A Storm Subsides*. He felt that that phrase had a negative overtone, and I now quite see that it does, but then I did not know better.[14]

Is there a shift evident round about this time: Nehru to Lohia, Anglophone elitism to Hindiphone majoritarianism? Student Union elections had a lighter side to them then, even if complicated forces played out within the practical operations. There were student leaders who were middle-aged and who had stayed on as 'students' by virtue of membership in some peripheral diploma course. There were others like 'dhakkan guru' who made capital of his tiny size, standing with folded hands atop an elephant as he went around canvassing. There was the doggedly optimistic neta who began his speeches with allusive references to the time when he had jumped off the Hindi department roof. He had come crashing headlong to the ground, before a dozen howling supporters flung themselves on his prone form, covering him with their piled up bodies to protect him from police lathis, a coup quickly clicked by waiting photographers.

This was a feat deserving of so much noisy accolade that for a few years thereafter it became the neta's formula for generating instant applause until no one remembered why he had jumped off the Hindi department roof in the first place! He had only to say: '*Us Hindi department ki chhat...*'[15] And thunderous clapping started, to the great disgust of a rival leader whose speech, even after forty years bristles with contempt: '*Hindi department, Hindi department, Hindi department! Main poochhta hoon, kya wah Hindi department ki chhat Waterloo ka maidan ban gayee aur hamare neta ji uske Napolean?*'[16]

At the other end of the spectrum was the highly focused Science Faculty, which had its own special mix of dedication and diversion documented by a student of the 1960s, Satya Deo Tripathi—a mathematician and one-time vice chancellor of a State University:

Inside Vizianagram Hall

When I joined BSc in July 1962, all the three departments, mathematics, physics and chemistry, had excellent reputations. R.N. Chaudhary (BA, Cantab) was the head of mathematics, Rajendra Singh was head of physics and R.D. Tiwari was the head of chemistry. The science faculty was located in the premises of the Muir Central College with its magnificent building. There was the beautiful Vijayanagaram Hall for cultural activities and the highly attractive Main Stadium for annual sports. It was fun, during the winters, to watch the annual athletic tournaments being held in the Main Stadium. One could attend one's classes and also enjoy, in one's free time, various athletic competitions going on in the stadium. The hockey match, the 100-metre race, 400-metre race and the marathon 10,000-metre race, etc. were indeed the great sports to watch from the gallery of the mathematics department or the zoology department.

Textbooks written by Gorakh Prasad in mathematics, Saha and Srivastava in physics and Satya Prakash in chemistry were very popular. These authors were very eminent teachers of the Allahabad University, but we didn't enjoy the privilege of being taught by them. During 1962–64, we had teachers like Murli Manohar Joshi, V.P. Gupta, Arvind Mohan, Ashok Mishra (in physics), A.K. De, Krishna Bahadur, Bal Krishna, S.P. Tandon (in chemistry) and T. Pati, H.C. Khare, R.C. Khare, R. Gupta (in mathematics). From the class work in the science faculty it was very clear that we had joined this University to learn our subjects well and prepare ourselves for all manner of exams. The general atmosphere was to complete university education and go for various competitions like the IAS, PCS, banks, the army, etc. and make our careers in those fields.

The reputation of the University of Allahabad was

already established since long for producing a lot of IAS and PCS officers to serve the government organizations, and I felt that this was really the case. However, there were some exceptions. Dr T. Pati in the mathematics department was dead against going in for the civil services. He would always plead, without being asked, that students go for research in the subjects of their liking. Very often he would devote more of his class time to denouncing the competitive exams, as well as the authorities of the University, for encouraging them. He himself, coming from the Arts Faculty (BA with maths, logic and Sanskrit), was a scholar with an amazing capacity to convince that 'students should be original thinkers, good writers, good historians, good academicians, and good scientists, rather than good civil servants'.

Dr Murli Manohar Joshi of the physics department, wearing a white dress made of khadi (kurta-dhoti), used to teach us optics, but would deviate from the subject to tell us that most of modern science was already known to our ancient Indian scholars. In particular, he would give us evidence to prove that much of science is already explained in our Vedas and Puranas, of course in Sanskrit. Professor H.C. Khare (mathematics, PhD from McGill, Canada) used to lecture in class in a uniquely melodious style as if he was singing; his writing on the blackboard was so nice that it looked as if it was printed. After solving a tricky exercise, he would always say: 'Practice alone will tell you how to find the trick!' Dr A.K. De, who wore a dhoti-kurta, though not of khadi, used to teach us inorganic chemistry quite impressively, but would leave the class fifteen or twenty minutes before time saying: 'It is rather hot today, we will now meet next time.'

When I joined my MSc in Mathematics in 1965, I found

the same atmosphere of intense teaching from the point of view of exams. The capacity to solve tricky problems in mathematics, regardless of the appreciation of concepts, was considered the measure of intelligence. Intelligent students secretly used 'keys', 'golden solved examples' and the like to prepare. As a rule, the toppers of the final exams were immediately offered lectureship in the department. Once appointed on an ad hoc basis, they would teach in the department, quietly appear in the competitive exams like IAS or the PCS and would quickly disappear. I myself was taught by four such teachers and don't remember their names except that they were extremely good problem solvers. There was little emphasis on doing research in mathematics at that time. Some of the teachers had amazing memories and they could solve any given problem instantly, but if asked a question which needed fresh understanding and ideas, they would toss it aside with the remark: 'This question is of no use.'

On the other hand, there were teachers like P.S.V. Naidu, G.D. Dixit and some others, who, though trained in classical mathematics, learnt and understood new courses very well. It was a pleasure to attend their classes because their emphasis was on understanding modern concepts and not problem-solving alone. There was hardly anyone who encouraged research in these new areas then. Banwari Lal Sharma, when he returned from Paris, was one of the first encouraging ones. Before his coming, Professor B.N. Prasad (PhD, Liverpool, and DSc, Paris) and Professor R.S. Mishra had been guiding some research, but most students preferred the civil services to a life devoted to mathematics or the pure sciences.[17]

The official overview of this period undertaken by the centenary souvenir published in 1987 lists development on all fronts. Between the years 1960 and 1987, the Allahabad University was documented as a highly energetic and eventful place, though the souvenir mentions the circumstances with predictable selectivity. In every department there had been umpteen conferences and colloquiums, symposia and seminars, training and development programs, workshops, summer and winter schools; projects and publications: books, monographs, and research papers.

An American researcher, Joseph Edward Di Bona, who studied the Allahabad University as part of a doctoral project for the University of California, at Berkeley in 1967, perceptively commented on the application of the British policy of giving primacy to teaching over research. The policy makers stressed 'the diffusion of knowledge' rather than the advancement of knowledge, as also evident from the Woods Despatch of 1854. We get repeated references confirming this. For instance, the 1903 convocation address of Sir James La Touche categorically affirms that, 'We must accept the view...that diffusion of knowledge rather than advancement of learning is, under existing conditions, the main function of our university.'[18] A discussion was on, then, as to the twin objectives of a university—the making of men and the making of truth. As far as AU was concerned, the former end dominated the latter in the early days, and the creative product of the original scheme, lived up to proving themselves as a class of men 'who may be interpreters between us and the millions whom we govern...'[19]

But by the 1960s, the University had slowly demonstrated a process of mutation from an exclusively teaching institution to a research institution. In the years that followed, there were creative collaborations with the Council of Scientific and Industrial Research (CSIR), the Indian Council for Cultural Relations (ICCR), the Council of Science and Technology, the University Grants

Commission, the National Council of Educational Research and Training (NCERT) and the National Physical Laboratory. There were academic exchange programmes with foreign universities, and enrichment and outreach programmes. New departments came up with new buildings to house them, and also to house some older departments. The number of seats for students had gone up, as had posts for teachers.

A medical college at Allahabad came up in 1961 and was recognized as a constituent college of the University. Its hospital, named after Swaroop Rani, Motilal Nehru's wife, is built on the site of the former Malacca Jail. Its teaching and hostel wings stand on the grounds of the demolished Government House, the location of the imposing residence of Sir William Muir and alongside what is now called the Darbhanga Colony. There is a new engineering college as well, named after Motilal Nehru, and recognized as an associate college of the University. With these the dependence on King George's Medical College, Lucknow, and the Thomason College, Roorkee, was over.

There is also a dynamic new department of psychology, founded in 1961 by Durganand Sinha. In 1968 it moved into a brand new building and very soon established itself as one of the prestigious departments of the country, recognized by the UGC as a Centre of Excellence in 1976 and granted the UGC's Special Assistance Programme. Subsequently it was upgraded to a Centre for Advanced Study in 1986. It has the best-groomed building. Its work culture is intensive and the staff work long hours, a far cry from the laid-back colonial English character. The psychologists have been engaged in studying social change in rural and urban settings, psycho-social stress and coping behaviour, social disadvantage and poverty, ethnicity and group relations, social influence and behaviour, pro-social and moral behaviour and cross-cultural psychology.

The Department of Defence Studies initiated MA classes and research facilities in 1965, and its courses have been used as standard models by the UGC to serve as benchmarks for diverse departments in other universities. In 1985, two departments were founded. A Department of Social Anthropology, dedicated to studying 'the peoples, cultures, economies and languages of the region', is now busy studying patterns of migration from the hills of UP to the plains, as also the problems of marginalized sections. The second, a Department of Geology and Geophysics is engaged in cutting-edge research. Its scientists have been absorbed in exploring the genesis of diamond-bearing rocks.

The older departments have been bustling with activity too. The Hindi department expanded its course choices to include several Indian languages: Bengali, Punjabi, Tamil, Telugu, Urdu, Maithili and Rajasthani, attracting many a foreign student from Britain, Russia, Japan and the Czech Republic. A whole crop of writers was fostered, many of national acclaim—Kamleshwar, Usha Priyamvada, Dushyanta, Doodhnath Singh, Sharad Joshi and some who technically belonged to the English department, like V.D.N. Sahi and Govind Mishra. Apart from the creative and critical journals published, such as *Aalochana*; *Nishak*; *Ka, Kha, Ga*; *Nayi Kavita*; and *Naye Patte*, two anthologies of Hindi literature have been issued by the department as well.

The garden of the botany department now possesses various species of plants belonging to different categories of life forms—'ecological groups and taxa ranging from algae to angiosperms'. It has acquired a glass house, a well-sized fern house, a nursery and a sixteen-acre farm at some distance from the campus. This farm is equipped with a custom-made lysimeter to enable the study of the nutritional index of plants.[20] The department publishes an annual bulletin and a bimonthly paper. It also has a very popular cafeteria haunted by students of both the arts and the science wings.

The JK Institute of Applied Physics has a central instrumentation complex and a central workshop; it also provides training in fabrication and maintenance of research apparatus. Aiming 'to bring into its fold the study of modern subjects like space physics and technology', it has already introduced courses in BTech, MTech and computer science, and also runs computer awareness programmes.[21] The department publishes a research journal, and its club, Vaichariki, is a prestigious platform for thinkers and scientists to meet and confer. The chemistry department has upgraded its laboratory and research facilities. The mathematics department has been occupied with fluid dynamics and differential geometry, with real, complex and fourier analysis and summability, cosmology, magnetohydrodynamics, plasma dynamics and astrophysics, topology and abstract algebra.

The Department of Ancient History, Culture and Archaeology (earlier only 'Ancient History') has distinguished itself as an eminent academic centre, selected by the UGC for departmental support in 1976, and then for the Special Assistance Programme. The historians are intensely involved in fieldwork, and provide practical training to the archaeological exploration in the Vindhya regions and the Gangetic valley. It is also collaborating with Soviet institutions in comparative archaeological and ethno-linguistic studies. The philosophy department has introduced innovative courses like Islamic philosophy, the philosophies of science and of living Indian thinkers. The geography department has refocused its subject content, transforming it into an analytical science from its earlier descriptive avatar. It has also redefined its goal as the training of geographers into social scientists.

The all-new proactive and cutting-edge Department of Commerce and Business Administration (earlier only Commerce) came into being at the behest of the legendary A.N. Agarwala. In 1961, his brilliant calculation vis-à-vis the devaluation of the rupee—to seventeen paise, at a conference in Cochin—earned him a breakfast invitation from Jawaharlal Nehru, who instructed his office to immediately contact the district magistrate of Allahabad to trace this economist. Ram Manohar Lohia had just about that time challenged Nehru, in Parliament, regarding the seventy-five big industrial houses feeding off the fat of the land while the poor man had grown poorer. And Nehru now needed a proper economic advisor. Whether Agarwala had occasion to advise Nehru we do not know, but he was certainly able to get all his projects for the commerce department passed. The department started an MBA course in 1965, and it now also possesses a research and statistical laboratory, an agro-economic research centre, and a publication and documentation centre.

The Department of Law has settled into its new premises in the Chatham Lines Campus, and has hosted dignitaries of the stature of V.V. Giri, G.S. Pathak, M.C. Setalvad, Niren De, V.K. Krishna Menon, P.N. Bhagwati, R.B. Misra and H.N. Seth. The painting cell is now the independent Department of Visual Arts and has introduced both BA and MA in Fine Arts courses; so also the music department, which has an MA course too, as well as a bonafide claim to its own building. The education department has designed a new MA course that aims at 'producing educational scientists and not schoolteachers'[22], and it has introduced innovations in examination patterns.

Several departments have come to possess their own museums. The ancient history department is also technically equipped for the conservation of antique artefacts; the Department of Commerce and Business Administration owns a commercial museum; and the geology and geophysics department has a modern museum with excellent rock, mineral and fossil specimens.

A correspondence course and distance education programme was begun which, up to the session of 1998–99, offered the same BA and BCom courses as the regular University did, but after 2000, ran its own academic programmes. An Institute of Gandhian Studies has been initiated, its foundation stone laid by Mother Theresa herself; and a journalism department started. Biotechnology and nuclear physics departments had been planned, as were a multimedia centre, a department of physical education, an institute of food technology and departments of planning and architecture, national integration, Vedic studies and chemical technology. (Only some of these plans came to fruition subsequently.)

The Athletics Association has given a good account of itself. A student of the University, Suresh Goyal, after helping the University team win the All-India-Inter-University Badminton championship in 1962–69, went on to become the national champion. In the juniors' section Sunjay Mehrotra became India's Number One in 1980–81.[23] In the lawn tennis Junior Asian Championship of 1980–81, Deepak Bhargava and Mayank Kapoor won the first and first runner-up positions, respectively. Two students, Deepak and Amit Bhargava, were part of the Indian University team at the World University Games held in Canada the following year. Between 1982 and 1985, AU tennis players won the Inter-University Lawn Tennis championship for three continuous years. Shooting, wrestling, volleyball, football and basketball have done creditably and a Physical Conditioning Unit was set up with a special UGC grant. The National Cadet Corps and the National Service Scheme have both excelled.

To conserve and maintain the great old heritage buildings, to get the clock started again and to extend, clean and beautify the University's campus area, a master plan was passed by the executive council. A Science Centre was envisaged in the Muir

Central College campus with a science library, a science museum and an auditorium for 250 persons. A Social Science Complex was likewise projected for the Senate Hall Campus, with spacious lecture theatres, seminar halls and teachers' cubicles. A large auditorium was outlined in the Chatham Lines campus; and a new guest house, sports complex, art gallery, new hostels for students and residential complexes for teachers lie in the blueprint stage, to see realization two decades down the line.

Professors from various departments have presided on plenary sessions of international conferences, be they of physics or of literature; and a commerce department faculty member, S.C. Kuchhal, joined IIM, Ahmedabad, as professor, finance. Prof. Krishnaji was honoured with the prestigious Raman Award, and Prof. Alok Gupta the Shanti Swaroop Bhatnagar Award. Geeta Banerjee received a gold medal and the title of 'Surmani' from the Sur Singar Parishad of Mumbai. The parishad conferred the 'Surmani' and the 'Taal-mani' title to three others of the Allahabad University as well—Girish Chandra Srivastava, S.K. Nahar and Vidyadhar Mishra.

The *Centenary Souvenir* of 1987 reads like a glossy advertisement brochure, taking the reader on a guided tour, department to department. Its self-laudatory inputs are its natural and understandable function as behoves, after all, an official record as against a critically objective analysis. Words like 'glorious tradition' occur with counter-productive frequency, and while it all sounds impressive in print, some of it was also genuinely so. However, it does studiously avoid reference to the slow systemic failure, manifesting in the institution in many ways. Neither does it mention the language riots of the 1960s, or the Emergency in the mid-1970s, or the student unrest that severely rocked the University in the late 1970s and early '80s, debasing it to a lawless and auto-destructing instance of institutional miscarriage.

This book, though, is not a compendium of annual reports (which, too, carry highly selective and distorted inputs, depending on prevailing staff politics in various departments), but a story of an institution's evolving profile. And so, it is imperative to examine each of these disturbances specifically and contextually. But while enumerating what is on the debit side of history's ledger, we must not omit to consider what exists inerasably to its credit, not of an official commemorative souvenir, but in the far more authentic register of the University's collective local memory of the 1960s and '70s. These comprise the names of great teachers who, by any standard, were superlative and remembered much afterwards:

G.C. Pande, B.N.S. Yadav, J.S. Negi, G.R. Sharma and Shibesh Bhattacharya of the ancient history department; Ram Kumar Varma—writer-critic, Hardev Bahri—the lexicographer, Paras Nath Dwivedi—whose Kabir translation exists in a Clarendon Press edition, Jagdish Gupt and Satya Prakash Mishra, in Hindi; that brilliant linguistics scholar, Mahabir Prasad Lakhera, in Sanskrit; Dr Rafiq in Arabic; R.N. Choudhuri, B.N. Prasad, Chandika Prasad, Pyarelal Srivastava, T. Pati and Banwari Lal Sharma in mathematics; A.D. Pant in political science; and Durganand Sinha in psychology; Krishnaji, Vachaspati, Bipin Kumar Agarwal and S.N. Banerjee in physics; I.K. Taimni and Krishna Bahadur in chemistry; S.S. Rai and V. Naravane in philosophy; D.D. Pant in botany; A.N. Agarwala in commerce; P.D. Hajela, J.S. Mathur, Ram Lohkar and S.L. Parmar in economics; Pundit B.A. Kashalkar and Pundit B.N. Thakkar in music; and professors Aejaz Hussain, Ehtesham Hussain and S.M.H. Aquil Rizvi in Urdu. There were also the younger teachers, some conservatively excellent, some intellectual mavericks and stylish role models to impressionable students.

But the presence of these extraordinary campus personalities notwithstanding, the University's institutional batteries had been slowly discharging, as anyone could sense—as could be sensed even in the late 1940s. Since then, alongside the indulgent and rapturous evocations of the 'glorious tradition' there was always a creeping feeling of disquiet; something rotten in the kingdom of Denmark, in short, as our routinely groomed Eng-Lit academics might put it. What is wrong with us?... seems to have been a persistent issue for introspection and discussion. Even in the high noon of the University's history, one can find this soul-searching in the writings of Amaranatha Jha (as an ex-vice chancellor, in the late 1940s), of Tara Chand (a functioning vice chancellor, of the same time) and of C.D. Deshmukh (chairman, UGC, in the late 1950s). I have also got here some inputs from students dialoguing over the university's condition in the early 1960s. Each one zeroes in on a special angle of the decline. Amazingly, though some things have changed, a greater number remain unchanged in essence, if not grown more aggravated in degree. I shall cite just a few samples of their rueful self-scrutiny

Amaranatha Jha expressed his dissatisfactions, much after leaving the University, in a piece entitled 'Role Of The Universities':[24]

> The main impression that I have formed is that, for a large number, University Education has no real significance. They have discovered that a degree is no guarantee for employment, and they feel that they have been cheated of their due. This gives, to life in the University, a distressing atmosphere of unreality, doubt, frustration, and even antagonism. They blame the University, their teachers, their courses of study... Too many students join the University without any clear idea of what they aim to get out of it. Some come to have a good time and spend a few years under agreeable conditions; there is no harm in this if they

can afford it. Some come from a genuine love of learning, in search of knowledge and scholarship; but their number is small. A few come in the expectation that they will equip themselves for some profession.

But a vast majority just drift in, not knowing what to do, faintly trusting that somehow, at some time, they will secure, with the aid of a degree, some occupation. These last, are disappointed at the end, disillusioned, disheartened, and go about dispirited, soured and embittered... Students flock to the Universities in such large numbers, because they find no other avenues open to them. They postpone until an undetermined future date, the decision about their career. It is not the lure of higher learning that attracts them; it is a blind groping in the dim twilight, for a gleam of light that may show them their further path.[25]

And that was the late 1940s. It is startling that what appears as a malady of more recent times, was present—almost exactly so—in the so-called 'golden era'. Tara Chand, with the perspective of a historian making a sweeping analytical survey, explains the restlessness:

The mind of India's youth (is) unsettled. Decades of defiance of authority, strikes, demonstrations, processions, and the mounting excitement of (the) 'Quit India' movement, had a deleterious influence upon discipline. Then, the freedom movement could not be confined to the field of politics alone. Anti-authoritarianism made inroads upon all settled beliefs. Morals, traditions, attitudes, manners and conduct—all came under criticism, and the sanctity of relations between old and young, teacher and pupil, received a mighty blow. The inevitable result was, that the University ceased to function normally. Disturbance became a routine. An unnatural gulf began to yawn amidst those, whom every conceivable consideration of morals and utility, obliges to work in harmony for the achievement of common aims. Relations between those whose function was to guide, and those who enjoyed the privileged status of pupils, became strained.[26]

K.K. Mehrotra, writing in 1958, is more philosophical and forgiving of the late 1930s and '40s: '…in the turmoil inevitable in the struggle for freedom, some values had to be sacrificed at the expense of others,' he reflects.[27]

> The ten years between the Golden and the Diamond Jubilee (1937 to 1947) were a period of agony and disruption for the whole world. The struggle for existence became harder; life was complicated by shortage and scarcity, and all kinds of controls, and in India the momentous struggle for freedom became another factor to throw academic pursuits into the background.[28]

It is a revelation, reading these expressions of dissatisfaction from concerned academicians, even in what we assume to be a 'golden era'. One recalls the hard-hitting admission made by M.G. Gupta in the same year: 'Our University is behind time in India by at least two decades, and behind the leading Universities of the West by half a century or more.'[29] The tranquil times lasted barely a decade, if even that, considering the politics of the time. The Convocation Address of C.D. Deshmukh, of 20 December 1958, is brutal in its clear appraisal of the situation:

> There can be no question that, as in other periods, this period (the 1950s) would also have produced its outstanding teachers, its brilliant scholars and its significant research work. But, if one considers the quality of the total

achievements in the light of the standards of achievement registered, and the quality of graduates produced, then one may perhaps have some cause for misgiving.[30]

Deshmukh does some plain speaking, unpleasant but accurate. The number of cases, according to him, 'about which one hears every year of the use of unfair means, not only by candidates, but also by teachers in colleges and universities, is only one aspect of the depressing situation.'

Then he goes on to utter a harder truth: 'The main reason... (is)... that persons in the academic world in India are not saturated with the true academic spirit and academic integrity.'[31] Teachers do not 'regard the pursuit of learning as one deserving the highest value.' And by pursuit of learning, Deshmukh means 'new ideas, new discourse, new points of view, deep study and expert knowledge.' In the great universities of the West, these virtues earn respect. The truth is that, apart from lip service, this cannot be said of Indian universities. This is the point Deshmukh makes, and follows it up with a few more punches: 'A wise and experienced Vice Chancellor can indeed do much to keep the University on the straight and narrow path of rectitude. But if he tries to, or is forced to, form supporting groups then, as many recent examples show, a University can go from bad to worse in no time.'[32]

As we read this, the essential immutability of the situation hits us. We've seen what happens to both kinds of vice chancellors—those who create support lobbies and those who strive to go it alone. And vice chancellors as a class seem to deserve more pity than censure, as a 1964 student's input amusingly states. (Of that presently). Deshmukh's final dart pierces home:

> The basic fact...appears...that we do not attach very high value to academic excellence, although cabinet ministers

> and other men in public life pay verbal homage to learned people, in season and out of season, and refer to the college and university teacher, as the maker of the future of the country and the builder of the new generation. The fact is that in our public life, a learned man does not count for much.[33]

This is the reason why gifted persons either do not join the University or, if they do, do so for a short while only, before joining some other better paying service. For in the 1950s too, as now, public esteem was about money, the power of enforcement associated with a chair—however temporary, the prestige of commanding visibility and the agency to do damage or to pre-empt schemes. A reputation for learning has no solvency in this scenario.

The conferment of central university status to the AU, followed by the implementation of the Sixth Pay Commission offering extremely good salaries to teachers, saw teeming numbers of ambitious and able aspirants vying for University positions. It furnishes food for thought regarding a differently manifesting syndrome in as great a departure from Deshmukh's description of the pursuit of learning as of a high value sufficient unto itself. This new syndrome is a form of intellectual consumerism, with most of the trappings of a generally consumerist society, in which quantity of production prevails over quality—and publicity, packaging and window-dressing of academic life compensate for absence of authenticity.

The point Deshmukh makes, late in the 1950s, is that few join the university from a sense of vocation; for most people it is a job like any other, and now, in our times—a comfortable, settled, well-paid job. The forms and motions of intellectual life are achieved through the fulfilment of professional requirements—even though the consequent attainments are largely spurious, just as better emoluments for research work have notched up scores of sub-standard PhD theses—benefitting only the scholar's CV.

Thus far for counter-histories; my purpose, at this point, is to represent the period of the 1960s and '70s not as a time of dismal unravelling of former excellence, but as the acceleration of processes that were in visible operation for decades preceding. Already in the early 1960s, students responding to a call for opinions in a symposium entitled 'My Idea of a University', held forth in interesting and perceptive ways.[34] Their observations make for lively reading half a century down the line. I quote from a few viewpoints expressed by what were called 'English medium' students, and they are stern and earnest. Class heterogeneity has been a reality of the AU campus, even more so then than now, the commonest agent of this disjunction being language. Another class of students might have different dissatisfactions, but I'm pretty sure language would have been a running theme. The year is 1964. While we may enjoy the charm of each one's particular precocities we must remember that these were elite students.

Krishna Chandra Srivastava of BA (Part Two) pronounces with dark severity: 'A university worth its name cannot make due contribution in the development of a nation with its unenthusiastic teaching staff, ill-equipped library and corrupt Students' Union.' Shishir Kumar of BA (Part One) lists concrete complaints: 'Nobody helps the students in the Registrar's Office… The students have no place to sit in their vacant periods—no common rooms, no chairs, no canteen and no bathrooms. My college where I used to study last year was, in this respect, ten times better than the university.'

Syed Saeed Ahmed of BA (Part One) speaks in dismal accents:

> Growing indiscipline and sporadic closure of universities have become the normal feature of our academic life. All indiscipline, however, deserves to be condemned in

> unequivocal terms. But mere condemnation will not solve the tangle, which has so far defied solution… Politics is the main rot that is eating into the very vitals of our academic life. The demagogues have defiled the temples of learning… Unions have ceased to be forums of debates and literary contests.

The young man has extreme but rather practical solutions: 'It is high time that we get rid of the evils of the students' union, and invest it with a sense of dignity by introducing drastic changes in its constitutions.' He ends with a resounding diktat: 'Pusillanimity, filth, dirt and squalor must be eliminated from the centres of learning.'

But Harish Kumar Trivedi of BA (Part One) speaks with breezy insouciance and with great point and cogency on vice chancellors in general. The vice chancellor

> …is supposed to be the head of the academic staff of the university and also something more, as the Hindi equivalent of his designation, Upa-kulpati, makes abundantly clear. But as it comes to happen, the academic side of the university looks upon him as an out and out administrator, and the administrative side as anything but an administrator. He admits no student to the university—that is supposed to be the business of the Registrar.
>
> But when a student has got to be sent down, the Vice Chancellor is the man to do it! This begets anything but respect for him. Moreover, the Vice Chancellor has the added disadvantage of not being an actual teacher and thus in not being in direct touch with the students. This only adds to the feeling of 'he-is-not-ours' which the academic side in general and [the] students in particular, come to have towards a Vice Chancellor. And, that is why, whenever

there is anything to be said against the administration of the university, it is the Vice Chancellor—we all have seen too well—who has to bear the brunt of the attack.

Which vice chancellor would stay uncharmed by this piercing analysis of his state of tragic exile!

The withering syllables of Alok Rai, BA (Part Two) survey the mess with messianic and metaphysical scorn:

> Rather than perpetrate something that must remain a mere flutter in the void, because of its lack of ballast, I prefer to criticise my own university, and trust that from these negatives a positive thesis of sorts may emerge... The recent disturbances should not be played up too much. Disturbance—even of such a nature—is one of the pitifully few alleviating features of the situation. For it is energy *misdirected*—but energy all the same. These are the few sparks left in a dying generation. These are the portents of hope for the future.

Apparently some bricks had been hurled at the vice chancellor's residence. The diagnostician of doom continues in ringing tones:

> A disease, a cancer is eating into our educational system... Our educators, God bless them, have caught the democratic virus. And this twentieth century tragedy is the result. Higher education is not meant for everybody and there is no reason why everybody should get it. We must not fight shy of the fact that even in this democratic age, abilities and capabilities have not all been reduced to the same level. Most people should be given professional training right after the Matriculation or Higher Secondary and immediately assigned useful positions. This would be in their interest also.

The foregoing lines have such an authentic ring of privilege and inherited colonial pragmatism that one might be given to understand by the young sage that 'most people' who are to be 'assigned useful positions' which would 'be in their interest also' are the hoi-polloi, the great unwashed, the plebian unteachables from Black Town; the natives, in short! But in a more serious vein, aside from the inherent attitudinal stance of the language, there was in the young scholar's prescriptions what a great many policy-makers were saying—a body of thought from which our great institutes of technology sprang. Higher education, declares Alok Rai in great wrath, has been turned into

> a cruel parody... where you train morons to become parrots. Universities are not, or should not be, factories maintained by the Government to keep the offices of the nation amply supplied with graduate clerks and post-graduate peons. And that is just what they are. And will remain so long as you compromise the sanctity of higher education with a lot of sentimental consideration for the mediocre demos which is more suited elsewhere...

The Parnassian sneer might prejudice acceptance, fifty years down the line, and there might be alternative ways of expressing it, but there is no denying the essential, if unpalatable, soundness of this perception. The young Jeremiah demands with intimidating ferocity:

> Now, what are we doing about these circumstances? Or have we left it in charge of the Divine Spirit that is moving everywhere—and appears to be as lazy as a Government Department...? ...How has this transcendent confusion reacted on the youth of India? Its fire and enthusiasm has been extinguished. It is without hope. Out of such uninspiring clods, you cannot produce a dynamic and living nation...[35]

After such turbulence, what temerity to demur, with the cautious, if craven, observation, that the youth of the 1960s Allahabad University circuit did pretty well for themselves, hopelessness and uninspiring clodhood notwithstanding! Rather than sustain a unifocal monologue of my own, I've tried to embed this analysis with recorded voices engaged in introspection, reflective reminiscence, brain-strorming, or candid critique. All of these reflect the troubled soul-searching of the 1960s and '70s, as the systemic failure manifested in its more destructive forms. When we scrutinize the lay of the land and identify the fault lines, we hone in on a few constants: breakdown of authority and uncontainable lawlessness, collapsing infrastructure, alienation between students and teachers, the declining image of the teacher, the intrusion of politics, and the irrelevance of degrees to employment. All of this, against the backdrop of the terrifyingly vast multitudes of new students pouring in every year, in a steady, ever-increasing and unmanageable human stream, as the higher education highway turned into the road to nowhere.

The word 'reorganization' pops up time and again in the University's trail; it was the holy grail sought by many but found by none. Panels of educationists, academics, policymakers and a number of commissions, singly and successively, addressed each of the issues, along with the most vexing of them all—the English language—encrypted into the DNA of this colonial university, within its founding vision. These attempts included the Abbot-Wood Report of 1936–37, the Sargeant Report of 1944, the Reorganization Scheme of 1948, the Radhakrishnan Commission of 1946, the University Enquiry Committee—also known as the Mootham Commission, the Education Commissions of 1964–66, the National Policy of Education of 1979 and 1986 and the Challenge of Education of 1985.

A silly joke of the 1950s, delivered by a dignitary after many clearings of the throat and apologies to the ladies present, was that the University 'bred too fast'. But it couldn't have been truer. As the years passed, if we scan the statistics, the hordes continued to descend in their hundreds, in thousands, until the old structures cracked under the sheer pressure of numbers. As several official reports cautioned, Indian universities were growing too large for their own good and there was no workable way to cope with the influx. The old 'unitary, residential, teaching' model could not be made to accommodate this enormous population surge.

To begin with, the vision of the University as a community in which teachers and students could live in close proximity to one another, in a fine fellowship of high learning and personal mentoring, could not work. The first thing to come apart was the tutorial system. The original idea was to have six students to one teacher. By 1926, as Di Bona's study states, it had climbed to fourteen students to a teacher; by 1941 'the tutorial program had largely disappeared, or classes called tutorials were so large they were conducted as lectures.'[36] The classes were so unwieldy and the number of teachers so inadequate, that individual attention to students was not feasible, and teaching became 'mass lecturing'.[37]

As for residential accommodation, the hostels were jam-packed, and soon enough the newly formed Delegacy had unmanageable numbers too. Building new hostels was a costly proposition, as was building larger classrooms. It has been traced, that after 1942, there was always a cash crunch. It was easier to throw in more beds, and squeeze in more benches.

> The Delegacy has come to symbolise the students who were poor, living in small rented rooms and struggling against great odds to secure an education. In many cases their parents had not been to university themselves, and they

were hard pressed to send their children there. While it is impossible to find socio-economic data on this group, it (has been) suggested that they represented the first influx of less than middle class youth into the University.[38]

The Great Indian Dream among the youth was to qualify for the Civil Services, and the university system had encouraged this dream from its inception. In his convocation address of 1893, as recorded in the minutes of the University, the vice chancellor, T. Conlan, had declared: 'the occupation, which is immediately available to those who have passed, or are passing through our University, is represented by the public service, and it is to this occupation that nearly all such persons look to (as) the end in view, and the reward of their labour.' But that was 1893. Fifty years, or even less, along the way, the 'immediate availability' of such services was a pipe dream even though there seemed to be few other optional illusions for most. Further, the hopes had been tempered down from the Indian Civil Services to any government service, failing which any other service, and as a last resort—a something-will-turn-up attitude—that propelled the crowds university-wards.

In former times, when the University's territories extended over a vast area—the United Provinces, the Central Provinces, Rajputana and even parts of Maharashtra—students qualifying in the tough entrance examination of Muir Central College were not 'representative of the general Indian population.'[39] They represented a select group, literate in English—a very tiny percentage of a province in which even vernacular literacy was very small. But as new universities came up—Nagpur, Benaras, Lucknow and Agra—it made better sense for students from those regions to head to a university nearest home. This was one reason for the shrinking in the number of quality students and the local regionalism that beset the nature of the student population. Also, for a great many students pouring in from Eastern UP, one of the poorest and least literate areas of India, a university education promised an escape from the village with its limited scope for better prospects in a town, whatever that might entail.

These possible ranks of students had always existed on the periphery of the founder-fathers' vision. A letter from Kempson, the director of public instruction, to C.A. Elliott, officiating secretary of the government of the North-Western Province, states: 'There are two modes of education—the first is intended for the benefit of the masses and is purely vernacular... The second system of education at work is that...in which English is the basis of instruction as the language of the governing class, the key to offices of trust and emoluments and the means of introducing Western science and philosophy.'[40] This clear distinction might have seemed practical to the British, but when it was confounded by the assumption of an ideal, egalitarian education for all, it could make that system crash. Not only were those from 'vernacular' secondary schools under-equipped to handle the demands of an elitist University, the poor standard of education in primary and secondary schools which sent up students for admission, was also greatly responsible for the mess.

As early as 1937, the idea of introducing vocational courses directly after secondary school had been proposed, with the idea of de-linking the graduation degree from the prospect of a job. The Abbott-Wood Report had recommended a complete set of institutions for vocational training to be set up in order to afford greater choices to students, and also to take the pressure off the universities. In 1944 it was suggested, in the Sargeant Report, that at the secondary school stage itself, there should be industrial and commercial courses. These were excellent proposals, but for one curious tendency in the provincial Indian mindset—to look down upon manual or technical jobs, and preferring the perceived respectability of a 'sarkari' one. In other words, it was better to be a clerk than a carpenter, even a prosperous one, and most definitely better to be a peon than a plumber or electrician.

It is amazing how many struggling, barely literate students pour into Allahabad University, entertaining dreams of white-collar jobs. In the old days, poor but able students—many who lacked even the most basic books—resorted to tutoring other students to earn their keep. Today there are several other earning opportunities while pursuing subjects like ancient history, education or even English literature. A young security guard who came to work for me would sit through the nights poring over notes. I learnt that he was a BA student. A newspaper delivery boy, likewise, would rush through his duties in the morning before tearing off to attend classes in the University.

I once made the students of a writing skills class describe a day in their lives, and it was moving to read through their submissions. In halting, broken English they recounted getting up very early in their cheap, uncomfortable, rented rooms, carrying empty buckets to the municipal taps on the road, filling and lugging them back, lighting their kerosene stoves and cooking their meal, then heading for some public park to study—all this before making their way to the University. It is a common sight to see economically disadvantaged students sitting alone under the trees in the Chandra Shekhar Azad Park, poring over their books. The difference between these students and those of the 1930s and '40s is that the latter could look forward to a reasonably comfortable and even bright future if they persisted long enough, while the new representatives of the 'masses' are less lucky.

Devanshu Gour, a young alumnus of the University, who now works as a senior monitoring journalist with the BBC at their New Delhi office, had a thought-provoking experience:

My first year at university brought me both shock and delight. The shock came first and took months to wear off. The school I had been to was an unimaginative institution run with unfeeling efficiency. It was also elitist in a narrow, provincial way: the message was drilled into us that it was the best school in Allahabad, and even—as one teacher told us—one of the best in north India. Looking back, I am inclined to exercise great wariness towards the first suggestion and entirely dismiss the second.

We were also trained in an attitude of snobbishness—indeed, of class discrimination—towards children from other schools, especially those from Hindi-medium ones. University was completely different. Allahabad University shook and weakened my elitism, and though I subsequently felt much the better for it, it was something of a culture shock at the time. The first day I attended a class in the English department, I found myself sitting next to a young poultry farmer from a nearby village. My urban middle class background and my school-induced snobbishness had not prepared me for interacting with someone so different. I remember not knowing what to say to him. Fortunately, over the next five years I spent at the university, I learnt a valuable life lesson: how to relate to people from backgrounds other than mine.

Years later in Delhi, I was one day accosted by a security guard at the office where I work. He had recognized me, he said, since he and I had been classmates at Allahabad University. I was embarrassed that he insisted on addressing me as 'sir' rather than by name. But I was grateful that I did not find myself in the position of the Harvard alumnus who wrote about the disadvantages of an elite education. He said that he discovered, to his discomfort, that he could not carry on a conversation with a man who came to repair the plumbing at his flat. Allahabad University offered me a strange petri dish of healthily disorienting experiences: a formerly elite institution now peopled with a large population of non-elite students.[41]

In a previous time foreign secretaries, who were Muir alumni, met at diplomatic summits and shook hands across the board, and a law minister rose from his chair in his ministerial chamber to salute a former superior at the University Training Corps. We've moved on since then, and who is to say that we've regressed? The country does not comprise foreign secretaries alone. In the embattled grounds and corridors of AU we see a new India taking shape and it is not an easy birthing. 'The mass enrolments, as well as the rural origin of students, has begun to alter the official culture of Allahabad. It is… less like an elitist British university, and more like a democratic Indian one. But the departure from an English model, which was associated with talent and achievement, has brought with it cries of "falling standards…"'[42]

It took an outsider like Edward J. Di Bona, studying the Allahabad University in 1967, to comment: '…this is the way things should really be in a new, secular, socialist and democratic society.'[43] But by the end of the century the over-crowding and infrastructural collapse had assumed nerve-wracking proportions. The young alumnus quoted above shares his experience of the stampede-like conditions that prevailed at the University counters:

> Getting the simplest tasks done—such as obtaining or submitting a form at a designated counter—was an ordeal. Not only were the clerical officials unhelpful, the students could also be violent. Through several unpleasant experiences, I learnt the best way to submit documents: put them securely in your pocket, reach the unopened

counter at least an hour before the crowd assembles, and most importantly—hold on to the bars of the window as tightly as possible. Not observing the last rule could mean you might be jerked away from the window. If, after all this, the official at the counter didn't send you back for more papers or photocopies—something they did routinely, as they never seemed to give out complete information—and if you finally got your precious enrolment form or identity card or whatever it was, your next challenge was to fight your way out of the crowd without the document getting torn or damaged...[44]

This turn-of-the-century chaos was the cumulative build-up of a half-century of steadily increasing enrolments, under the pressure of numbers churned out from the hundreds of secondary schools spread over the region. Attempts had been made to arrest or channelize this runaway growth as early as in 1948, with the appointment, by the Government of India, of the University Education Commission. Under the chairmanship of Dr Radhakrishnan (henceforth known as the Radhakrishnan Commission), it had looked into that part of the problem, which related to the poor educational grounding provided at the primary and secondary school level. And, in 1951–52, the UP government constituted what was called the Allahabad University Enquiry Committee under the chairmanship of Justice O.H. Mootham (hence its name, the Mootham Commission). It recommended that under no conditions should the total number of students in the University exceed 5,000. This is odd because by 1952 the number was already well over 6,000!

To cope with the large numbers, the Enquiry Commission emphasized the urgent need for more hostels, more Delegacy lodges and extensions to existing buildings. It pointed out that students had no facilities on the campus to make their study hours attractive or even tolerable, no common rooms to sit in, poor library and reading room arrangements, no system in place for obtaining food, a too-limited dispensary and inadequate medical arrangements. These necessities were imperative for the proper physical and mental health of students. In their absence, students put in the barest minimum hours—just enough to achieve the requisite attendance—and then left the campus. But, seeing as even in the hostels, lodges and most private homes, good conditions for study did not exist, the Enquiry Commission—after an extensive review of all these conditions—recommended strong measures. It also looked into the plight of teachers, their salaries, prospects, and perks...but of that subsequently.

Failing infrastructure was one of the primary areas of redressal. Inadequate facilities did not impact students alone. Speaking as a female teacher, I can cite a case of glaring insufficiency in the first two and a half decades of my service. Within the atmosphere of genteel etiquette prevailing in the English department, we demure lady academics displayed stupendous self-control, both over our behavioural airs and graces as over our unacknowledged bladders. There existed the remains of washrooms, possibly from the time of King Edward of merry England or, at a more conservative estimate, the coronation of Queen Elizabeth II, but they had been imperially colonized by the men. The ladies were left in a state of decorous denial of any such crude emergencies as might possibly exist, such as the sudden and distressing need to powder our noses. It was only on this side of the millennial divide that a washroom for all staff members was refashioned out of the Edwardian ruins, a gesture of egalitarian solicitude that's prompted me to frequently suggest the installation of a plaque, honouring the perceptive head who built this monument to equality.

But in a more serious vein, the issue of the swelling numbers posed a problem particularly resistant to any solution. One answer was to outsource teaching to the local affiliated colleges. Much earlier in 1932, affiliation had been granted to the Allahabad Agricultural Institute, established in 1911 by Sam Higginbottom (after whom it is currently named). The institute is built on a 610-acre plot across the Yamuna, in a beautifully designed campus funded by American missionaries. The process of affiliation was continued, when in 1950, the Allahabad University had accorded recognition to the Chaudhari Mahadeo Prasad Degree College, founded by and named after the philanthropist and patriot of the same name. In 1951, a similar recognition was extended to the Ewing Christian College, founded by the American Presbyterian missionary Reverend Arthur H. Ewing. In 1956, approval for affiliation was granted to the Agrawal Vidyalaya Intermediate College, founded in 1926 by the philanthropist Kashi Nath Ji Agarwal and renamed the Allahabad Degree College.

It must be noted that the edifice was fissuring—or extending—along religious or caste denominational lines. Initially there was a spirited debate over whether affiliation should be allowed at all; it was felt that outsourced teaching would compromise the integrity of the 'unitary, residential, teaching' model. It was even suggested that all local colleges should be affiliated to the Agra University instead. However, in view of the uncontainable influx of students keen to have an Allahabad University degree, it was resolved that colleges situated within 10 or 16 kilometres (another debated matter) of the Senate Hall, should be construed as falling within Allahabad University's jurisdiction.

In course of time, more local intermediate colleges were upgraded to BA degree status. These included Ishvar Saran Degree College in 1970—founded in 1933 by Munshi Iswar Saran, well-known associate of Mahatma Gandhi, and a dedicated social worker committed to 'Harijan' uplift; Arya Kanya Degree College in 1975—originally part of the Arya Samaj circuit; Hamidia Girls' College, in 1975—founded by Begum Khursheed Khwaja, daughter of Hamidullah Jung, law minister to the Nizam of Hyderabad and wife of Khwaja Abdul Majid, barrister and freedom fighter; Jagat Taran Girls' Degree College in 1975—founded in 1919 by the freedom fighter, Major Baman Das Basu; Rajarshi Tandon Girls' Degree College in 1975—founded by Purushottam Das Tandon in 1882; Sadanlal Sanwaldas Khanna Degree College in 1975; Shyama Prasad Mukherjee College in 1997; and the KP Training College, part of the KP Trust—originally founded by Munshi Kali Prasad Kulbhashkar in 1873, and affiliated to the Allahabad University when it became a central university in 2005. As may be noticed from this list, the large majority of these colleges, after the first spurt of the 1950s, were affiliated in the mid-1970s.

The University Grants Commission Act of 1956 had 'been authorised to recommend to the Central Government, to declare by notification in the Official Gazette, that any institution for higher education other than a University, shall be deemed to be a University for the purpose of the Act.'[45] Accordingly, some colleges, for example, the Agriculture Institute (now named the Sam Higginbottom Institute of Agriculture, Technology and Sciences), the Motilal Nehru Regional Engineering College and the Ewing Christian College, became autonomous. The University has developed into a federation, like Delhi University. The act's provision for deemed universities opened the possibility for the Allahabad University itself to be upgraded, and deemed a central university. The twentieth century ended on this hope. It would materialize five years into the twenty-first.

The next step in decentralizing teaching was suggested by the National Policy on Education in 1986, which 'recognised the need for providing autonomy to such of the colleges as have inter-alia the capacity to undertake innovations, design curricula, evolve methods of teaching and learning, frame their own rules for admission, prescribe…courses of study, and conduct examinations.'[46] Part V of this policy envisaged the development of associate colleges into autonomous institutions, and some colleges did indeed achieve this end.

In the decades that had passed since the early days of Muir Central College, the position of the teacher had also changed. The legendary first-generation teachers had a paternalistic relationship with their students, both morally and materially. Quite obviously, their own material conditions, as members of the Imperial (or subsequently the Indian) Educational Service, and its local brand—the Provincial Educational Service, put them in a position of prosperity, reasonable enough to allow for personal comfort and pecuniary generosity. Even as academics in the University, they continued drawing salaries in the IES and PES grades.

But teachers appointed directly to positions at the AU received more modest remunerations. A study reveals that in 1926, their average salary was ₹448. Thirty years later, in 1956, it had climbed to an average of just ₹489. Actually, a uniform pay scale specifically for university teachers did not exist till much later. Faculty members from the IES drew related scales—even when working as professors in the University—and those employed through the PES were paid according to their calibrations. Since the latter were recruited in India, their remuneration was less than the IES, and so a cause for some heartburn. Lecturers were absurdly underpaid; in 1948 they started at ₹250 and could go up to ₹450 a month. Those few professors who were directly appointed, however, were paid in the range of ₹800 to 1200. There were always very few readers, just a handful, and they were in the ₹450 to 800 salary order.

After a great many technical discussions, the proposals of the Enquiry Committee were put into effect in 1962. Accordingly, professors came in to the ₹1,000 to 1,500 pay band; readers, ₹700–1,100; but lecturers remained stuck at ₹400–800. The committee also suggested that the middle rank of reader, or associate professor, be altogether abolished, and merged with the lecturer or assistant professor grade. But this remained a proposal on paper, despite some canvassing from teachers' groups who, from time to time, raised a demand for a single running grade, which, in their view, would pre-empt unwholesome rivalries and a vitiation of academic atmosphere.

It was a curious break-up: professors of the old IES/PES drew much higher salaries, lived in enormous bungalows with several acres of garden area, holidayed in Mussoorie in the summer months and drove around in their European or American cars. Even their subsequent avatars, the ones who drew university grades, received four times more than the lecturers. In 1964 there were fourteen professors out of a total of 274 teachers, only 8 readers and 252 lecturers. There seemed to be little chance of moving up. Most lecturers could see themselves growing old and retiring in the same position at a salary of ₹800 per month, at the end of a long career. Such a state of affairs could engender two mindsets: (a) it could generate an idyllic, non-competitive state of well-being, in which general good fellowship prevailed, since none were more equal than others (as described by my senior colleague at the beginning of this chapter) (b) it could demotivate and foster a state of academic stagnation, arresting the progress of knowledge.

As it turned out, both states could work to the detriment of the institution. Of course, there were always those individual teachers, extraordinarily gifted, nonetheless committed to their subjects and to the joy of teaching. But as Edward Di Bona's shrewd outsider's eye observed, the emphasis in AU in the 1960s was on the examination and the degree, and not the growth of the student's mind. And courses and examination papers maintained a certain monolithic uniformity over long periods, quite out of step with the development of disciplines the world over. It is no wonder then, that only a few good students opted for the teaching profession as a permanent choice and if they taught for a while, it was only to buy time before their appointments to more lucrative jobs at the earliest opportunity. There was a lot of talk about the widening gulf between teachers and students, but in their underpaid, overworked state, teachers possibly did not—or could not—give of their best.

The historian Tara Chand wrote an accurate, if slightly melodramatic, description of the plight of the AU teacher, from which I quote:

> Relations between those whose function was to guide, and those who enjoyed the privileged status of pupils, became strained. The only remedy which could mitigate the unsatisfactory state, was a transformation of the University teacher in response to this challenge. Although some individuals did rise to the occasion, it was unrealistic to expect everyone to undergo an inner revolution. Nor did conditions encourage a development of this nature. The teacher was involved in conflicts and grievances, which intimately affected his life and career. For the vast majority—low incomes with increasing burdens of rising prices and growing families; lack of social recognition and esteem; inadequacy of means and instruments, for scholarship and research; heavy teaching duties, and increasing numbers in classes—these and other factors combined to make him ineffective, a helpless mariner on a rudderless craft buffeted by winds and waves, carried up and down streams, unable to control his boat, and incapable of steering it towards the destination.[47]

Tara Chand was writing his tribute to Amaranatha Jha in *Amaranatha Jha: A Memorial Volume,* edited by K.K. Mehrotra. Jha, himself a far more forceful and pointed speaker, spoke tersely on the matter, in a convocation address delivered on 4 October 1952, at the Maharaja Sayajirao University of Baroda. Parts of it bear repeating in this context. Speaking of intellectual and political freedom, Jha qualified:

> In order…that this academic freedom should flourish, it is of the utmost importance that teachers should be free from financial worries… Teachers' salaries in our country are so low, that one wonders whether the powers that be realise how seriously they are damaging the future of the country, at its fountainhead. A discontented teacher, almost always on the verge of want, is a grave menace to the community, a greater menace than an inefficient teacher… It should cause anxiety, to watch the reluctance of able persons to join the teaching profession, and the readiness with which they seize any opportunity to leave it… It is all very well to preach the ideal of plain living and high thinking. But too often it amounts to living in want and no leisure for any thinking at all.[48]

Happily, this is now in the past, as present-day pay scales show. When I joined in 1977, as a permanent lecturer in what was called a substantive post (just after the declaration of my MA results), things were already marginally better, with the lecturer now starting in the ₹600–700 pay band. The Mootham Committee, or as it was officially known, the University Enquiry Committee, had suggested measures for the relief of the teaching community in 1952. These included: relaxing the rules of subscription to the provident fund, study leave provisions, life insurance, medical benefits, better service conditions and residential accommodation. All of these saw implementation in the course of time.

Personal promotion and subsequent career advancement schemes enabled upward mobility, and obviated demotivation and stagnation. Demands for parity—in payment of allowances and facilities—with teachers of central universities, had been very much a part of the AU Teachers' Association's agenda since the early 1980s. The upgrade to central university status, in conjunction with the implementation of the Sixth Pay Commission's recommendations, proved a veritable windfall both for the coffers, as well as the social position of AU teachers.

But whether good salaries and benefits guarantee better commitment to profession is another matter. Many alumni from the 1960s, up until the '90s, recall that some malaise seemed to afflict the teaching profession. What seemed missing was the spark of passion for subject and vocation—what Amaranatha Jha has elsewhere called 'the swell of soul'[49], and the qualities of 'zest, enthusiasm, ardour'—as distinct from imitative book learning that could be regurgitated. There were always memorable examples of teachers whose classes promised intellectual excitement and discovery, but—for the most part—lectures prepared long ago were repeated, and sometimes dictated, with lacklustre recurrence year after year. What was being undertaken was a routine grind, a necessary evil to earn a salary, even though a better one than previously. C.D. Deshmukh's severe indictment of spurious academics has already been cited, and the teacher's absence of interest was eminently transparent to students.

As the organizational failure slowly imploded the institution, especially in the disturbed 1980s and '90s, an atmosphere of laxity spread to the teaching community as well and accountability became an individual imperative alone. In a system where there have been too many malpractices in the selection of teachers, bitterness and a spirit of vendetta breed, often with a caste angle to it. The rise of the 'teacher-politician', the one who dabbles in power games on the campus for personal and caste advantage, has not helped matters. An upgrade of one's own knowledge threshold is rare, although there is often a bustling parade of it.

Then there are teachers who should not have been selected for the profession to begin with. There are teachers who are eminently suited for the profession, but who choose to flaunt a lofty disdain for their rustic students, for a decaying university and towards their middle-brow colleagues. Even preferring to deny their classrooms the honour of their presence, they appear only to sign salary bills, or put in minimal token appearances. These incumbents, too—passengers who steal free rides on public transport and then curse it for its faults, as one alumnus described—have liberally contributed to AU's fall from its high estate, as much as the other obvious forces of demography or social change.

Amaranatha Jha's strong reprimand, uttered in 1952, has continued to have enormous topical relevance:

> Teachers have some grave obligations and also some rights. They should have the right to conditions of work that will enable them to function efficiently; for instance, leisure for preparing lessons, and manageable numbers in class. They should have the right to a salary that will reflect their professional status, the right to protection against dismissal without just cause, the right to professional freedom... All these rights must be safeguarded, but they must first be *earned*. Certain duties have also to be performed, some obligations fulfilled. Responsibilities must be assumed...[50]

Jha speaks of 'the uncertainty, the drift, the absence of ideals in the teaching profession'.[51] To those of us who have been borne along on this drift, 'the absence of ideals' has surfaced time and again. When merit is mysteriously passed over, when documents disappear or are doctored, when crass cronyism shows itself in the allotment of positions, when opponents are manhandled, when CVs are manipulated and certificates forged, when strategically interpreted and ill-thought out norms effectively filter out the names of able candidates before selection—and we are not even touching upon the matter of money flows—then the toxicity of the festering environment induces both suffocation and cynicism. Let me go back to Jha one more time, to some lines of a poem by Mildred Howland, which he read or maybe quoted from memory in 1952, at the convocation at Baroda University:

> How shall we teach
> A child to reach
> Beyond himself and touch
> The stars
> We who have stooped so much?
> How shall we tell
> A child to dwell
> With honour, live and die
> For truth,
> We who have lived a lie....

In case this is taking an overly bleak view of the situation, something must be said on behalf of those teachers who continue to work to the best of their power, albeit in meeting a different kind of need; but who still find the quality of their performance deteriorating, because of the constituency they serve. A very substantial scholar of history shared his disturbance on this point, saying that the nature of students is such that there is absolutely no element of stimulating challenge for the teacher; one has to habitually perform beneath the level of one's natural capacities. Delivering something old anyhow, in the desperate hope of achieving some description of intelligible communication, the teacher fills serious gaps in secondary and even primary education, in students who have muddled through school without learning very basic things.

Over a period of time, the absence of challenge and the pressures of under-performance lead to a general degeneration of intellectual muscle, a tragic dumbing-down, which results in a quality of output which quite often cannot measure up to national standards. Every earnest teacher in the Allahabad University has felt this at some time or the other—barring those fortunate enough to labour under comfortable delusions of self-worth—and the usual self-defensive, maybe unconscious, reflex is provincial arrogance and insular complacence. This is one of the saddest fallouts of the decay, quite like the discoloured, mouldering walls of the noble buildings.

Still, there are teachers who are able to break through this handicap too. I shall cite the accounts of two alumni, the first one by Ashok Kumar Barat, the chief executive officer (CEO) of a well-known multinational company, who was a student in the commerce faculty in the mid-1970s:

> One of my first memories of the University is our encounter with Professor B.B. Lal, who taught us accountancy. He was a sharp-witted but fastidious person, given to paranoic displays of his obsession with grooming, hygiene and discipline. He was always impeccably dressed in a suit, despite sweltering summers and the long hours of power cuts that the University witnessed routinely.
>
> Since there were a number of students who had come with a science background, accountancy was an alien subject for them. The curriculum assumed the students to have come with some degree of knowledge about the subject. However,

Professor Lal, realizing this inadequacy, planned a few sessions on the basis of accountancy. His opening comment was that the double-entry bookkeeping was nothing but a commercial adaptation of the adage 'as you sow, so shall you reap'. He went on to explain, philosophically, the balancing influence of good and evil deeds in one's lifetime, and how these translated to a fundamental principle of every debit having a credit, and vice versa.

The other professor who made a distinct impression on his students was Professor J.S. Mathur, an ardent and practicing Gandhian, who taught us economic history. He left no opportunity to pepper his discussion with what Gandhi would have thought or done, if he was faced with similar situations in history. I must confess that in school I had developed a distaste for the subject, because of the manner in which it was taught—cramming up dates and events only, thereby representing the historical characters as devoid of life, emotion and thought. My exposure to economic history through Professor Mathur whetted my appetite to look at history not merely as a chronicle of events, but also as a portrait of people thinking, responding and acting. I was also enlightened to the knowledge that many of those events had a high probability of recurrence, albeit under different circumstances and manifested differently, and therefore those who ignored it were condemned to repeat it...[52]

That was surely a syllabus-surpassing bit of learning!

The other quote is from Devanshu Gour, a student of the University in the late 1990s:

The teachers ranged from very poor to very good. The very good ones are memorable, and though the syllabus was outdated, their mastery over it was so thorough that it used to be a real pleasure attending their classes. Sitting in the high-ceilinged classrooms of the English department while Professor Manas Mukul Das would, in his leisurely fashion, make Eliot or Hardy or Yeats come alive—quoting them from memory with the natural ease of someone who had closely known the lines for decades—one would feel transported from the broken desks and neglected old building.

Indeed, the very neglect of something so grand and noble, now fallen upon adverse days, lent the setting of these electrifying lectures an air of great authenticity. In the well-tended classrooms of St. Stephen's, or the colleges of Oxford, I could not imagine my poultry farmer or security guard classmates passionately following a lecture on Eliot. It was fascinating to see how Professor Das, lecturing entirely in English, was able to powerfully convey the thrill of the poems to a classroom full of students who did not know basic English. I recall how, on one occasion, after the class ended, one of my classmates got up and told me in Hindi: '*Yeh to mehsoos kara dete hain* (He makes you experience it).'[53]

Maybe that's what Amaranatha Jha meant by 'the swell of soul'.

Teaching was inextricably tied up with the vexing language question, brought to a boil in the 1960s, when the Angrezi Hatao agitation erupted. But angrezi was, as I have written earlier in this chapter, encrypted into the DNA of this colonial University. Macaulay had prescribed an educational system designated to create 'a class of persons Indian in blood and colour but English in tastes, in opinions, in morals and in intellect'.[54] In keeping with that, William Muir, guiding spirit of Muir Central College, had declared that he 'would not support any scheme which did not make proficiency in English a condition of obtaining degrees'.[55] As Di Bona put it in his 1967 study, 'the single most important element of culture transfer was the English language. It was seen as the necessity for clear thinking, moral training, occupational success'.[56] It was not merely language proficiency that was considered imperative for moulding a new kind of native mind; it was reckoned important to expose the Indian mind to English literature as a manner of psychological grooming.

It is interesting to know that English literature as a subject of study was not taken seriously in Oxford and Cambridge in the nineteenth century. The respectable subjects there were the Classics, which meant texts in Latin and Greek to be learnt by 'construing', that is, comprehension, followed by exact translation, and finally by committing to memory. It was only when the ICS examinations were introduced to select men for professional government service that an intensive knowledge of English literature was thought desirable. In fact, English became 'a core subject' in the Civil Service examinations, and British universities were compelled to introduce an organized English literature syllabus. 'Foremost among these subjects we place our own language and literature', as the conceptualizers of the ICS put it.[57] The function of this introduction was bifocal: to give the Englishmen coming to India a sense of their own literary heritage and a consciousness of imperial identity, and subsequently—as we shall see later—to fashion the native mind in an English mould.

There is a powerful ongoing discussion about the way English language and literature were used, to engineer social control in influencing Indians towards giving psychological consent to British rule; as a political instrument. The choice of authors and texts in the Calcutta University courses would not entirely support a political agenda other than providing concentrated exposure to a particular culture. It is interesting to glance through a couple of Muir Central College's English literature question papers. The BA paper of 1889 has questions like: 'Discuss Shakespeare's portrayal of the common people in *Coriolanus*.'; 'Is the name Butler's Sermons a misnomer? To what extent are they polemical? How is his style affected by the nature of his subject and his mode of treating it?' The MA question paper of 1893 is scarcely less formidable. It includes questions like: 'What are the limits to which Law and Public Opinion may use coercion to promote virtue—with reference to Mill's *Liberty*?'

Through this exhaustive culture transfer, a version of Indian personality resulted, of which Amaranatha Jha would be the perfect exemplar—a competent, intensively exposed Eng Lit man who was, counter-intuitively, something of a divided soul. The language issue was very much in Jha's mind even when AU was at the peak of its Anglophone and Anglophile phase. At the Baroda Convocation, Jha made a powerful case for English, while simultaneously making a clearer claim on behalf of the Indian languages:

> It cannot be gainsaid that to the English language we owe much. We found inspiration in our national struggle in the writings of Burke, Godwin, Shelley, Mill, Morley and Swinburne. The annual sessions of the National Congress could, in the earlier years, have been conducted only in English. Dadabhai Naoroji could have conversed with W.C. Bonnerjee through English and not through any Indian language. Among the forces that united India and made us one nation, English must be reckoned to have been one of the most powerful. English was the only language in which the Legislative Assembly or the All-India bodies could conduct their business...
>
> But that cannot make us forget that it is a difficult tongue and a foreign tongue, that it must always remain alien,

> that only a few of us can use it. Its importance in the international sphere cannot be minimised... But surely it offends all educational principles to make a foreign language the medium of education. Every child has the right to be taught through its mother tongue. In the secondary stage and at the university the regional language should be the medium of instruction...[58]

Many scholars then made a case for multilingual proficiency. But the English question hasn't only been about speaking, teaching or examinations. It was about class and power, and it later got willy-nilly mixed up with a subsequent nationalist agenda—the ensuing sequel to the early days of Nationalism, enabled by the very language noisily decried in the turbulent agitations of the 1960s. The issue had gathered much before the '60s, as the British presence on the AU campus slowly reduced. Edward Di Bona has tracked this withdrawal:

> Until the administration of G.N. Jha in 1923 practically all the Vice Chancellors had been Englishmen, and these had been connected with the High Court located in Allahabad. Two exceptions were Sir P.C. Bannerjee and Sir Sunder Lal, both Justices themselves. Registrars were all drawn from Principals of Muir College, with which the university shared offices. In 1896, the composition of the Boards of Study showed 37 Westerners, and 6 Indians in the University. This general pattern was followed in the case of examiners, Deans, teachers and others connected with the University. In sharp contrast to the period we shall deal with subsequently, the list of persons who addressed the Convocation between 1887 and 1929 were again almost entirely Western.[59]

In 1923, with the election of Ganganatha Jha as vice chancellor, the long line of British top administrators came to an end, and after 1920, all registrars have been Indian. From 1923 the deans of the science faculty are all Indians too; for commerce, with one exception, the year is 1929; arts, 1930; and law, 1931. In other aspects as well, the University was able to demonstrate its independence. Sir William Hailey was the last foreigner, in 1929, to address the convocation. So far as the teachers are concerned, a few Englishmen remained in service—S.G. Dunn in the English department until at least 1930, and Sir Charles Weir in law until almost 1937. But these were exceptions, and by 1941, all the teachers listed in the calendar had Indian names.'[60]

The demand to include Hindi as a medium of instruction was examined by several commissions as the process of Indianization overtook the University, and as the origins and class character of the students changed. The Reorganization Scheme of 1949 had suggested the introduction of Hindi as a compulsory language at all stages, and also the abolition of the distinction between Hindustani and Anglo-Hindustani schools. But it had also suggested the retention of English at the secondary stage. The Radhakrishnan Commission had likewise suggested a balanced approach to the language issue. The University Enquiry Committee of 1951–52 had proposed that the regional language be adopted as the medium of instruction at the undergraduate level, and English be phased out slowly over a period of ten years. It had put forward elaborate plans for setting up translation bureaus for 'producing the needed literature in the Indian languages; advised the retention of English at the postgraduate level; but was silent on the language of Ph.D. theses.'[61]

Edward J. Di Bona's table of popular courses in AU reveals that in the years 1927, 1932, 1937 and 1940, English kept its position as the first choice of students. In 1962, it disappeared from the chart. Hindi as the first choice, followed by philosophy and ancient history, took its place.[62] Di Bona also states that in

1951, teaching in Hindi had started in several departments—including in science, which after some experimentation gave it up. Slowly, a bunch of Hindi-medium BA courses held the majority of students, with only one English-medium section for those who preferred their lectures in English.[63] On the campus, the language used between students was Hindi rather than English, as they came from Hindi-medium secondary schools, and this posed a great handicap and an intensification of antipathy.

The AU student had, and continues to have, a love-hate relationship with English. In 1937, records show a loud student demonstration insisting, and succeeding, in the matter of inviting Madan Mohan Malaviya to address the convocation, which he did—in Hindi—something unprecedented in AU. About ten years after Independence, the statue of Queen Victoria was removed from its marble pedestal in the Alfred Park (now Chandra Shekhar Azad Park). I have yet to find out whether or not Victoria's nose was actually smashed by passionate patriots or if that is only a rumour. But even in our times, the park witnesses a comic if lesser-known tradition of anti-colonial zeal in the third week of February, during that so-Brit spring event, the Annual Flower and Dog Show. Students of the Hindu Hostel, that bastion of classic nationalism, invade the show with their own entry—an Indian mixed-breed stray dog wearing a garland—who, at their aggressive insistence, is actually made a contestant, and carried in by these ardent patriots in a boisterous procession. It is usually a terrified pup because carrying about a grown street dog, who might just express his dissent in unwelcome ways, is a daunting prospect, even for the sternest hostel patriot.

Deciding which language should replace English was always an embattled question. In AU, it inevitably turned into a Hindu-Muslim issue, as arguments in favour of Sanskritized Hindi and Persianized Urdu were hotly supported, and so much heat was generated at the meetings of the University Court that the matter was dropped. I recall having heard a fervent student language-activist thunderously describe Bharat Mata in a quite literally spectacular optic metaphor, with Sanskrit as her third eye; Hindi, India's official language, her left eye; and the language of the region, her right eye. English is depicted as a pocket-telescope to view the big world far, far away! It would have been inappropriate to have asked the speaker whether Bharat Mata's saree had pockets.

The Hindu–Muslim standoff that had come to exist in the Congress party had not yet overtly percolated AU's academic domains, although both Sir Shafaat Ahmed Khan and Pandit Madan Mohan Malaviya had put forward cautionary complaints, that the 'other' sectarian group was being favoured. The fallout of the language impasses was that neither Hindi nor Urdu could be called the language of the region. As for Hindustani, that elegant and natural-blended combination that most people used—that both Gandhi and Nehru favoured, and that Lohia certainly did not frown upon—it had its vehement purist-critics who condemned it as an ersatz and unworthy form. Jha himself was a severe critic of Hindustani, preferring the pure and parallel coexistence of Sanskritized Hindi and Persian Urdu to any 'unholy' mixture of the two. The language question, as a facet of identity politics, mirrored many complex issues of ethnicity, class, and territory in the 1960s, leading to inflamed passions in political communications and public spaces.

'Legislatures have walked out of the Assembly Hall in Lucknow over minor linguistic issues, and politicians have generally been uncompromising in their efforts to do away with English as soon as possible.'[64] In 1963, that iconic socialist, Ram Manohar Lohia, who had been a frequent presence at the Allahabad University Union, uttered a protest call to students to abandon their classes, and not come back until all books had been translated into Hindi. The following year C.B. Rao, retired ICS member and famous AU alumnus, urged students to demand that all classroom teaching be done in Hindi. The demand for translated books did not take into consideration the fact that 'a lot of such (translated) literature was already available but rotting in the stock rooms of granth academies, Hindi samitis and Urdu academies'.[65]

Strong words passed during debates in the Constituent Assembly, and Hindi supporters like Seth Govind Das and Purushottam Das Tandon won the field. The government of independent India, accordingly, stood committed to the use of Hindi as its official language, with the temporary and time-framed continuance of English to be phased out, and eventually given up in 1965. It was a decision fraught and problematic, because it antagonized the thousands of South Indians who had learnt Hindi under the aegis of the Dakshin Bharat Hindi Prachar Sabha in their nationalist impulse, but who now saw their own considerably rich languages relegated to the minor status of regional languages.[66] As soon as the Angrezi Hatao Movement[67] began in 1967, anti-Hindi demonstrations burst into flames in South India. 'It took 66 deaths and 10 self-immolations in the anti-Hindi student agitation of Tamil Nadu, for the government to realise that a language could not be imposed on any people against their wishes.'[68]

In Allahabad, an anti-English agitation broke out. Some shop signages in English were disfigured or smashed. In English, lecture-class sounds of shoes scraping against floors erupted intermittently to disturb teaching. There were a few comic incidents too. A Hindi activist approached a senior teacher of the English department and declared wrathfully: '*Aapke scooter ka ank-pat angrezi mein hai. Kyon na main ise aag laga doon?* (The number plate on your scooter is in English. Why don't I set fire to it?) 'The English teacher, always quick on the uptake, retorted: *'Aapki ghadi ke ank angrezi mein hain. Kyon na main ise pehle phod daloon?* (The numerals on your watch are in English. Why don't I smash your watch first?)' But while there was a Hindi word for 'watch', there wasn't one for 'scooter'. There is a postscript to this laughable exchange. Some years later, the activist met the academic and gave him his visiting card. The don was quietly delighted to notice that the card was in English!

One consequence of turning AU into a primarily Hindi-phone institution was the exodus of students from other states of India, coinciding with the founding of the Jawaharlal Nehru University (JNU) as also the heightened eminence of Delhi University. Within a short time, the crowds of Civil Service aspirants from distant regions of the country, who had earlier flocked to AU because of its reputation, preferred to head for Delhi. The river had changed its course, and what was left to Allahabad's portion was a thin trickle of residual local streams that fed a stagnant pool. The age of parochial localism now commenced, but it took some time to register. By then the changes had become irreversible.

An attempt was made by the Executive Council on 16 June 1984 with a grandiose declaration. Resolution No. 131 announced that

> The Executive Council of the University of Allahabad viewed with concern, the falling of educational standards all round, and (the) increasing tendency among Indian universities to localise and regionalise themselves, leading to inbreeding in the academic system. Therefore, keeping in view the past tradition and high reputation of the University, the Council resolved to recapture its past glory by declaring the University of Allahabad a National and Equal Opportunity Institution of Higher Learning in the

> country. The Executive Council directs various university bodies and offices to work towards the implementation of these objectives...[69]

This diktat has the boom of a royal fiat uttered by a disempowered monarch who finds his delusions of grandeur failing. As per this decree, henceforth 25 per cent of seats would be opened to students from other states. It was all to no avail. Too much water had flowed down the Sangam. Very few students were interested in coming to Allahabad, even when lured by cutting-edge subjects like geophysics and microbiology. A few straggling foreign students from countries with less developed educational infrastructure than India's come annually, only to discover a different idiom of inefficiency and anarchy than the kind back home.

As for the place of English, history has this counter-intuitive way of overleaping, even mocking human expectation. The leading lights of the Angrezi Hatao Movement could not possibly have known that they were historically positioned on the leeward side of a massive storm that would leave the world transformed—that of the digital and cyber revolution and the onset of globalization. These would re-implicate English in the lives of ordinary Indians in a neo-colonial incarnation, with American commercial imperialism counter-weighed by Asian self-confidence, so that far from being a symbol of privilege and power, English would turn into an appropriated, culturally morphed and convenient tool.

There's poetic justice as well as comic relief in the situation. The city is now dotted with private English teaching 'institutes' with curious names like Trounce, Lingua Franca, Stratford Academy and Oxford Classes. Like the ghost of Banquo, English is there and not there, present in the widespread hankering to speak it well, absent in the equally widespread mongrelizations in which it clothes itself. For my part I find myself holding forth to my BA students, much to my colleagues' unspoken disapproval: '*Jab Macbeth ki antar-aatma vidroh karti hai, tab uski kalpana-shakti teevra ho uthti hai. Usay bhram hote hain, drishya dikhai dete hain, aavazein sunai deti hain...*'[70]

But how in tarnation do I translate 'three witches'? Not 'teen chudail' surely! So I go into a lengthy explanation about women energy healers, and the opposition of organized religion and heresy, and the church and the seventeenth-century witchhunts. All this has nothing to do with the BA examination, but my students are patient and suffer my excesses, if not gladly then at least with indulgence.

7
WANING DAY

Through the 1950s and till the early '70s, student unrest on the Allahabad University campus manifested itself through a curious and altogether inconsistent combination of pious Gandhian fasting and noisy vandalism. In fact, the many ways in which Gandhi's vocabulary has been appropriated and his idiom pantomimed by Indian politicians of all stripes and seniorities, would make for a piquant study.

As early as 1948, the University witnessed a conflict in the Students' Union, regarding the legitimacy of certain elections. The following year there was an uprising, defying the proctor's orders against an increase in hostel fees. The same year, there was also a demonstration against the education minister of UP who had come as a guest of the University. Then a two-year lull followed till 1951, when chaos reigned in an examination hall during a tough economics paper, its nature somewhat closer to the agitations of the late 1980s. 1951 had already had its share of political unrest at the campus, when Sri Golwalkar of the Rashtriya Swayamsevak Sangh (RSS) was invited by the Students' Union president to lecture the students, and a clash broke out between his loyalists and opponents. The following year, the Students' Union took issue with Eleanor Roosevelt's visit to the University, and demonstrated against it. Between 1952 and 1953, records reveal, there were three different incidents of violent protest.[1]

Although there is a University Ordinance stating that anyone engaging in a hunger strike must be expelled, in practice this does not happen because of the Gandhian association of sanctity it commands. Records show that hunger strikes were most common, and students in AU agitations regularly used the bhukh-hartal—in 1955 by one Lakhan Singh, 1959 by Badri Vishal and 1964 by Mirza Hussain.[2] Hussain was forced to give up his strike and removed by armed police in the middle of the night. It was not uncommon for proctors and other university functionaries to ritually capitulate before a student on hunger strike by offering him his first glass of juice.

It is amusing to read how, in a 1959 protest demonstration against the vice chancellor, students sang '*Raghupati Raghav Raja Ram*' at the full force of their lungs outside the VC's bungalow.[3] (They had recently gone around offering posies of flowers, in Gandhigiri, to functionaries of the University administration—possibly including one whom they had once bathed in coal tar.) Their demands were frequently very mundane, but the Ram-dhun soundtrack gave it dignity and an aura of high principle.

The 1960s had been a time of language wars. The central episode of the 1970s was the Emergency. On 12 June 1975, the Allahabad High Court quashed Indira Gandhi's election to the Lok Sabha for technical election irregularities. On 26 June, the country awoke to read the word Emergency splashed in bold type on the front pages of newspapers, suddenly guarded in tone as they reported the events. At the stroke of the midnight hour, while the world had slept, the president of India, S.S. Ray, had quietly and without demur signed the declaration of Emergency that his imperious lady prime minister had brought to him.

It took some days to register this suspension of fundamental rights, the discontinuance of the Habeas Corpus Act. Allahabad had earlier had its political dissenters, those out of sympathy with the ascendant Indira Gandhi legend and the parliamentary pantheon made up of her coterie. There had been some healthy challenging in public deliberations of the 'Durga-in-conflict, Kautilya-in-counsel' stardom, the 'Indira-is-India and India-is-Indira' sycophancies, and the 'only-man-in-a-Parliament-of-women' fanfare. In particular, the Jayaprakash Narayan Movement had strong links with Allahabad, which had always been an argumentative city, and the Allahabad University crowd was prominent amidst the circle of dissenters. It was the Allahabad High Court's historic judgment that had triggered off these events.

The country had never been as superficially disciplined as in the eleven months that followed. While trains ran on time, streets were clean and government functionaries always present, punctual and polite. There was also something sinister and abnormal in the paeans of praise pouring out of both the state-authorized media and the private-run magazines, including very respectable ones like *The Illustrated Weekly of India*. There were, of course, worthy exceptions like the plucky little paper *Himmat*.

Saplings were planted along major streets. Some slums were cleared. And then rickshaw-pullers, small-time vendors, construction workers and even beggars began running for their lives as the vasectomy teams started targeting 'volunteers'.

When the state of Emergency was declared, the University was in the middle of its examinations. In class, no matter what the topic, the discourse turned warily to the subject of freedom and democracy, and what they involved. Those with socialist leanings talked socialism, and right-wingers spoke of Ram Rajya. In my MA (Previous) English literature classes, a teacher talked incessantly of the Courts of High Commission, and the Star Chamber in Tudor England and the subsequent Civil War. The talk turned inevitably to the American and French Revolutions, the Rights of Man, the Boston Tea Party. I don't think our teachers were en masse on a crusade to educate the young in the vocabulary of rights as much as giving vent to suppressed personal indignations of their own.

Then abruptly the talk stopped and the rumours began. So-and-so had received a warning, such-and-such had been asked to be more mindful of his own safety. By now the dreaded Maintenance of Internal Security Act, or the MISA as it was called, was in force. People were picked up without warning, sent to jail without trial. Some High Court lawyers boldly represented the detenues picked up under the MISA. Of the eight people arrested in Allahabad, four were university teachers—Dr Banwari Lal Sharma, Dr Murli Manohar Joshi, Dr Krishna Lal and Dr Raghuvansh. Dr Sharma was closely linked to Jayaprakash Narayan's movement, Dr Raghuvansh was a Lohia supporter, Dr Joshi an RSS sympathizer, and Dr Lal—who was not political to the best of his colleagues' knowledge—was jailed for stray remarks. As one retired professor told me, 'No one will ever know why these four were picked up.' Of the four, Dr Raghuvansh's case was the most bizarre. He was jailed on the trumped-up charge of stealing telephone wires!

The University functioned with uncanny efficiency and a few token meetings were held purporting to condemn the events. The campus seemed intent, its articulations coded in ambiguities. Beneath the surface, old smouldering animosities used the Emergency to settle personal, and possibly caste-lobby, scores, threatening or out-manouevring campus opponents. There were some who played a mysteriously ambiguous role, affecting to be champions of democratic protest, while receiving some secret assurance of immunity from arrest. There were others suspected of being informers. Some functioned as undercover hosts to wanted persons, but most maintained a subdued caution. When a particular teacher parked his scooter with its front facing the gate, people guessed that he'd received a tip-off and was ready to take flight, though nobody said anything. When the scooter was parked facing the building, people knew there was no cause for the teacher to be anxious that day.

To students, much of these goings-on were peripheral. That academic year of 1975–76 was a concentrated one for me, unbroken by student unrest, closures or postponed examinations. So the uproar that broke out on the night of the Janata Party's victory at the polls is something unforgettable. Slogans rang out in the normally still and patrolled nocturnal streets, which were now milling with crowds till very late hours. No University classes were held the following morning. Peeping into the staffroom, we saw the chairs around the twin tables full, the atmosphere charged, as multiple simultaneous conversations buzzed in the kindled air. The most frequently used word I recall hearing was 'she'.

As soon as the Emergency was lifted, the dam burst. The campus was once again the anarchic battleground of competing self and group interests that it had slowly become, now only more so than before. It seemed as though the months of forced discipline were being reversed with a perverse vengeance. It's not that student unrest was unknown to the University; there were many instances of violent student agitation, as has been recounted at the beginning of the chapter. Yet, the virulent nature of law and order breakdown that overtook the AU campus after the withdrawal of the Emergency would initiate another phase of disintegration, destined to definitively alter the character of university culture for a time. 1979–81 is a case study in microcosmic realpolitik, played out with all its subtle overt and covert power calibrations in a colonial-turned-parochial space. If one lists the sporadic flare-up of student agitation on the campus, one must come to the disquieting deduction that it seems to be a spillover from the civil disobedience days, a habit learned and repeated with compulsive and expedient regularity.

More seriously, there have been situations when Gandhians of established reputation, persons who lived the Gandhian values in their personal lives and engaged in Gandhian fasts for substantial causes found themselves out of sync with the environment. They were bogged down by the subterranean play of campus politics that reduced them to the position of public mascots, in a larger, less value-assertive power game. The reason why these later Gandhian activists found immediate concrete goals eluding them, despite their sincerity of involvement, is that possibly they did not have the hard-nosed pragmatic brinkmanship of Gandhi himself.

Also, the larger crowd of so-called supporters—outside of committed central groups—only mimicked the moral pitch, the sacred cause and the motivational drive and was compromised at the core by objectives no different from those of quotidian power politics. Any history worth its name has no space for decorous evasions, and the piercing truth is that Gandhian methods, if not bolstered by supporting conditions, all too frequently lapse. Irom Sharmila's is a case in point.

Gandhi's own idealpolitik had a certain overarching ethical reference, a powerful conscience-quotient that gave it its high public profile. This, in turn, fired the imagination of people and mobilized the numbers, giving an emotional charge to causes and movements, and fuelled acts of courage and sacrifice in stirred sensibilities. Further, Gandhi's success with the Independence achievement was possible not exclusively due to his novel methods, but also because of the special situational complex of the times.

The period following the Emergency is variously described in records as 'mobocracy', 'goonda-ism', the 'reign of terror' etc. In a column, 'Baat ki Baat', published in the Hindi daily *Amrit Prabhat*, the Hindi writer Lakshmikant Verma wrote: 'The purity of life on the campus has got destroyed and from 10.00 a.m. to 5.00 p.m. the campus is used like a public park... Today, unsocial elements have a mafia-like hold on the University. Such elements appear more active on the campus than either students or teachers...'[4]

It was not unusual to see rifle-toting bikers tearing around the campus. Nor were shootouts unheard of. Students in the commerce faculty once cowered in fear as gunshots boomed in the quad between the medieval history and economics departments. Bombs exploded off and on in the campus, sending the old windowpanes rattling. After a fracas with violent students in February 1978, the vice chancellor stayed away from the campus for long months on end, preferring to conduct university duties under police protection, specifically the Provincial Armed Constabulary (PAC). His retreat to his distant bungalow and his self-imposed exile under armed guard sent all the wrong signals to the lumpen elements on the campus. The withdrawal of the highest authority left the field open for riot and rampage, and it was frequently heard that office assistants and counter clerks were beaten up, teachers threatened and abused during examinations, and the silent majority of passive students terrorized.

In the University's long history, 1979–81 was when it touched rock bottom.

A news report, which appeared on 31 October 1979 in *Northern India Patrika* is entitled: 'Teachers hurt in Exam Violence in ECC'. A paragraph reads as follows: 'The examinees who were detected copying, left the examination hall and forced other students to walk out...They indulged in breaking furniture, created pandemonium and gherao-ed the teachers who had caught them using unfair means. Some of the invigilators were injured, it is gathered...'

The conditions in the degree colleges were no different. The newspaper reports of the time carry shocking accounts. Here is one titled 'Hooliganism in Exam Office', which appeared in *Northern India Patrika* of 6 November 1979:

> Detection of a case of using unfair means in the C.M.P. Degree College examination hall resulted in disturbance in the examination office. This happened just after the examination was over on Monday morning. At about 11.20 a.m. an unruly mob of candidates, protesting against the detection, forced its entry into the examination office where the answer books were being collected. These students, about 100 in number, took recourse to hooliganism when their talk with the college authorities regarding settlement of the case failed. They threw the answer books here and there in the office. This reporter found answer books lying all over the office floor. The office staff were busy collecting them and setting them right...

The news report goes on to say that the principal of the college, by his own accounts, had 'repeatedly requested the police official to deploy (an) adequate number of police personnel at the college gate and the gate of the examination hall. But there was no police arrangement... He alleged that even the inadequate police staff which was posted around the college remained a silent spectator to the incident...'

The role of the University administration was odd. They chose to ignore the cheating and hooliganism, and to go on with the façade of examinations and results. If a walkout occurred, the examination was held again. If a student was caught cheating, he paid a fine of ₹25 only, and was let off. On one occasion the functionary-in-charge of the Flying Squad at the Ewing Christian College chose to take on the duties of a centre superintendent when regular invigilators had left in protest, and allowed the mass copying to go on. There were other exam irregularities too. Papers were leaked in advance. Some daily-wage temporary clerks, who were given the duty of preparing the mark-sheets, made their pile raising the marks of candidates for a consideration.

If we comb through the minutes of the Allahabad University Teachers' Association meetings and the newspaper reports of the time, the reasons for this administrative collapse do not readily recommend themselves to observation, until we read between the lines and resort to the recountings of witnesses and participants. The underlying reality has as much to do with specific personality clashes as with the classic pattern of political pressure lobbying—the formulaic binary of ruling group and opposition—in this case largely, though not necessarily, founded on caste affiliation.

Teachers were under a shadow. Not only were they a demoralized lot, but they were exposed to flak from the state government as well. The session was running scandalously late. Examinations that should have been over in April were nowhere near ending. Some examinations were stayed by court orders; many had been cancelled and needing to be rescheduled. To add to it all, floods in North India had led to a suspension of classes. Spokespersons of the education ministry in Lucknow were known to have uttered defamatory statements about AU teachers in general: they were held responsible for the mess, said to do no work, deserving to have their salaries withdrawn and needing to be transferred out of their comfort zones.

On top of this, the decision-making powers of the academic community had been irreversibly eroded by the introduction of government-appointed administrative functionaries—a registrar, a deputy registrar and a finance officer. Many of them did not belong to the University and were birds of passage, without any emotional connection with the institution they temporarily served.

All of this—in conjunction with the lawlessness on the campus and the breakdown of teacherly dignity and moral authority—had left the teaching community in a state of ignoble passivity and simmering helplessness over the dishonour of their position.

The education minister came to call, and as is the way with our elected representatives, spoke words of cloying humility. He claimed to be a dwarf elevated to a high throne.[5] He came seeking the superior guidance of seasoned gurus. He wished to make a difference to higher education; he was going to make that difference. Any society, which did not accord respect to its teachers, was doomed to perish, etc. Consider our ancient epics, cited the minister: when Drona 'was employed as a servant by the Kauravas, the Kaurava dynasty got wiped out; when Vasishtha was respected as Kulaguru, Ramrajya was established.'[6]

Ministers are known to cite scripture for their purpose, but that vice chancellors should require the PAC for theirs was something that rankled most, and teachers identified this single fact as the central cause for their ignominy. Bringing this to the notice of the government was useless, as were theoretical clarifications about the unconnected-ness of teaching and delayed examinations. Sooner or later, a nascent impulse for moral self-assertion had to take shape in the private and public communications between members of the teaching community, and it did.

It took the form of a Gandhian protest—the Silent March of 11 April 1979. The idea came from Banwari Lal Sharma. A hardcore mathematician with a Sorbonne degree, he spoke French like a Frenchman, but in Allahabad spoke chaste, softly modulated Hindi and wrote fine, underplayed English. I always saw him dressed in a crisply starched snow-white khaddar dhoti-kurta, and his spare, slightly built form conveyed the essence of a lifestyle specifically chosen and devoutly practised. He had been active in Jayaprakash Narayan's movement, spending the Emergency months in jail. There were rumours that he had faced some custodial torture, but that may be a campus whisper. All his life he represented the conscience of socially concerned sections of the university community, editing a journal dedicated to social causes, organizing unaligned reflection groups, leading peace marches and being the public face of Gandhian movements in the city.

He did not seek to lead the Teachers' Movement but inevitably found himself spearheading it. A close associate recalls how in the middle of a conversation, Banwari Lalji said thoughtfully: 'Kuchh karna chahiye.' And from this mild resolve was born the Silent March. A meeting of teachers was called in the English department on 9 April 1979. Banwari Lalji was the president; 126 teachers attended. Among the resolutions passed was the one cited below:

> This body resolves that on April 11, 1979, the teachers of the University of Allahabad participate in a silent procession which will start at 12.00 noon from in front of the North Hall, Senate House, to emphasise the unity of students, teachers, and the non-teaching staff of the University, to condemn violence in whatever form, and to ask for peace on the campus.[7]

I quote the account published in *The Allahabad University Magazine* verbatim, to preserve the spontaneously generated Gandhian flavour of the movement:

> Accordingly, on April 11, 1979, two hundred and fifty teachers collected before the North Hall for the Silent March. Among them were some forty lady teachers. The teachers walked in a silent procession from the Arts Campus

to the Science Campus and back, choosing a circuitous route in order to pass by the side of every department. The procession which started around 12.00 noon returned to its starting point at 1.30 p.m. At this peak rush hour of the University, hundreds of students watched as the procession went by carrying banners and placards, but not speaking a word. The atmosphere was surcharged. There had been rumours. Some teachers and students suspected that the procession had been engineered by the Vice Chancellor and his supporters. There were chances of confrontation with students. It was said some would lie down before the procession. There were rumours that stones would be thrown. There were even rumours that firearms had been collected in a hostel.

The police was tense. They informed the Vice Chancellor, the Proctor, and one of the organisers of the procession, that Section 144 had been imposed, and the teachers should not move out of the Arts Campus. Banwari Lal Sharma decided not to obey. He asked the younger teachers to be in front, the lady teachers to be in the middle, and the older teachers to bring up the rear. It was announced—since this was a silent, non-violent march, meant to arouse consciousness— even if there was a violent attack on the processionists, the peace marchers would not retaliate, not even in words. The procession must remain silent and disciplined. The feeling of those in the procession was later expressed by a young teacher: 'It felt as if you flowed into the procession and the procession flowed into you.'

Student leaders had called a meeting at 11.30 a.m. near the Hindi Bhavan, about 100 yards from the North Hall and, over loudspeakers, were denouncing the procession that would start at 12. When the procession started and the students read what was on the banners and the placards, they were dumbfounded. As the procession passed by the place where the student leaders had called a meeting, a student walked up to Banwari Lal Sharma, who was leading the procession, and read aloud what was written on the placard he was carrying: '*VC ke Ghar se PAC hatey*'. And he moved aside. The previous night Sharma had said to the organizers, 'We are against violence in whatever form. The PAC too is a form of violence. It must go. You cannot fight violence with violence.' And Sharma had decided what would be the slogan of the leading placard. There were four banners and twenty-six placards in the procession.

The banners read: '*Prayag Vishvavidyalaya ke Adhyapakon ka Maun Juloos*,'[8] 'We are for Students', '*Shikshak, Vidyarthi, Karmachari Zindabad*,'[9] '*Hum Adhikar ke Liye Nahin Kartavya ke Liye Sadak par Aaye Hain*.'[10]

On the placards the slogans were: '*VC ke Ghar se PAC Turant Hatey*',[11] 'Withdraw PAC from VC's Residence', 'Who Gains from Anarchy? Students? Guardians? Teachers?', 'We Condemn Violence in the Campus,' 'Peace, not PAC'.

There were many more placards declaring the same pacific intent. The scene reads like some classic replay of a period novel; its impact on students, like a demonstration of instantaneous moral conversion. There is a slightly heightened emotional pitch to the saga, akin to the collective exaltation of Gandhian movements. The article recounts how students 'walked behind the procession all through' and 'some silently cleared the way'. There was a discreet police presence too. 'Police marched 100 yards ahead of the procession, and a police truck moved slowly', but the 'law-breakers' who 'defied Section 144 (were) not arrested'. The local press gave huge coverage to the march. There was abundant reference to 'purity of purpose' and the fact that 'our teachers stepped on the roads not to demand their rights but to perform their duties.'[12]

The vice chancellor—when the teachers met him with the request that he have the PAC removed from his residence—complimented them for their admirable show of moral force, but politely refused to accede to their appeal. In his considered opinion, the teaching community should carry on with their attempts to transform the moral climate of the campus; he, for his part, was liaising with ministers and high-ups to de-politicize the environment. He stuck to his 'three-pronged' solution: 'moral force + physical force + depoliticizing'. It was at this time that an essential Gandhian tenet came under trial—whether moral force could overcome physical violence, or was physical force a necessary evil, indispensable in critical conflicts? The vice chancellor plainly favoured the latter view, and absolutely refused to have the PAC removed. The teachers undertook to return to him with written assurances of peace from student leaders.

The word 'dialogue' now dominates the account preserved in the AUTA's (Allahabad University Teachers' Association) minutes. There were lengthy discussions with student leaders lasting till late at night. There were representatives of various affiliations—the All India Students' Federation (AISF), the Akhil BharatiyaVidyarthi Parishad (ABVP), Yuva Janta, etc., and these no-holds-barred dialogues frequently lapsed into eminently censorable profanities. The students' objections to the vice chancellor and his policies were virulent to the extreme. The vice chancellor was past dialoguing with, they declared. Indeed, reading over the records, the intensity of negative passions aroused by a mere vice chancellor seems astonishing, if not amusing. In their arguments they make him seem like the dictator of a police state, and a fit candidate for assassination at the hands of some student martyr!

But negative passion, by some curious play of conscience, turned into positive submission to Banwari Lal Sharma's reasoning. The dialogues ended in an overwhelming flourish of magnanimous trust—through the offering of a blank sheet of paper signed by all the student leaders, with the humble request that Sharma write anything he wished over their signatures. Whether lions had turned into lambs events alone would reveal, but this disarming development only goes to prove that in any Gandhian experiment the personality factor outweighs most others.

With the fait accompli of a written assurance of 'non-violence', the teacher-representatives made another attempt to persuade the vice chancellor. But they were turned down again by a vice chancellor weary of the subject, and closed to all discussion on it. One might be led to think that this was the dead end for this particular issue, but something inexplicable happened. The vice chancellor, paranoid all along about giving up police protection, surrendered to the temptation of suspending his disbelief in moral force and drove to the campus to attend a function. He had left his PAC guards behind. He was assaulted, either pushed into his car, or kicked by a minor student leader.

The 'incident' ruptured that moment of tenuous trust that had materialized, first with the student leaders on account of their blank signed sheet, then of the vice chancellor who had suspended his apprehensions and taken the risk. That single moment of trust *had* manifested, even if it was fractured by a decisive breach of faith.

It was Sharma's 'Chauri-Chaura' moment. The AUTA minutes record it:

> An emergency meeting of the General House was called on July 21, 1979 at 3 p.m., in the North Hall of the Senate House, to discuss what the teachers of the University should do—in the situation created by Sri Banwari Lal Sharma going on an indefinite fast from the morning of July, 20th—for 'starting

a process of self-purification through introspection in all members of the University community...'[13]

'The hall was packed to capacity by teachers and students. Many stood outside in the verandahs. Cyclostyled copies of Sri Banwari Lal Sharma's statement (entitled 'Purification Fast for Peace on University Campus'), explaining the purpose of this indefinite fast were distributed.'[14]

In that statement he outlined the history of the atmosphere of impunity and intimidation on the campus, mentioned the Silent March and dwelt on the signed and unconditional assurance of peace, given in the form of a blank sheet of paper to teachers by the student leaders:

> When, after receiving such assurance from the students, of their trust in teachers and of their faith in maintaining peace on the campus, the teachers met the Vice Chancellor; he agreed to contribute towards the creating of goodwill on the campus, on the eve of the Student Union Elections—by staying the action he had taken against student leaders, and restoring them as students of the University. For a day it appeared that the campus was moving towards normalcy, but day before yesterday evening an ugly incident took place—in which some students manhandled and even kicked the Vice Chancellor—and thereby broke their trust with teachers, and scuttled the process of bringing peace on the campus, which had been started.
>
> Perhaps now there is no other way but for everyone to look within, to try and find an answer. There is need for introspection by all members of the University community... This indefinite fast is undertaken for creating a spirit of goodwill and self-purification through introspection. I earnestly beseech each member of the University community

to take it in this spirit and to contribute what he can to make this intention succeed.

Politics is a complex of heterogeneous stratagems, and pledges of honour have unequal sanctities for unequal persons. Gandhian methods involved both, pressures on conscience, and unerring situational assessment. In the case of the VC's assault, one tiny element had escaped unanticipated. The assurances of peace had been given by the major student leaders, the misbehaviour perpetrated by one very minor one, eager to achieve an upgraded stature in the unofficial hierarchy of student leadership, for his act of brash daring.

While Sharma fasted, his close supporters collected 8,000 signatures from students, assuring peace on the campus and urging him to break his fast. Student leaders took the microphone and delivered lengthy harangues for hours. After four days, Sharma agreed to break his fast. But there were very complicated forces working at a subterranean level, all through the Teachers' Movement, and even before that during the anarchic months. They were in the form of retributive caste politics, against the actions of the vice chancellor during the Emergency days, when he had enjoyed the assured protection of New Delhi. There were subtle incitements to violence, efforts to aid and abet campus vandalism, and disturbances to university functioning—in a move to discredit the vice chancellor and his coterie.

The entrenched caste lobbies, an ever-present and vicious reality of UP, operated in many insidious ways, and the return of peace to the campus would not have been welcome to certain groups. Even the Teachers' Union, before Sharma's election as president, had been torn by a centuries-old schism—between a Brahmin clique and a Kayastha, the two dominant oppositional caste groups. One called itself the AUTA, the other, the Teachers' Forum. By virtue of their unaligned position, the press often referred to Sharma and his supporters as the Third Front, although the group itself emphatically disclaimed that epithet. The two former groups were persuaded to merge, and Sharma was elected president of the single entity called the AUTA, immediately after the Silent March.

The covert chess moves and counter-moves of the caste lobbies played the game of realpolitik, while Sharma and his crusaders organized a Gandhian march, undertook an indefinite fast, spoke earnestly of moral pressure and of purity of motives. Like all genuine Gandhian exercises, the gain, as a result of Sharma's fast was subtler. It injected an incremental element of rectitude, in a campus poisoned by factionalism and violence, even if that element was short-lived and limited to only a few. A grudging concession to idealism from hardened lobbyists and cynics was a triumph wrested by the so-called Third Front activists, and there was, if not a change of moral climate, at least a positive micro-shift. The fight was to go on. There were still the issues of unfair means in examinations and the diluted penalties for cheating.

The way examinations took place has been described. At the rate at which mass copying went on, the AU degree would soon be discredited beyond redemption. Time and again the teaching community had urged the students that it was in their best interests to desist from copying, and the administration to enforce penalties strictly. The atmosphere of flagrant impunity in the examination halls, the complete disregard for rules, and the underlying assumption of institutional consent to corruption, had a vitiating effect on the general values of the institution. The situation had reached uncontainable proportions.

There was nothing for it but another Gandhian protest. Minutes of the 4th General House Meeting of the AUTA, held on 12 September 1979, reveal the following decision on the part of the teaching community: 'The House resolved that in case students resorted to using unfair means defiantly and on a large scale, and teachers as invigilators were not able to check them effectively and without police help, they would dissociate themselves en bloc from invigilation work.'

It was resolved that the university administration was to be strongly urged to cancel those examinations in which mass copying had occurred. Furthermore, re-examinations in papers where walkouts had taken place—a pernicious consequence encouraging the practice of copying, and having led to the delayed session—also had to stop. If these demands were unmet, the entire teaching body would abstain from invigilation work, from setting question papers for re-examinations and from correcting the answer scripts of such examinations. Normal teaching and research would carry on as before but—as both the minutes of the fifth AUTA meeting of 10 October 1979[15] and the report published in the 12 October 1979 *Northern India Patrika* declared—teachers 'will not remain mute spectators to farce'.

The University administration, headed now by a different vice chancellor, initially dragged its feet, but under threat that the teachers 'would dissociate themselves completely from the examination work from November 7',[16] buckled down and complied. A statement to the press, printed on 1 November 1979[17], announced that there would be no more re-examinations in papers in which candidates had staged a walkout. A letter dated 6 November 1979 to the AUTA president from the registrar confirmed that the Executive Committee meeting of the same date had taken the decision that 'the examinations of centres from where there are reports of mass copying (would) be cancelled'. Also, that there would be no re-examinations in papers 'in which walk-out is staged by the examinees'. Accordingly, amidst general congratulations and much celebration, the AUTA and the

Allahabad University College Teachers' Association announced their decision to withdraw their earlier ultimatum to boycott invigilation duty from the following day.

Their victory was illusory. In a volte-face quite unexpected, the executive council at its meeting held on 13 January 1980 reversed its earlier decision, and it was resolved 'that re-examination in the walkout papers of BA (I) be held'. Further, that 'the examinations which had been cancelled, as the proper atmosphere for the conduct of the same did not prevail in the examination halls because of large scale defiant copying, be also re-held.'

This was the second time, that session, that the Teachers' Movement ran into a roadblock because of a breach of faith, this time on the part of the University's highest decision-making body. There was worse to come. The next meeting of the AUTA witnessed scenes of chaos. Students barged in, asking by what right was the association holding its meetings on the campus, and raising 'Shikshak Sangh Murdabad' slogans, until the meeting ended in confusion. The sabotage was planned in advance, and the Students' Union president's comment—while condemning the incident—was that groupism among teachers had been behind the disturbance.

Banwari Lal Sharma called another General House meeting to discuss the recent setbacks to their position, but no consensus could be reached as to the next step to take. The Teachers' Movement lapsed into a faction and clique-ridden body for the next year or so. As an article by R.U. Govindan stated: 'The second meeting...proved infructuous because of a split among the teachers. Ever since, the teachers of the university, by and large, seem to be licking their wounds and drifting on the river of discontent...'[18]

Examination time was especially horrific, mass copying the

order of the day. As one contrite article, printed in *Northern India Patrika's Sunday Magazine* section of 23 March 1980, described:

> Invigilators having been suitably cowed down, examinees make hay while the sun shines. Candidates are known to walk in and out of examination halls at will. Invigilators cower in a corner. Cases of examinees going away with their answer books to hostels and returning them after three hours are widely talked about. Many a time the water boys are the only representatives of the administration.

R.U. Govindan, the author of the article, sardonically describes how examinees 'have more than one book open in front of them. If such candidates fail, the fault must be that of the books.'[19] Invigilators who tried to prevent cheating were abused and threatened with dire consequences. In one case a chair was hurled at an invigilator, cracking his skull.

After a year in this slump and with characteristic Gandhian obduracy, the Teachers' Association raised the issue of punishments once again. Although exact rules were laid down for redressal in cases of unfair means, the penalty, due to student pressure, had come down to a small fine. This made the whole idea of culpability and correction ridiculous, the teachers seeing it as 'dilution amounting almost to nullification of punishment.'[20]

On 16 February 1981, after talks with Student Union leaders had failed, and after an advance notice of forty-eight hours, a general strike of teachers was announced. It was to last a week but not before significant disturbances, and also notable achievement. The very first day of the strike, students pounced on a young political science teacher and AUTA Working Committee member, Devi Prasad Tripathi, pushing and throwing him on the ground and kicking him too. This incident occurred at 11 a.m., just before a scheduled Teachers' Association Meeting in the political science department's lecture theatre. Tripathi, himself a former president of the JNU Students' Union, was later to become a member of an astute think-tank for senior political figures, in mainstream Indian politics, and a member of the Rajya Sabha.

If violence against him was intended to intimidate teachers, it proved counter-productive. By now the campus satyagrahis had learnt the practicality of defensive violence, a tactic that Gandhi had vigorously upheld . A crowd of teachers 'intervened to wrest Tripathi from the hands of the hooligans and they answered the vile, anti-teacher slogans raised by a mob of 25 with a counter slogan: "Hooligans and dacoits, retreat. Long live the unity of students and teachers".[21]

With the temperature soaring, a mood of epic battle seemed to enter into the conflict, conveyed in the ringing pledge taken by the teachers at the meeting that day:

> We as teachers of the University of Allahabad, holding the solemn trust of our student community in our hands, do hereby take a pledge to remain united in upholding the honour, the dignity, the reputation, and the credibility of the University, by maintaining academic standard, honesty, integrity, peace and harmony on our campus, and for this purpose, we shall do everything we can, democratically, to resist coercion, violence and intimidation on the campus.[22]

Leaflets were printed, and advertisements released in newspapers, from money raised during a meeting of 17 February 1981. It was decided that the silent majority of unorganized students who had watched from the ranks and were not only apolitical but inarticulate would be targeted and mobilized for collective protest. Teachers visited hostels and delegacies in small groups, on scooters, rickshaws or on foot. They explained their stand, sought feedback from the students, drew them out, struck chords in perplexed minds and succeeded in creating a climate of opinion regarding the penalty for cheating. More than 5, 800 signatures were collected, appealing for eradication of violence on the campus and supporting sterner punishments for unfair means in examinations.

The cumulative impact of this prolonged exercise was to bear fruit with the coming of the next vice chancellor, U.N. Singh, who did not take to the complicated caste tribalism of the campus. His strong moves succeeded in mitigating the problem considerably. Slowly, over the next decade the law-and-order situation was contained, though it has always remained a fragile peace. The session was salvaged, though that too, is a contingent position, dependent on many fortuitous factors. If for the next few years, we worked in a relatively more peaceful campus, it was due to administrative measures such as the presence of security guards, the system of identity cards and barriers to stop vehicular movement. Very helpful were a stricter system of punishment for unfair means and a ban on the Students' Union that lasted some years.

I have covered this particular period in some detail because of the way it reflects a thwarting of ideals confounded by the perennial play of political moves—a national neutralization of ethics reduced to the scale of a single campus. The manner in which factional campus politicians commandeered a campus movement from the control of local Gandhians replicates the way in which the original nation-building exercise was hijacked from Gandhi's grip, by the smooth manoeuverings of divisive politics. There were scores of other agitations, and permanent issues remained to instigate further turbulence: students' elections, legitimacy of candidatures, admission cut-off marks, deadlines, examination dates, fees, hostel occupancy, availability of conveniences like ambulances and common rooms.

This is noisy democracy, warts and all, fraught and compromised, which does not claim to have all the answers, but is at least theoretically committed to enabling everyone to put their own answers to the test. And if, in those testings, there are unfair means practiced, and insufficient penalties applied, that too has a procedure, however problematic, for correction, and voices to agitate for it. The conflicts on the Allahabad University campus mirror this democracy-by-default in full gallop, headed in the same indiscernible direction that the country is.

8
REAL TIME

The Mad Hatter told Alice that he was busy putting together a list of words starting with 'em'. For us, in brave new India, the triptych of Mandal, Mandir and McDonalds were the three necromantic 'ems' that whisked away a world and replaced it with another. Those who lived out their lives on the right side of the 1990s had absolutely no idea what the country was going to be like a decade down the line. Allahabad University partook of such changes as were inevitable, though in retrospect it is fair to say that the University's engagement was quite contained, if not detached—surprising when the rest of India was on the boil.

The implementation of the proposals of the Mandal Commission (spurred on by Vishvanath Pratap Singh, Allahabad University alumnus and prime minister of India) did lead to a furore of protests. Reservation for the Scheduled Castes (SC), Scheduled Tribes (ST) and Other Backward Classes (OBC) came to be strictly applied 'in the sequence of the Roster prescribed by (the) U.P. Public Services Act 1994'.[1] As I write this, in June 2013, newspaper reports state that AU has 'got its first set of Scheduled Tribe teachers, drawn from all over the country. The report goes on to say that although the reservation policy was implemented right from 1994, it is only now that recruitment could take place owing to failure to find any suitable S.T. candidate.

To students henceforth categorized as 'General', that is, belonging to the so-called 'upper castes', this meant stiffer competition, exclusion and deprivation of rightfully secured places. But rightness itself became a compromised category, challenged by a powerful discourse against privilege and hegemony. To those students who belonged to the 'reserved' categories it proved a turning point, a window of opportunity in recompense for ancestral denials and a definitive expression of social justice, entitlement and inclusion.

Although new tensions broke out with this hitherto unprecedented development in Indian history, as far as the University was concerned, the clashes between the oppositional classes did not initially get out of hand. If it entirely altered the composition of university students over a period of time, it also blunted the sharp rancour that had existed amongst the upper castes themselves, who were now compelled to draw closer together to confront a common threat they had never envisaged. Caste groups still banded together in clusters of kinship and cronyism but there were more extensive frontiers to patrol now and more allies needed—and an attitudinal shift is to be sensed in the bitter caste politics of the campus.

As for the desperate boys and girls who protested against reservation, they were numerically at a disadvantage and born on the wrong side of history. Their crusade had no essential and defensible principle to anchor their protest on, save that of the old order that had afforded them better chances, but which was now insufficient against the fait accompli of the act. They agitated against the impending injustice they foresaw, but it is one of the insolubles of the situation that you cannot barter injustice for justice, but only one kind of injustice for another kind. They were hounded by the police, beaten down and dispersed. Some immolated themselves. One died. The University looked on, out of its depth. The protest spread to areas of the main city and was put down with severity.

While the ethnic profile of the student community has changed, the teaching body is still largely dominated by Brahmins, Thakurs, Kayasthas, Vaishyas and other sub-groups categorized under 'caste Hindus'. The reservation policy ensures slots for the reserved categories also in appointments to teaching and all administrative and ministerial positions. If the well-intentioned idea was an eventual levelling-off into a utopian classlessness, I'm not sure if I see that happening in the foreseeable future. In UP, it is more about sustaining a precarious balance between different orders of dominance, if not retributive dominance, in a slow, on-going covert class war.

I once asked a Dalit student why he opted for English literature as a subject, so dated and so distant from his world, and his answer was, in halting English: 'In my village I get honour when I tell people I am studying English in Allahabad Univeristy.' I do not know what the nature of this species of 'honour' is, but it seems suspiciously close to class advantage.

Coming to the second 'em' in the triptych, Mandir, and the forces of communalism it let loose, by and large, Allahabad University has been a wholesomely secular space. Although hostels were built along communal lines, often funded by religious trusts and patrons, this was more because of the strictures on commensality than on any oppositional stances. Mention has been made of the anxiety felt by a British principal of Muir Central College, as recorded in the principal's report of 1907–08, which states: 'The growth of irreligion is a dangerous evil. I believe that the appointment of a Pandit and a Maulvi whose sole duties should be religious and moral instruction in the Government and the Muhammadan Hostels would be purely beneficial and I earnestly advocate that the experiment be made. Attendance at their lectures should be compulsory.'[2]

It wasn't a new anxiety. Seven years further back, in the 1900–01 academic session, another principal had noted: 'In the Musalman Boarding House, the Superintendent reports that there was a good attendance at prayers during the month of Ramzan; but in the other months the Boarders did not offer their prayers regularly, and the attendance was rather poor.'[3] In an interview with the superintendent of the Hindu Hostel, in November 1964, Edward Di Bona noted a similar laidback attitude to religion. He writes:

> In the Madan Mohan Malaviya Hostel (the Hindu Hostel), which has always housed the most orthodox Hindus, morning communal prayers have been abandoned for lack of interest. The Superintendent complained that a large number of Gitas that had been donated to the library, had never been opened, and that he could count the number of students who went to the Sangam to bathe regularly on one hand (out of 250 hostellers).[4]

Di Bona had other observations based on direct investigations. In the late 1940s, the andawalla (egg-seller) was 'forcibly expelled from the Madan Mohan Malaviya Hostel, but today he can freely sell his eggs to the boys. So long as food is consumed in the privacy of their rooms, even meat may be taken.'[5] This is in the 1960s. Indeed, it all seemed to be more about eating than about praying. Of course, meat could not be cooked in the kitchens of the Hindu, GN Jha and Jain Hostels, but it was cooked in the Muslim Hostel and Holland Hall, the perceived Christian territory. In the last two mentioned, it could be eaten in a common dining area, despite that odd incident in Holland Hall Hostel referred to in an earlier chapter, when Hindu students would not sit down to eat with their English warden because he was, in their eyes, a mlechcha!

I've picked up these telltale details because they are clues to an institution's climate, which was healthily indisposed to make an issue out of religion. But Edward Di Bona does mention that at the level of the ministerial staff in the 1960s, there did seem to exist a pervasive prejudice against Muslims.[6] If we consider the dress worn by teachers and students between 1895 and 1916, we notice a variety of dress styles. In late nineteenth- and early twentieth-century photographs beards, narrow Aligarh pajamas and shervanis are seen, and the turban, fez and dhoti-kurta are also common. European staff can be made out by their suits, ties and sola topees. By the 1960s, all the Indian dress codes had disappeared, and the uniform shirt-trouser preference gave a sameness to the look of the boys.

As for women's dresses, there is no question in the late nineteenth and early twentieth centuries of any campus record, because at the turn of the century there *were* no women on the campus, although one would imagine that in the 1930s and '40s they were generally saree-clad. As with the boys of the 1960s girls, too, now had a couple of Indian options besides the saree—the comfortable salwar-kameez or the churidar-kurta. The Bollywood films of those decades are fairly reliable markers of the dress codes of the campus. But whichever fashion was dominant—and there was a 1970s phase of the cosmopolitan bell-bottom, flared pants and flowery lounger-trousers with short, fitted tops for girls—the fact remains that it was hard to tell Hindu from Muslim.

One way was perhaps by accent and vocabulary, and maybe by Muslim girls often preferring the salwar-kameez over the saree, which was midriff-exposing. But this was by no means a general attitude. Muslim girls seldom wore burqas once they were in the campus; they would take them off and fold and put them away in their shoulder bags as soon as they alighted from their rickshaws or other vehicles. The burqa and hijab were for the satisfaction of their orthodox neighbours, not for the campus—which signified mingling and merging, and even perhaps a homogenizing modernity.

Even in the crisis preceding Independence, when Muslim mobs wandered the lanes of the old city shouting: *'Ladkar lenge Pakistan, hanskar lenge Hindustan!'*, the Muslim population was sharply divided into Congress Muslim and League Muslim while the Hindu Mahasabha too made its presence felt, these issues did not affect the University. It stayed largely a peaceful campus, though it would be too much to say that a state of high-minded harmony and sweet solidarity existed between Hindus and Muslims on the campus. 'Pakistan' became a code word for the lavatory among the boys of several hostels. Very early in its history, Sir Shafaat Ahmad Khan had voiced his grievance that Muslims were being discriminated against, while Madan Mohan Malaviya had protested that Muslims were being cosseted and appeased. The two stalwarts seemed to have uttered one of Uttar Pradesh's core paradoxes. Yet even during Partition, the atmosphere in the campus and the hostels stayed benumbed into inaction, shell-shocked by the news of the widespread killings on the part of both communities.

In the 1960s, as part of the annual Holi celebrations, there was a 'gaali' competition between students of the Muslim and Hindu hostels, when inmates outdid themselves shouting abuse at one another, with insults that were richly incestuous and creatively scatological. I don't know if there was a prize and who usually won, and whether the sporting contestants shook hands and embraced later, saying: *'Bura na mano, Holi hai'*,[7] a standard line for mediation and merry-making during Holi. All this was 'good fun' and not serious, though it may have been noisily cathartic and therapeutic too.

But when the Babri Masjid was razed to the ground in December 1992, there was no noise but a dark silence. Even then, there were no serious clashes in the city of Allahabad, only a sinister sense of gathering unease, before which the happy-go-lucky 'gaalis' of Holi paled into childish babblings. Friends fell speechless or changed the subject to safe topics. Some struggled to arrest the widening fissures, but were met with strained faces and a discomfort so deep that everyone knew it would be difficult to sound the right chord. Shortly afterwards, the Mumbai riots took place and then came the era of bomb blasts, airport security checks and policing of places of worship. Against the gathering silence boomed the sound of headlines, the IC-814 aeroplane hijacking, 9/11 and the Godhra riots in February 2002. Through all this, Allahabad University maintained a cool distance, although Murli Manohar Joshi, prominent right-winger and cabinet minister, who had been, as mentioned, a teacher of the University before he entered politics, had a loyal following here too.

Of course, with the hardening of private stances, there was a certain shift from mature neutrality. Some heads of departments took to chanting mantras to Shiva before staff meetings, during which the scanty or solitary representatives of Islam or Christianity sat in quiet pique. Suddenly we had turned into 'majority' and 'minority'. Suddenly we were talking busily of our ritual fasts and ceremonial foods and various pujas and hours of prayer. Suddenly it was all a big deal. If a picture of Saraswati was put up in a chamber, it now turned into an issue. It would never have earlier. If a lamp was lit and a Saraswati Vandana sung at a function, a Sikh chief guest would be miffed. The tectonic plates had shifted, overthrowing old and settled sanities. We had no one to blame but ourselves.

Fortunately, this unwholesome surge of identity politics did not last long on the Allahabad University campus. Sometimes the now-banned Students' Islamic Movement of India's (SIMI) name appeared, painted on walls or on pasted posters here and there, but soon disappeared. A functionary of the University in charge of student matters once mentioned that some radical pamphlets had been seized from the rooms of hostels, but students did not get radicalized. And when there were small 'incidents', peace marches organized by University teachers from both communities—Banwari Lal Sharma, R.C. Tripathi, O.P. Malviya, S.M.H. Aquil Rizvi and others—restored common sense.

I heard one such account of a classroom episode, told to me by a senior teacher of my department. It was the morning after a major riot, maybe in Gujarat, the teacher couldn't quite recall where. He had gone up to room number 18, on the first floor of the English department, on its north-facing flank. A few paces short of the door, where the large old stone staircase ends, he got the feeling that no students had come to class that day. The classroom, usually buzzing with voices before the teacher's arrival, was absolutely silent. He walked in and was surprised to find a full class, the large room packed to capacity, but no one speaking. He also noticed that all the Muslim students sat in a cluster in one corner, and all the others sat a little apart, bunched together.

He told me later, that the frightening silence of that classroomful of students had left him momentarily stunned. 'I said to myself, I can't teach this class,' he recalled. But teach he did, relying on his well-established command over his students. He did not teach them English literature. Instead, he began speaking of the essential unity of all religions, of the politicizing of religion and the abuse of faith. He spoke for the entire fifty-minute span and came away feeling that towards the end, the tension had relaxed somewhat.

I owed him an episode in return for this one. So I told him my recent experience in the same room on the first floor. There, I teach a BA class *Macbeth*, and my students sit in clusters too. Only, this is a gender-based division—the boys in one bunch, the girls in another. But on one bench, the first from the right, a boy and girl sit together, always. They seem to have only one copy of the book between them. In fact, I remember having asked those who had come with books to share them with those who hadn't, and this twosome obediently complied.

Sharing a book affords proximities rich in possibility, which poets might anticipate better than lecturing dons. When, after many months of teaching, Birnam Wood had come to Dunsinane with MacDuff close at hand, I noticed the two still together, still sharing the same book. I looked up their names in the attendance register. It was better than I'd expected, she a Muslim and he a Hindu, both probably lower middle class. My class was the only place they could meet to read out of a common book, sitting side by side on a common bench, the first bench from the right. When I asked them a question about Lady Macbeth's sleepwalking scene, they hung their heads and couldn't answer, and no wonder. They just weren't listening, those two sleepwalkers. They kept silent and I fell silent too, recognizing this silence as something of a different register, fragile and sacred. I don't know what became of them.

In 2013, the campus seems to have large numbers of burqa-clad girls, my MA classroom benches and examination halls included. It wasn't this way a decade back, but it's still not an issue here either. Allahabad University has witnessed many forms of unrest, but never about religion.

The third 'em' in this triveni, McDonalds, to my mind the international badge for globalization, assails me on all sides now. The dress code has changed to jeans and T-shirts for most of the boys and a good number of girls, with the perennial salwar-kameez having given way to tights, leggings and tops in interesting designs and colours. Universal mall-wear walks the ramps of our corridors. In the sun, faces conceal themselves behind expertly knotted scarf-masks, as ozone layer awareness has grown. The omnipresent cellphone or iPod plugs are firmly clamped to ears.

But globalization notwithstanding, they're brisk feet-touchers, a custom that did not exist on such a stupendous scale before. It is the local overcoming the global. A student has only to come in front of you that he stoops to lift the dust off your toes to his heart chakra. No amount of protests will discourage these respectful zealots. This is our tradition, our culture, they reprimand me sternly if I ask them not to.

As for classroom situations, the experiences can be pretty hilarious. To illustrate, I'm having problems with the name MacDonwald, the fellow who had led a rebellion against Duncan, and whom Macbeth had 'unseamed…from the nave to the chops'. I wonder if kitchen scenes haunt my students' imaginations too, as I read out this bit. One student actually said 'Lay on, McDonald,' in the course of an answer. Spelling and grammar having receded into colonial history, it is not at all beyond the bounds of possibility that some students, busily scribbling notes about Macbeth meeting the three witches on the heath, may write in the following shorthand: 'Mcbt send msg 2 lady mcbt dat he met 3 witches in heat'.

As for computer programs, our students are still a tad behind other campuses, though they've learnt enough to cut-paste their assignments, and even their dissertations, into curiously uneven texts. Broken English prose flowers into passages of tangled postmodern jargon, then goes all Brit, then lapses into ponderous Indianisms, before falling back into its original grammatically challenged, spelling-slaughtered state. I get hordes of Facebook friend requests from names whose photographs resemble faces

I have seen in class. Social networking seems to have initiated a new politics of popularity and self-marketing chumminess, with some teachers indulging in inane pontificating, students clicking 'like' and slavering with sycophantic applause. And campus politics has taken a whole new form, with teachers blocking other teachers from friend lists as alliances change with the seasons!

But when, entering into the spirit of the age, I read out to my students passages from that irresistible work of genius called *Twitterature*, a sparkling compendium of 'The World's Greatest Books Retold Through Twitter'[8], I have them in a condition described as ROFL. Those initiated into this cabala know this to mean 'Rolling-On-The-Floor-Laughing'. Here's Macbeth, in 140 characters' long Twitter soliloquies. It's the Banquet Scene and after, and these are Macbeth's tweets:

> Everyone is leaving the party! What? WHAT? Does no one else see BLEEDING DODDAMN BANQUO AT THE TABLE?
>
> I'm trying to sleep. Will someone please shut this wino up? I'm the king goddamn it, can't I get a reliable porter? Seriously.
>
> Old hags say Macbeth is killed by no man of woman born. Relieved. The Terminator not invented yet.
>
> My enemies and their families keep dying randomly! This is beginning to get out of hand.
>
> Maybe not. Wife is having mid-life crisis or woman troubles. Bitch is nuts.
>
> @Lady Mac: THERE'S NOTHING ON YOUR HANDS, YOU'VE WASHED THEM 100 TIMES ALREADY!
>
> People found out about the whole murder thing; they're all pissed. I say everyone must chill out and stop blowing shit out of proportion.

> Armies moving against me, Queen's dead. Life is nothing but a lone poster, tweeting his time upon the stage and then he tweets no more!

Amazing that this generation, groomed in a culture of international text-messaging codes, finds all this perfectly accessible, far more than the Bard's original expressions. But this is tragedy, not comedy; I threaten the class when the ROFL-ing gets out of hand. It's supposed to induce pity and terror, not crazy laughter. I am driven to thunder. Then a boy asks soberly (it's the one who gets honour in his village from the study of English literature, and who drops his aitches as North Indians who speak dialect Hindi can, so that both Shakespeare and Vishal Bharadwaj share a common plight on his lips): 'Ma'am, why is it that Sakespeare's Macbeth makes us feel sadness and ijjat while Visal Bharadwaj's *Maqbool* only gives us pain?' I look at him closely and stop laughing, all of a sudden awed by the chastening knowledge that we're all somehow muddling through! This, as a central university in its quasquicentennial year (and no, that's not a Twitter cryptolinguism, but pedigreed Latin straight out of the Vatican scrolls! It means a hundred and twenty-five years) we have the honour and privilege of doing.

Over the last quarter century, and especially after 2005, the Allahabad University did indeed transform. It was accorded the status of a central university in 2005 after a prolonged campaign which began in its centenary year, 1987, ran into several roadblocks but eventually did get the Government of India's nod in December 2004. The bill presented in Parliament had also proposed declaring the University of Allahabad an Institution of National Importance. Both Houses of Parliament passed the University of Allahabad Act in May 2005, the president of India gave it his authorization on 23 June and the University of Allahabad began functioning in its new capacity, as central university, from 14 July of the same year. The first ordinances were put into effect from 9 February 2008; they were also translated into Hindi, and have since become standard models for the new crop of central universities that have come up in the last few years, in various Indian states.

Becoming a central university meant that an institution cash-strapped since the early 1940s and forced to cramp its style was now flush with funds. At its inception as central university it received, under the Non-Plan Grant, ₹2,815,876,000, and under the Plan Grant, ₹1,040,513,462, amounting to ₹3,856,389,462. In its new avatar, it was also temporally located in a brand new century, in a country that was no longer the colony of an imperial power, nor economically diffident. India had lately forged a new identity for itself as a representative of Asian renaissance, in a world in which Europe and the US were both in recession and engaged in horrific wars on terror.

How would this relic of the Raj reinvent itself? Globally, the frontiers of knowledge had expanded at mind-boggling speed, and there were areas of study undreamt of. The technological revolution had created new ways of accessing, storing and engaging with fresh knowledge fields. The uses to which this knowledge could be applied had generated alternative vocations. Also, learning was more collaborative than ever before. There were alliances between disciplines and between physically far-flung institutions, unthought of in the old days. Specialized knowledge was now the common preserve of clusters of disciplines and each branch of knowledge had multiple custodians.

The challenge of remodelling itself was exciting, but also daunting. In the wake of the worldwide revolution in information technology, it will be appropriate to use a tech-analogical metaphor. An institution has its metaphoric hardware and its metaphoric software, roughly a matter-mind binary. The hardware consists of the buildings, grounds and amenities, all of which comprise its physical structure. It was refreshing to see the old buildings being given a makeover, carved stone-work repaired, cast-iron fences painted, glass panes replaced and neon flood-lighting installed. By night a pearly moonwash bathed the gracious old monuments, a lovely spectacle from the roads outside. Even the hands on the old clock-face kept real time, giving voice to its forgotten mellow, bell-metal chimes—albeit for a short while. Walkways were repaved. The gardens grew lush and flower beds bloomed.

Suddenly, walking from the newly-laid-out parking lot to the English department, I grew conscious of the light meshing through stonework lattices and leaf canopies, the flowers in abundance in the lawns and the birdsong too. The Senate Hall campus is one of the most gracious and pleasing in the country, although the Muir College campus has its own stark majesty. A stonemason might be busy with mallet and chisel somewhere; a new cafeteria might exude the smell of fresh paint, along with the savouries it served. The Indira Gandhi Social Sciences Complex, which for years had stood empty, looking for all the world like the conical ribcage of an Egyptian pyramid, is now fleshed out in glass and fibre panel, corrugated shuttering and smart grille-work.

Measures have now been taken for the restoration and maintenance of the grand old heritage buildings. The addition of mezzanine floors for older buildings is being considered so as to optimize space without disturbing old structures. Startling was the transformation of the old Pioneer Press building across the road, the place where Kipling worked for a short while, and which the Government of India acquired and turned into the Food Corporation Office. A derelict old shell of a red-brick bungalow, lost in its vast, unkempt compound, it had its scary legend of a headless angrez who was sighted by night.

Corridors of the Senate Hall

On that note, the English department building, too, has its ghost story. Late evening or very early morning walkers in the University grounds claim to see a bunch of grapes dangling from the middle of the ceiling of its long west-facing first-floor veranda. Whether it is the play of light or some illusory entelechy of residual Western civilization in pristine Grecian manifestation, I don't know. My informer was an old peon, Chhote Lal, who has since passed on. He swore he'd seen the headless angrez, the bunch of grapes and even a tall lone form standing motionless in front of the north door of the head's room, room number 5. The heads, it goes without saying, have not appreciated this piece of helpfully volunteered information on my part. University ghosts are one of my abiding interests. In a hattrick, there's 'Lord Friday', who paces the terraces of the Hindu Hostel, like Hamlet's father on the battlements—or so I am told by a senior teacher.

The former Pioneer-Press-turned-Food-Corporation site is now a massive state-of-the-art academic complex, still incomplete but promising to become the new location for undergraduate classrooms. The University and RITES (formerly Rail India Technical and Economic Service) have signed a Memorandum of Understanding to launch large-scale building projects, and to draw up a comprehensive master plan for the three campuses— Senate Hall, Muir College and Chatham Lines, with adjoining properties (where constructions have proceeded apace). Systematic utilization of empty lots, lying unused for lack of funds, are now being creatively and gainfully developed, either for construction or for garden spaces. Some of the achievements are there for all to see, for instance, a whole new floor added to each of three faculty buildings—physics, home science and law. There are four more new buildings, one each for e-learning, a laboratory, an employment bureau and the Teachers' Academic and Cultural Centre.

New hostels include a 250-bedder for boys, named after Dr Sarvapalli Radhakrishnan, and the Shatabdi Boys' Hostel with thirty beds. Older hostels have been modernized with crumbling electrical fittings repaired, better drinking water and sanitation systems arranged, water huts, washroom complexes on campus, a common room and recreation centres for hostels like Sir Sunder Lal and P.C. Bannerjee. For girls, there are two new ones—Kalpana Chawla Girls' Hostel with 130 beds and a 100-bedder near the Priyadarshini Girls' Hostel. The provision of a Women's Advisory Board building, a cafeteria and a well-equipped gym for girls are new acquisitions of the Women's College premises. Residential accommodations for staff have also been built—150 quarters each for teachers at Beli Farm and for administrative staff on University land near Govindpur-Shivkoti.

The departments, too, have undergone a welcome makeover, with new glass and fibre-glass cabin spaces, computerized work stations, new classroom appurtenances and better fittings and furnishings in staffrooms in general. The resources of the central faculty and departmental libraries have been upgraded, with significantly increased numbers of books and journals, and reading spaces, including one for differently abled students. A campus-wide fibre-optic network, linking all the campus libraries, now exists, and a digital-electronic library is being developed. Internet-abled terminals have been installed, and memberships in INFLIBNET and UGC INFONET consortiums have been initiated. Furthermore, a new IT-enabled and digital technology system has been provided to all departments.

Administrative and office spaces, likewise, have been modernized and made physically comfortable to work in, with modern office technology and computer systems introduced. A central data and implementation monitoring facility is envisaged, with databases of all the proceedings of committees and other University bodies, and recorded information covering all possible details, in addition to those related to admissions, fee collection, examinations, etc. With 100 computers, the e-learning facility opened on 18 October 2008.

A major hurdle in these systems working smoothly is the issue of electricity. Power supply in Allahabad is interrupted daily from 10 a.m. till 1 p.m., the peak time for University functioning. No matter how ambitious our e-learning plans and new technological set-up, it all comes to nothing in this dismal power situation. To solve this, the University has taken steps through UGC's intervention to install a 33/11 KV substation connected with the nearest grid for uninterrupted power supply. Giant generators were installed, but when some departments and functionaries—unmindful of the needs of the entire campus—overdraw on power resources by running air-conditioners in power-rostering hours, other departments are affected.

Everything has been upgraded, updated, retrofitted, except the people whose mindsets, work disciplines, technical knowledge and civic accountabilities lag far behind. So once a sophisticated piece of equipment breaks down, it stays non-functional for weeks, even months, putting the clock back in an institution where it is a never-ending battle against inertia.

To return to the old techno-metaphor of the university's hardware and software, the knowledge generated and imparted in the physical framework that has been given a fresh lease of life, is the true object of the immense enterprise. The University now has thirty-eight departments distributed across the four faculties of arts, science, commerce and law. In addition to these, it has three University institutes: inter-disciplinary studies, professional studies and the National Centre of Experimental Minerology and Petrology. The Institute of Interdisciplinary Studies has, in its ambit, centres for studies across the disciplines: biotechnology, bio-informatics, film and theatre, women's studies, Gandhian thought, globalization and development studies, material science, nano-technology application and environmental sciences. There are two centres named after two of AU's iconic men of science—the Meghnad Saha Centre of Space Studies and the K. Banerjee Centre of Atmospheric and Ocean Sciences. The Institute of Professional Studies has, under its banner, the centres of food technology, computer education, media studies, fashion design and technology and e-learning initiative.

Apart from the three University colleges of William Holland, Madan Mohan Malaviya and Kayastha Pathshala, there are eleven constituent colleges, some of which have achieved autonomy. There is also a Constituent Institute and the Gobind Ballabh Pant Social Science Institute, supported by the Indian Council of Cultural Relations (ICCR), but offering academic and research programmes geared towards a degree from the University of Allahabad. The Harish Chandra Research Institute of Mathematics and Mathematical Physics, the Kamala Nehru Post-Graduate

Medical Institute and the Motilal Nehru Medical College have been withdrawn by an amendment of the Allahabad University Act. The Motilal Nehru Regional Engineering College too has been transferred to the state government. Many departments have received support from the UGC's Special Assistance Programme—the Assistance for Strengthening of Infrastructure for Humanities and Social Sciences Programme, and also the DST's Fund for Improvement of the Science and Technology Infrastructure Programme.

It will be seen that the University has come a long way from being a nursery for producing potential civil servants. The professional studies' centres groom students for meaningful vocations, and the inter-disciplinary centres focus on new and emerging areas of knowledge like behavioural and cognitive science, and intellectual property rights. In recent years, academic sessions have become regular, common all-India entrance tests have been reorganized in six centres and more foreign students from Asian and African countries have been accommodated. Enormous efforts have been made to cater to the needs of students through a grievance cell—a unit devoted to differently abled students—and a Women's Advisory Board to look after issues concerning female students. Additionally, a very successful Placement Cell and an Employment and Information Bureau were begun, as also a unit to help Dalit students prepare for public service examinations.

Some recruitment of teachers has also taken place but a great many posts still lie vacant. A few incumbents are drawn from distant parts of the country and from the weaker sections—women and minorities duly having received representation. Opinion is divided as to the justice of the recruitment procedure, but that is a perennial feature of academic life. Once, years back, when I was passed over in a selection, I was placidly told not to be so naïve as to use words like justice.

There is finally an anti-ragging cell in place, which till the last session had such a charming punitive procedure that I have left it for the last. Raggers were made to write book reviews and submit them for appraisal! Now who is to ensure that the raggers will not outsource the punishment to the ragged, as a fresh piece of ragging? Also, whoever thought of this severe penalty must definitely be of the opinion that reading a book and writing about it is a most punishingly painful job!

If there is a flipside to all this proactive growth, it lies in the inertia referred to earlier. Rebooting a slow system is no easy job, and no amount of financial largesse will pump oxygen into work procedures polluted by decades of deprogramming. Large chunks of the annual grant revert to the funding bodies for want of intelligent and practical utilization. C.D. Deshmukh had spoken about it in 1957, when he revealed that out of the ₹70 lakh allotted, only 7 lakh was utilized.[9] The situation is no different now, only the scale is larger. Shortage of funds is not the problem. Somewhere there has been a breakdown of efficiency and imagination, although there are always some extraordinary extenuating factors cited.

Alongside all its twenty-first century makeover, if there is one single agent of regression, it is the problem of student unrest, which persists in its constitution like a rogue gene. This quasquicentennial year has been a turbulent one. Students' Union elections were allowed to take place after a long gap, under the qualified conditions of the JM Lyngdoh Committee's regulations. Student unrest has witnessed tempestuous clashes at this time, and the 2005–06 academic session was extremely disturbed. The Allahabad High Court Judgment of 23 November 2005 questioned the soundness of the Students' Union elections of that year, vitiated as they were by the gross violation of rules and code of conduct norms, and even the murder of a candidate.

This anniversary year, likewise, witnessed eruptions of violence and large-scale disorder, starting with resistance to hostel evacuation, to measures by University authorities, and ending in a fresh intervention by the Allahabad High Court. This called in question the University's efficiency in the screening of prospective candidates prior to elections, to be given a rejoinder by the panel of teachers concerned, that their decisions were altered by some mysterious supervention. The grand 125th Foundation Day festivities were called off at the last minute because students threatened to disrupt the function over the murder of a student at a private party a couple of days earlier. The beautifully illuminated heritage buildings stood desolate as last-minute faxes and phone calls called off the event.

I maintained a Calendar of Unrest for a month in the 2012–13 academic session, and it makes for revealing reading. It starts on 1 March, and is made up of snippets from the *Hindustan Times*, reporting on university matters. As the mammoth Kumbh Mela, organized on an unprecedented scale, drew towards its last phase, the University witnessed its own unprecedented cycle of events. I transcribe exactly from the newspaper reports. The language is shaky and repetitive, and the grammar sometimes awkward, but I have not tried to correct or fine-tune anything. I have only omitted the names of the persons involved. The information in brackets is my own:

> 1 March 2013: AMU, BHU Get ₹100 crores to Foster Excellence. (The last NAAC accreditation score given to AU in 2010 was B+++.)
>
> 1 March: AU Scientist Bags INSA Medal.
>
> 2 March: AU Students Make Immolation Bid. Enraged over their expulsion from the university on charges of attacking the vice chancellor's steno some time ago, two Allahabad University student leaders attempted self-

immolation on the university campus of Friday.

The two students…first doused themselves in kerosene and were about to light a matchstick when some students and policemen present there stopped the duo from setting themselves afire. The incident took place outside the vice chancellor's office. Following it, some students indulged in vandalism in the North Hall, breaking windowpanes there. This resulted in total chaos on the campus and the situation remained tense till evening… A group of students took out a procession and forced closure of offices later. They also went to different departments and forced suspension of classes going on there. According to the students, the two students won't be able to appear in their exam starting on March 5, if their expulsion was not taken back. On their part, the university authorities said, since the VC had expelled them, he alone could revoke the expulsion…

3 March: AU Chief Proctor Locked in Office for the Day. Angry students create ruckus, force closure of all offices on campus. Allahabad University students created ruckus on the campus for the second day on Saturday and locked Chief Proctor, Professor—and Security Officer—in office. The students were angry that the university had not responded to the request to allow expelled student leaders to appear in the examination commencing from March 5, and to withdraw their expulsion. The Chief Proctor remained confined to his office along with the Security Officer for hours. The students sat outside the office, not allowing anybody to release him. A police force stood on the scene, watching the angry students… Students scheduled to appear in the examination from March 5, could not get their admit cards. As a result the AU authorities were forced to upload these cards on the website so that the students could download their cards.

4 March: Students Threaten to Lock AU Gates Today. (A photograph shows the Chief Proctor holding a glass of fruit juice to the lips of a student leader sitting up in what seems to be a hospital bed.)

Students of Allahabad University... have threatened to lock all the gates of the university on Monday and stop commencement of annual exam on Tuesday. This was decided in a meeting of students at the union hall on Sunday. On Sunday there was a heavy deployment of police along with fire tenders on all the gates of the varsity. The district administration had taken the measures after anticipating that students could go on a rampage, as a reaction to the forcible release of varsity's Chief Proctor from his chamber on Saturday night...cops brought him out at 9.30 p.m. Agitated students on Sunday informed that they would stop the Registrar, Dean Students Welfare and Chief Proctor, besides other staff, from entering the university by locking all the gates on Monday morning....

The inset with the photograph states: Expelled student leader_____ who was on fast-unto-death for the past three days, was forcibly admitted to a hospital on Saturday night. Medical test reports on Sunday morning revealed that the student leader had developed swelling in his kidney, which the doctors termed as serious. However, students protested when the police tried to forcibly make him drink fruit juice to break the fast. The students wanted a teacher to make the student leader break his fast, after which the Chief Proctor arrived in the hospital and offered fruit juice to_____.

5 March: Expelled Students Allowed to Appear in AU Exams Rider: results will be withheld till disciplinary action. The Allahabad University administration on Monday

granted conditional permission, to expel student leaders to appear in the annual examinations of the varsity scheduled to begin from March 5. As per reports, the decision was taken at a meeting of varsity officials held under the chairmanship of (the) Vice Chancellor…The decision… would not only provide relief to student leader _____ who had misbehaved with the VC but also… (those) accused of roughing up of VC's steno and security guard. It would also benefit the 10 students…accused in ragging case.

The inset states:

Contractual Workers on War Path: Contractual workers of Allahabad University demonstrated on its premises on Monday in protest against non-disbursement of salary since past five months. The employees raised slogans… and also staged a sit-in…

There are two photographs, one showing a large procession of students tearing forward, arms raised in the air, heads lifted in an attitude of shouting, the other of a group of men and women, sitting in a cluster, also with arms lifted and heads raised in the same attitude of shouting!

6 March: AU Women Footballers to be Feted Today. Athletic Association of Allahabad University will give University Football Colour Award to three women football players of varsity football team on Wednesday… Recently AU (women) football team reached the quarter finals in the North Zone Inter University Women's Football… Championship 2012-13 held in Delhi.

6 March: City Researchers Do It Again. Competing against best scientists, eight of them, including five from AU, bag projects worth ₹70.99 lakh.

7 March: Fashion Kumbh Begins at Varsity: Fashion Kumbh, an exhibition-cum-sale displaying a mind-boggling range of products created in the theme of ongoing Kumbh by students of Centre of Fashion Design and Technology of Allahabad University, began on Wednesday.

10 March: AU, IERT Students Go on Rampage. Students of two institutes of higher education in Allahabad went on the (sic) rampage on Saturday on different issues. While students of Allahabad university hurled crude bombs and indulged in stone throwing during distribution of forms for state government's free laptop distribution scheme, students of (the) Institute of Engineering and Rural Technology were involved in arson at teachers' colony over poor results in their diploma exams... At AU, the trouble began around noon when a large number of students, most of them in their first year of undergraduate courses, thronged the counters to obtain forms for availing the scheme introduced by state government, wherein free laptops are to be distributed to those who have passed their Intermediate examinations.

A quarrel erupted between two students of different hostels in which an inmate of KPUC Hostel got hurt. Enraged over this, the inmates of KPUC Hostel assembled in front of AU's Registrar's Office and allegedly thrashed inmates of Tara Chand Hostel. An inmate of Tara Chand Hostel...who is also the District President of Samajvadi Chatra Sabha, was seriously injured in the incident. In retaliation, inmates of Tara Chand Hostel too indulged in violence. Both parties pelted each other with stones in which two passers-by were also hurt. Around a dozen students and six security personnel sustained injuries. A few crude bombs were also hurled by the warring inmates close to

KPUC Hostel. Later security personnel had to use baton to quell the mob. Proctor--- termed the incident as 'a shameless violent act' by some students, and said that an unnamed FIR against 50 students had been lodged by the varsity, and efforts were on to identify the troublemakers after which they would be served show-cause notices.

11 March: Allahabad University and IERT Students Continued to Indulge in Violence on the Second Day on Sunday. Like Saturday, police had to intervene and also use force to stop the situation from going out of hand at both places… Dozens of inmates of AU's Tarachand Hostel attacked inmates of KPUC Hostel late Sunday night with crude bombs. The loud sounds…attracted the attention of Colonelgunj police station cops nearby… The hostellers dispersed on seeing the cops… The clash that began between inmates of Tarachand Hostel and KPUC Hostel during distribution of forms for free laptops continued…

At around 8 p.m. a group of residents of Tarachand Hostel attacked KPUC Hostel under Colonelgunj police station. A number of crude bombs were hurled at KPUC Hostel which created panic in the area. Taken by surprise KPUC inmates retaliated and throwing of stones ensued on both sides. Police from Colonelgunj police station reached the spot and first pushed Tarachand Hostel inmates back inside their hostel premises, and then chased away the KPUC inmates. The incident led to pandemonium that lasted for around two hours… Later as a precaution, a large number of PAC and police personnel were stationed near both hostels.

(The photograph beneath this piece showed policemen in full riot gear, helmeted and armoured in commando fatigues, lathis in their hands, striding down a paved pathway.)[10]

Another little inset has a highlighted item:

> The Allahabad University will prepare a formal proposal highlighting the short-term, medium term and long term measures for optimum utilisation of the National Knowledge Network. This proposal will then be implemented by the varsity. A decision in this regard was taken during a meeting of the members of the task force for Internet, website and e-governance held recently under the chairmanship of (the VC). NKN is a state-of-the-art multi-gigabit pan-India network for providing a unified high-speed network backbone for all knowledge related institutions in the country. AU is poised to set up many information and communication technology related facilities.[11]

Finally, cheek by jowl with this inset there's another news item: 'Recruitment for Non-teaching Posts in AU Yet to Begin. It may be facing shortage of non-teaching staff but Allahabad University has not started the recruitment process for around 80 'Class C' posts even after a year of the University Grants Commission sanctioning these posts under the OBC grant...'[12]

> 14 March: AU Authorities, Admin Must Take Jt. Action: HC
>
> Taking exception to incidents of indiscipline on and around Allahabad University campus, the Allahabad High Court has directed the District Administration as well as AU authorities to make joint efforts to see that the students are not permitted to take the law in their own hands... As per previous direction of the Court, the District Magistrate and Senior Superintendent of Police Allahabad, appeared before the Court and filed their respective affidavits. They assured the Court that all appropriate action shall be taken and law and order shall be maintained on AU campus... The Court was informed that deployment of two companies

of PAC shall serve the purpose. On this the Court directed SSP Allahabad to do the needful and if required, he may approach the state government for providing the force required immediately.

15 March: Hindu Hostel Students Batter IPS Students. Rowdyism was seen at its peak in the Science Faculty on Thursday after a group of inmates of nearby Hindu Hostel battered students of Institute of Professional Studies. The scared students ran for their lives inside classrooms and canteen but were chased and beaten up badly. A number of students sustained injuries in the incident. The hostellers also allegedly vandalised the canteen and some classrooms and ran back to their hostel after scaling the boundary wall of the Science Faculty. The incident occurred when some girls and boys of the Institute of Professional Studies were sitting on the lawns and talking. At this point a group of Hindu Hostel inmates crossed over the boundary wall, carrying sticks and other blunt weapons. As they attacked the students, the latter taken aback, ran for their lives but were still given a sound beating. According to reports, the attack was a sequel to an altercation when the boys of the Institute of Professional Studies confronted some hostellers who had behaved indecently with a girl belonging to their department. At that time the Hindu hostellers had gone away, following intervention by some teachers but today they returned to avenge the humiliation…

16 March: AU's Online Admissions Delayed. Separate bank account yet to be opened, problem likely to be solved by Tuesday. Allahabad University's online admission process would take a few more days to kick off. Though the process was scheduled to start from Friday, it could not begin owing to certain 'technical hurdles'…

16 March: Campus Violence Raises Queries in Lok Sabha. Repeated incidents of violence in Allahabad University, and questions on the varsity's students union have found mention in the Lok Sabha. After different MPs raised these issues, the Union Ministry of Human Resource Development asked AU officials to provide information regarding the questions raised so that it could reply to the queries of the MPs... University officials have informed about the various incidents of violence that occurred on the campus, including the one in which students of the Department of Arabic and Persian allegedly manhandled the Vice Chancellor, and lodged an FIR against the VC at Colonelgunj Police Station. AU officials have also mentioned the incident in which AU officials, including Registrar... Proctor... Security Officer... and the entire staff of the Proctor's Office was kept locked for over ten hours by a section of students.[13]

The 22 March issue of the *Hindustan Times* has a photograph showing a horde of young men, naked to the waist, some greened and encrimsoned and wildly empurpled, dancing boisterously in the street. The news item reads:

> Defiant Hostellers Take Out Holi Procession. Inmates of Holland Hall, G.N. Jha hostels cock a snook at recent varsity notice banning Holi processions, lewd behavior. Cocking a snook at the order issued by Allahabad university warning inmates of its various hostels against taking out processions and indulging in lewd behavior on the main roads in the name of Holi, inmates of Holland Hall and GN Jha Hostel took out a procession with loud blaring music on Thursday. The inmates danced bare-bodied on the roads and tore away each other's clothes while shouting obscenities and making lewd gestures, especially when close to the varsity's Women's

College campus which houses all girls' hostels... AU Proctor—said he had come to know about the development and immediately informed the Colonelgunj Police Station.

23 March: Firing, Crude Bomb Blasts Rock AU Hostel. Four sustain pellet injuries in clash involving BPEd students.

A violent clash involving students of Bachelor of Physical Education of Allahabad University resulted in injuries to four students at Radhakrishnan Hostel at the university on Friday. The students created panic in the area as they burst crude bombs and opened fire from a country made gun. As per reports, the incident was a fall-out of a minor scuffle between two students of BPEd in the classroom and resulted in outsiders, armed with hockey sticks and rods, barging into the hostel and indulging in violence. Three students sustained pellet injuries in the clash... The incident took place at around 1.30 p.m. when over half a dozen outsiders armed with rods, hockey sticks, crude bombs and country made weapons, barged into Radhakrishnan Hostel.

When the guard demanded that they enter their names in the visitors' register, they reportedly started bursting crude bombs. These students then entered the room of BPEd student—and started assaulting him. Hearing his cries for help, his neighbor and fellow student—came out to investigate but was also targeted. In the meantime the commotion and sounds of crude bomb explosions brought out a large number of students of Radhakrishnan Hostel and nearby PC Bannerjee Hostel. They chased the attackers. While most of the attackers managed to flee from the spot on bikes, one was nabbed by the students and given a sound thrashing...[14]

25 March: Project to Restore Heritage Structures of Allahabad University. Allahabad University, which turned

> 125 last September, has set in motion the renovation of four of its national heritage buildings [...] the Vijayanagaram Hall, [...] designed by [...] Sir William Emerson, known for designing the Victoria Memorial in Kolkatta, and inaugurated by Viceroy Lord Dufferin in 1887...RITES Limited, under the Ministry of Railways, is the varsity's management consultant for the project [...supported by...] an expert panel from INTACH [...] Delhi Chapter, and the Archaeological Survey of India... The other heritage buildings that are lined up for conservation are the Senate Hall, the Darbhanga Hall and the English Department Building. [...] designed in the Indo-Saracenic style by Sir Samuel Swinton Jacob and are known by their imposing facades, adorned by domes, cupolas, towers, ornamental columns and railings.[15]

The climate of Allahabad is one of incredible extremes. In summer, temperatures rise to 46, 47, even 48 degrees Celsius, and we have even touched 50 once. In winter, the mercury plunges to 1 or 2 degrees Celsius, and we've sometimes gone down to 0 as well. If we consider the AU, or as it is now called, the UoA's general existential state, it does seem to reflect the same extremes.

It is October 2013 as I write this. The academic session that ended in May was a special one. It was the quasquicentennial year and many celebrations were planned. But none of that could take place, so disturbed was the year, and especially its last trimester. Living in real time, the extreme binaries of AU's character have been internalized by many of us. We seem to be ensnared in two different time grids coiled together in an incredible double helix.

Admittedly the month of March covered was unusually disturbed, even by our current standards of disorder. Yet, it carries a faithful picture of the lived reality of an institution of singular learning, architectural beauty, cultural aristocracy and magnificent memories, struggling to negotiate times that lie quite outside the scope of its founding vision, or its former character. If anything seems visually true to its contemporary essence, it is the masterpiece created by a student of the visual arts department, alongside the wall of the University branch of the State Bank of India.

The model of a cowherd's hut

It is a life-sized model of a cowherd's hut in front of which a shaggy buffalo is tethered, and a herdsman hunkers down on his haunches, milking it, while close by stands a little calf, its body playfully tensed in mid-prance. The muscles on the herdsman's back, the matted streaks of the buffalo's coat and the mud-plastered wall of the little home exude an authenticity that seems to rise from the mental field generated by the collective sensibility of the new social class, to which the University caters, bravely teaching the first generation of students to come for higher education from humble origins outside the pale of educational opportunity all these centuries.

The doodhwala's bulging sinews, the buffalo's lazy patience, the calf just poised to spring, the cottage façade with its cowpats and palm prints might well serve as the new emblem of the region at this moment of its history as well as the aspirational fantasy of the student who created it, his imagination breaking through the glass ceiling of caste and class and culture. Indeed the history of the Allahabad University seems to be a legacy of mutating aspirational fantasies. It began as the aspirational fantasy of one race and class, morphed to accommodate that of another, and it must now fulfil the aspirational fantasy of yet another, larger, more diverse and more challenged by historic disabilities.

The legendary bargad, or banyan tree

If one walks down the shaded university route, past the old Hindi department well—one-time site of such resounding eloquence—past the newly laid garden areas and the modern Indira Gandhi Social Sciences block, and takes a turn to the left, one comes up behind the heritage Senate Hall block, and directly in front of the legendary bargad. It stands sentinel, like the guardian soul of a kindly ancestor, spreading its robe of shade around a large girth of garden, behind the old basin of its fountain. To say that this fountain works would be an exaggeration. A weak squirt of water occasionally goes up in a thin skein, bravely defying gravity before it falls, spent, into the pool. Mostly the fountain is dead and the water in the basin stands motionless. The bargad can't possibly figure out its face in the tinted glass of that drowsing pool. What it needs is a real looking glass. It's what I've tried to make this book—a mirror. Especially in this quasquicentennial year. 'Celebrations are the time to exhume from history, charismatic characters, unexpected trajectories and great struggles', as Giulia Bonaci put it.

As I walk down each morning past this iconic area, I often hear slogans and shouts and run into processions, effigy-burners and banner bearers, rights roarers and police vans, and I wonder what exactly is going on in this besieged space. Is it to become the site for missions forfeited, teachings unlearnt and causes trashed? Who is winning or is everyone losing? Or are only private priorities being cannily served, while the monumental structure sags? I honestly don't know.

I only know that when I see a rustic-looking boy absorbed in his new laptop, sitting hunched in the grass with a friend—and for a moment I imagine it's a farmer's child or a newspaper vendor's or a rickshaw-puller's—I see in a flash what is being won and at what great cost. But it's a winning all the same; and that's what these soaring arches and lofty halls and carved cupolas and colonnades and pigeon-haunted vaults celebrate and bless. I don't have a clue where all this is leading to, but you, who write a history of the Allahabad University in its 150th year, might know what happened next. In keeping with the literary training I received in my particular time at this one-time bastion of high learning, to you I say: if truth be the leaven of your history, write on.

ACKNOWLEDGEMENTS

This book could not have been written without the generous help of my teachers, Manas Mukul Das and Hemendra Shankar Saxena. To the former, I owe a very large part of the material on which I based this history. From the latter, I received a rich repertoire of anecdotes and memorabilia that have helped enliven and personalize this narrative. Much more than these has been the encouragement they have quietly given to all my efforts, which has seen me through the most demanding periods of research and writing.

I am grateful to Harish Trivedi, John Harrison, Ram Lohkar, Satya Deo Tripathi, Avinash Pandey, Ashok Barat, Ajoy Chakravarti, Naimurrahman Farooqi, Neerja Sachdeva, R.C. Tripathi, Gangeya Mukherji and Devanshu Gour for their inputs. To Keki Daruwalla for his kind support at all times, Kanishka Gupta for his appreciation and efforts, Ravi Singh for his faith in my work and Amrita Mukerji for her painstaking attention to detail. Writing this book would never have occurred to me had the then vice chancellor of my university, Prof. A.K. Singh, not thought of it first. He wanted to find the right person to take up this project in the University's 125th year and assigned to my colleague Rakesh Singh the daunting task of persuading someone to undertake it. I thank them both for starting me on this venture. I thank my children for their brisk photography and technical support.

And, as always, I thank Sudhanshu Gour, my husband, for patiently listening to my vocal voyagings, deliberations, discourses, discoveries, my exultations and my agonizings, as I wandered my way through this work.

COPYRIGHT ACKNOWLEDGEMENTS

Extracts and photographs from the *70th Anniversary Souvenir* (1958), the *Alumni Convention Souvenir* and the *Centenary Souvenir* of the University of Allahabad have been used with permission from the Vice Chancellor, University of Allahabad.

Extracts from 'Professor Ranade - Wisdom Incarnate' by V.S. Naravane (6 March 1998) and 'Journeying with a Professor' by H.S. Saxena (11 October 1998) have been used with permission from *Northern India Patrika*.

Extracts from *In the Afternoon of Time: An Autobiography* by Harivansh Rai Bachchan, edited and translated by Rupert Snell, (Viking, 1998) have been used with permission from Penguin Books India.

Extracts on pages 342–351 have been used with permission from the *Hindustan Times*.

ENDNOTES

Chapter 1: The Muir Overture

1. Amaranatha Jha, *A History of the Muir Central College*, The Indian Press, 1938.
2. Ibid., p. 4.
3. Ibid., p. 1.
4. *The Allahabad University Magazine*; Vol. 1, No. 1, October 1922, p. 19.
5. Motilal Bhargava, *Hundred Years of Allahabad University*, Ashish Publishing House, 1987, p. 318.
6. Jha, op. cit., p. 3.
7. Jha, op. cit., p. 5.
8. Quoted from *The Pioneer* of 9 December 1873, by Amaranatha Jha.
9. Manas Mukul Das, 'Banyan Tree', *Allahabad: Where The Rivers Meet*, edited by Neelum Saran Gour, Marg Publications, 2009, p. 129.
10. Ajoy Chakravarti, 'Some Legends and Lores about AU', *The Hindustan Times*, Allahabad Page, 2 February 2008.
11. Das, op. cit., pp. 129–130.
12. Ibid., p. 130.
13. Chakravarti, op. cit.
14. Amaranatha Jha, *A History of the Muir Central College*, The Indian Press, 1938, p. 7.

15. Jha, op. cit., p. 84.
16. Jha, op. cit., data taken from 'A Year-to-Year Chronicle—The Principal's Reports.', pp. 111–114.
17. Jha, op. cit., quoting Mohan Lal Hukku, p. 12.
18. Jha, op. cit., p. 13.
19. Jha, op. cit., Quotation from an essay by J.G. Jennings, p. 78.
20. Jha, op. cit., p. 79.
21. Jha, op. cit., Quotation from the reminiscences of Rai Bahadur Shyam Lal, p. 28.
22. J.G. Jennings, *The Lost Ring*, Indian Press, 1903, p. 7.
23. Jha, op. cit., p. 16.
24. Jha, op. cit., Quotation from an essay by J.G. Jennings, p. 85.
25. Jha, op. cit., p. 83.

Chapter 2: Act Two

1. K.K. Mehrotra, *University of Allahabad 70th Anniversary Souvenir*, 1958, p. 6.
2. Ibid., p. 6.
3. 'The Hermitage of Bharadwaja', *The Allahabad University Magazine*, Vol. III, No. 1, October 1924, pp. 68–69.
4. *University of Allahabad 70th Anniversary Souvenir*, 1958, p. 237.
5. Mehrotra, op. cit., p. 7.
6. Ibid., p. 8.
7. Ibid., p. 9.
8. Manas Mukul Das, 'Banyan Tree', *Allahabad: Where The Rivers Meet*, edited by Neelum Saran Gour, Marg Publications, 2009, p. 128.
9. R.N. Deb, 'Allahabad through the Ages', *70th Anniversary Souvenir*, 1958, p. 71.
10. Ajoy Chakravarti, 'Some Legends And Lores about AU', *Hindustan Times*, 2 February 2008.
11. Motilal Bhargava, *Hundred Years of Allahabad University*, Ashish Publishing House, 1987, p. 56.
12. Ibid., p. 69.

13. Ibid., p. 71.
14. Ibid., 9. 73.
15. Ibid., p. 3.
16. Ibid., p. 4.
17. Ibid., p. 15.
18. Ibid., p. 89.
19. Ibid., p. 113.
20. Ibid., p. 113.
21. Ibid., p. 113.

Chapter 3: High Noon

1. R.N. Deb, 'Allahabad through the Ages', *70th Anniversary Souvenir*, 1958, p. 74.
2. Rajeshwar Dayal, *70th Anniversary Souvenir*, p. 115.
3. K.K. Mehrotra (ed.), *Amaranatha Jha: A Memorial Volume*, University of Allahabad, 1957, p. 147.
4. Bishan Tandon, *Alumni Convention Souvenir*, University of Allahabad, 2008, p. 61.
5. *70th Anniversary Souvenir*, p. 114.
6. One of the founders of the Friday Club of the English department.
7. *Centenary Souvenir*, 1887–1987, University of Allahabad, p. 50.
8. K.N. Katju, *70th Anniversary Souvenir*, p. 92.
9. *Centenary Souvenir*, 1887–1987, University of Allahabad, p. 50.
10. *70th Anniversary Souvenir*, p. 132.
11. Ibid.
12. *Centenary Souvenir*, 1887–1987, University of Allahabad, p. 27.
13. Ibid., p. 66.
14. *70th Anniversary Souvenir*, p. 122.
15. Bishan Tandon, op. cit., p. 60.
16. *70th Anniversary Souvenir*, p. 116.
17. *Alumni Convention Souvenir*, 2008, p. 53.
18. *Centenary Souvenir*, op. cit., p. 59.
19. Ibid., p. 71.

20. Amaranatha Jha, *A History of the Muir Central College*, The Indian Press, 1938, p. 29.
21. *Alumni Convention Souvenir*, 2008, p. 53.
22. *70th Anniversary Souvenir*, p. 114.
23. H.S. Jevons, 'The Subject Matter of Economics', *The Allahabad University Magazine*, October 1922.
24. *Centenary Souvenir*, op. cit., p. 39.
25. Principal's Reports, Jha, p. 122.
26. Ibid., p. 126.
27. Ibid., p. 126.
28. Ibid., p. 136.
29. Kanhaiya Lal Nandan, *Alumni Convention Souvenir*, 2008, p. 81.
30. Ibid., p. 135.
31. Savitri Varma, 'Ab Tak Shesh Hain Ateet Ki Smritiyan', *Alumni Convention Souvenir*, op. cit., p. 52.
32. L.L. Mehrotra, 'My Allahabad Years', *Alumni Convention Souvenir*, op. cit., p. 68.
33. S.K. Mishra, '...And I Became Princess', *Alumni Convention Souvenir*, op. cit., p. 66.
34. D.D. Khanna, 'Seminar Classes—A Unique Opportunity', *Alumni Convention Souvenir*, op. cit., p. 59.
35. Shiva Adhar Pande, *70th Anniversary Souvenir*, p. 99.
36. Ibid., p. 100.
37. S.G. Dunn, 'Universities Past And Present', *The Allahabad University Magazine*, Vol. II, No. 2, p. 22.
38. Jha, op. cit., p. 100.
39. Ibid., p. 100.
40. Ibid.
41. *Centenary Souvenir*, op. cit., p. 96.
42. P.C. Gupta, *70th Anniversary Souvenir*, p. 120.
43. H.S. Saxena, 'The Dons Deb and Dustoor: Remembering Old Allahabad', *The Sunday Patrika*, May 1998.
44. V. Rajamani, 'University's Co-curricular Activities', *70th Anniversary Souvenir*, op. cit., p. 193.

45. P.C. Gupta, *70th Anniversary Souvenir*, op. cit., p. 119.
46. Dhanesh Mandal, 'Tab Union Bhi Bahut Kuch Sikhati Thi', *Alumni Convention Souvenir*, pp. 70–71.
47. H.S. Saxena, op. cit.
48. Ibid.
49. V. Rajamani, op. cit., p. 193.
50. Jha, op. cit., p. 95.
51. Tandon, op. cit., p. 61.
52. V. Rajamani, *70th Anniversary Souvenir*, op. cit., p. 195.
53. H.S. Saxena, 'The University Road', *Northern India Patrika*, 17 May 1998.
54. Ibid.
55. Ibid.
56. Ibid.
57. Ibid.
58. Back cover full page, *The Allahabad University Magazine*, December 1923.
59. V. Rajamani, *70th Anniversary Souvenir*, p. 193.
60. Rajeshwar Dayal, *70th Anniversary Souvenir*, p. 116.
61. *The Allahabad University Magazine*, Vol. 4, December 1925.
62. Ibid.
63. Jagat Mehta, 'University Had a Magic', *Alumni Convention Souvenir*, pp. 56–57.
64. Bishan Tandon, op. cit., p. 60.
65. *The Allahabad University Magazine*, December 1932, p. 127.
66. Ibid., October 1933, p. 56.
67. Ibid., December 1933, p. 15.
68. Ibid.
69. Ibid., December 1933, p. 44.
70. H.S. Saxena, *Allahabad: Where the Rivers Meet* edited by Neelum Saran Gour, Marg Publications, 2009.

Chapter 4: Tidal Wave

1. Amaranatha Jha, *A History of the Muir Central College*, The Indian Press, 1938, p. 22.
2. Ibid., p. 133.
3. Ibid., p. 146.
4. Shiva Adhar Pande, *70th Anniversary Souvenir*, University of Allahabad, 1958, p. 99.
5. B.N. Lahiri, *70th Anniversary Souvenir,* op. cit., p. 110.
6. In fact, he lectured in a tennis court.
7. Shiva Adhar Pande, op. cit., pp. 101–103.
8. K.K. Mehrotra (ed.), *Amaranatha Jha: A Memorial Volume*, University of Allahabad, 1957, p. 129.
9. Ibid., pp. 127–128.
10. Quoted by Motilal Bhargava, *Hundred Years of Allahabad University*, Ashish Publishing House, 1987, p. 205.
11. B.N. Lahiri, *70th Anniversary Souvenir*, p. 110.
12. Ibid.
13. Ibid.
14. Ibid.
15. Bhargava, op. cit., op. cit., p. 206.
16. *Centenary Souvenir,* 1887–1987, University of Allahabad, p. 96.
17. Ibid, p. 96.
18. *70th Anniversary Souvenir*, p. 236.
19. H.S. Saxena, *Allahabad: Where the Rivers Meet*, edited by Neelum Saran Gour, Marg Publications, 2009, p. 103.
20. Ibid.
21. Gangeya Mukherji, *Allahabad: Where the Rivers Meet*, edited by Neelum Saran Gour, Marg Publications, 2009, p. 160.
22. *Alumni Convention Souvenir*, 2008, p. 70.
23. Ibid., p. 46.
24. Bhargava, op. cit., p. 210.
25. Ibid., p. 212.
26. *Alumni Convention Souvenir*, p. 46.

27. Ibid., p. 46.
28. *Centenary Souvenir*, p. 97.
29. *Alumni Convention Souvenir*, p. 46.
30. K.K. Mehrotra, op. cit., p. 154. p. 154.
31. *Centenary Souvenir*, p. 97.
32. Ibid., p. 97.
33. Ibid., p. 97.
34. *Alumni Convention Souvenir*, p. 56.
35. H.S. Saxena, *Allahabad: Where the Rivers Meet*, p. 104.
36. Ibid., p. 105.
37. Amarkant, *Alumni Convention Souvenir*, p. 63.
38. Tridip Suhrud and Peter Ronald DeSouza, *Speaking of Gandhi's Death,* Orient Blackswan, 2010, pp. 13-14.
39. Ibid., p. 14.

Chapter 5: Picture Gallery

1. P.G. Wodehouse, *My Man Jeeves*, George Newnes, 1919, p. 6.
2. K.K. Mehrotra (ed.), *Amaranatha Jha: A Memorial Volume*, University of Allahabad, 1957, p. 141.
3. Ibid., p. 141.
4. Ibid., p. 142.
5. Bhuvaneshwar Singh Gehlot, *Ve Din Ve Log*, Raka Prakashan, p. 68.
6. K.K. Mehrotra, op. cit., p. 237.
7. R.N. Deb in K.K. Mehrotra (ed.), *Amaranatha Jha: A Memorial Volume*, University of Allahabad, 1957, p. 48.
8. Motilal Bhargava, *Hundred Years of Allahabad University*, Ashish Publishing House, 1987, p. 101.
9. Gehlot, op. cit., pp. 70-71.
10. Ibid., pp. 72-73.
11. G.D. Karwal in K.K. Mehrotra (ed.), *Amaranatha Jha: A Memorial Volume*, University of Allahabad, 1957, p. 61.
12. Harivansh Rai Bachchan, *In the Afternoon of Time*, translated from

the Hindi by Rupert Snell, Penguin-Viking, 1998, p. 254.
13. K.K. Mehrotra, op. cit., p. 126.
14. Ibid., p. 141.
15. Ibid., p. 150.
16. Ibid., p. 158.
17. V.S. Naravane, 'Professor Ranade—Wisdom Incarnate', *Northern India Patrika*, 6 March 1998.
18. Ibid.
19. Ibid.
20. Gehlot, op. cit., p. 82.
21. Ibid., p. 85.
22. Rajeshwar Dayal, *The Last Bungalow*, ed. Arvind Krishna Mehrotra, Penguin India 2007, p. 173.
23. Saeed Jaffrey, quoted in *The Last Bungalow*, ed. Arvind Krishna Mehrotra, Penguin India, 2007, pp. 222–223.
24. Gehlot, op. cit., p. 92.
25. Ibid., pp. 91–97.
26. S.K. Ghosh, *Allahabad University Alumni Meet Souvenir*, pp. 64–65.
27. Ibid.
28. Gehlot, op. cit., pp. 150–154.
29. *The Allahabad University Magazine*, Vol. XLI, No. 3, March 1964, p. 50.
30. Ibid.
31. Bachchan, op. cit., pp. 298–299.
32. Ibid., p. 298.
33. Ibid., p. 298.
34. *Allahabad University Alumni Meet Souvenir*, p. 70.
35. Ibid., pp. 49–50.
36. A financial dole to poor and deserving students.
37. *Allahabad University Alumni Meet Souvenir*, p. 52.
38. Ibid.
39. Ibid., p. 55.
40. Ibid.
41. Ibid.

42. Ibid.
43. Shared by a close neighbour.
44. Shamsur Rahman Faruqi, *Allahabad: Where the Rivers Meet*, ed. Neelum Saran Gour, Marg Publications, 2009, p. 154.
45. Gehlot, op. cit., pp. 150–154.
46. Bachchan, op. cit., p. 200.
47. H.S. Saxena, 'Journeying with a Professor', *The Sunday Magazine, Northern India Patrika*, 11 October 1998.
48. Bachchan, op. cit., p. 123.
49. Ibid.
50. Ibid., p. 124.
51. Ibid., p. 125.
52. Ibid., p. 193.
53. Ibid, p 220.
54. Ibid., p. 251.
55. H.S. Saxena, op. cit., 11 October 1998.
56. Bachchan, op. cit., p. 299.
57. Ibid., p. 364.
58. Ibid., p. 364.
59. Ibid., p. 368.
60. Gehlot, op. cit., pp. 101–105.
61. Bachchan, op. cit., pp. 295–296.
62. Ibid., p. 296.
63. Gehlot, op. cit., p. 105.
64. Bachchan, op. cit., p. 296.
65. H.S. Saxena, *Allahabad: Where the Rivers Meet*, ed. Neelum Saran Gour, Marg Publications, 2009, p. 113.
66. Gehlot, op. cit., pp. 102–103.
67. Govind Mishra, *Allahabad University Alumni Meet Souvenir*, pp. 76–77.
68. Ibid., translated by Neelum Saran Gour.
69. H.S. Saxena, op. cit., 11 October, 1998.
70. Ibid.
71. *Allahabad University Alumni Meet Souvenir*, p. 77.

72. H.S. Saxena, 'The Dons Deb and Dustoor: Remembering Old Allahabad', *The Sunday Patrika*, 1998.
73. Govind Mishra, *Allahabad University Alumni Meet Souvenir*, pp. 76–77.
74. Ibid., p. 76.
75. Ibid.
76. Bachchan, op. cit., p. 297.
77. Manas Mukul Das, *Allahabad: Where the Rivers Meet*, p. 127.
78. Ibid.
79. Ibid.

Chapter 6: Autumn Afterglow

1. Saeed Jaffrey, quoted in Arvind Krishna Mehrotra (ed.), *The Last Bungalow*, Penguin Books India, 2007, p. 222.
2. Ibid., p. 250.
3. Letter written by Professor Manas Mukul Das to the vice chancellor, 20 December 1993.
4. Ibid.
5. Ibid.
6. Ibid.
7. Harish K. Trivedi, *The Allahabad University Magazine*, Vol. XLVI No. 1, November 1967, p. 34.
8. Ibid., p. 57.
9. Mehrotra, op. cit., *The Allahabad University Magazine*, Vol. XLVI No. 1, Nov 1967, p. 58.
10. Mehrotra, op. cit., p. 1.
11. Arun Kumar Bhattacharya, *The Allahabad University Magazine*, Vol. XLVI, No. 1, November 1967, p. 35.
12. Ibid., p. 39.
13. Ibid.
14. Harish Trivedi, written for this volume.
15. 'That Hindi department roof'
16. 'Hindi department, Hindi department, Hindi department... I'd like

to ask, did that Hindi department roof turn into the battlefield of Waterloo and our leader its Napoleon?'
17. Dr Satya Deo Tripathi, Harish Chandra Research Institute, Allahabad, ex-vice chancellor, Rewa University, written for this volume.
18. 'Allahabad University Minutes 1903', *The Allahabad University Magazine*, LI–II, III.
19. Thomas Babington Macaulay, quoted in *The Allhabad University Magazine* LI, II –III p. 3.
20. *Centenary Souvenir*, 1887–1987, University of Allahabad, p. 32.
21. Ibid., p. 47.
22. Ibid., p. 39.
23. *Centenary Souvenir*, p. 100.
24. K.K. Mehrotra (ed.), *Amaranatha Jha: A Memorial Volume*, University of Allahabad, 1957, p. 253.
25. Ibid., p. 253.
26. Ibid., p. 21.
27. Ibid., p. 13.
28. *70th Anniversary Volume*, pp. 12–13.
29. M.G. Gupta, *70th Anniversary Souvenir*, p. 28.
30. *70th Anniversary Souvenir*, p. 224.
31. Ibid., p. 226.
32. Ibid., p. 226.
33. Ibid., p. 227.
34. *The Allahabad University Magazine*, Vol. XLI, No. 3, March 1964.
35. Ibid., pp. 42–48.
36. Edward J. Di Bona, *The Allahabad University Magazine*, Vol. LI–II–III, p. 20.
37. Ibid., p. 21.
38. Ibid., p. 22.
39. Ibid., p. 12.
40. Ibid., p. 9.
41. Devanshu Gour, senior monitoring journalist, BBC, written for this volume.

42. Edward J. Di Bona, op. cit., p. 26.
43. Ibid.
44. Devanshu Gour, op. cit.
45. *The Allahabad University Magazine*, Vol LI, II–III, p. 321.
46. Motilal Bhargava, *Hundred Years of Allahabad University*, Ashish Publishing House, 1987, p. 321.
47. Tara Chand in K.K. Mehrotra, op. cit., p. 21.
48. K.K. Mehrotra, op. cit., pp. 225–226.
49. K.K. Mehrotra, op. cit., p. 254.
50. Ibid., p. 227.
51. Ibid.
52. Ashok Kumar Barat, CEO, Forbes India, ex-president of the Bombay Chamber of Commerce and Industry, written for this volume.
53. Devanshu Gour, op. cit.
54. Thomas Babbington Macaulay, *Prose and Poetry*, Selected by G.M. Young, London: Rupert Hardt-Davis, 1952, p. 729.
55. Di Bona, *The Allahabad University Magazine*, Vol LI-II–III, p. 9.
56. Ibid., p. 8.
57. J.B. Harrison, 'English as a University Subject in India and England'. Paper read at a workshop on *Purposes of Education and Information*, 16–18 December 1991, School of Oriental and Asian Studies, London, p. 3.
58. K.K. Mehrotra, op. cit., pp. 228–229.
59. Di Bona, op. cit., p. 10.
60. Ibid., p. 17.
61. Bhargava, op. cit., p. 235.
62. Di Bona, op. cit., p. 29.
63. Ibid., p. 29.
64. Ibid., p. 31.
65. Bhargava, op. cit., p. 235.
66. Rama Kant Agnihotri, 'Stories They Tell About Languages', *The Hindu*, 5 May 2013.
67. 'Remove English'
68. Kuldeep Kumar, 'Official Language or National Language?', *The

Hindu Friday Review (Allahabad edition), 24 May 2013.
69. Bhargava, op. cit., p. 281.
70. 'When Macbeth's conscience rebels his imagination intensifies. He has hallucinations, visions, hears voices.'

Chapter 7: Waning Day

1. Motilal Bhargava, *Hundred Years of Allahabad University*, Ashish Publishing House, 1987, p. 299.
2. Ibid.
3. Edward J. Di Bona, 'Change in A.U.', *The Allahabad University Magazine*, Vol. LI— II–III, p. 37.
4. 'The Silent March And After', *The Allahabad University Magazine*, Vol. LV, I–III, 18 April 1979.
5. AUTA Minutes—First meeting of the General House, 26 June 1979. Visit of Dr Shivanand Nautiyal, minister of higher education, UP.
6. Ibid., p. 3.
7. 'Campus News: The Silent March and After', *The Allahabad University Magazine*, Vol. LV, Nos. 1–2, 1978–79, p. 95.
8. Silent March of the Teachers of the Allahabad University.
9. Teachers, Students and Workers Unite.
10. We have Taken to the Streets Not to Demand our Rights But in Answer to the Call of Duty.
11. The PAC Must Immediately Withdraw From the Vice Chancellor's Residence.
12. 'Campus News: The Silent March and After', published in *The Allahabad University Magazine*, Vol. LV, Nos. 1-2, 1978–79, p. 99.
13. Second Meeting of the General House, 21 July 1979, AUTA Minutes, p. 36.
14. Ibid.
15. Joint AUTA and AUCTA meeting, 10 October 1979.
16. 'Teachers Issue Ultimatum to Allahabad VC', *Northern India Patrika*, 31 October 1979.
17. *Northern Indian Patrika*, 1 November 1979.

18. R.U. Govindan, *The Sunday Magazine*, *Northern India Patrika*, 23 March 1980.
19. Ibid.
20. M.M. Das, 'Teachers' Fight For Academic Values', *Mainstream*, Vol. XIX, No. 29, 21 March 1981.
21. Ibid., pp. 20–24.
22. Ibid.

Chapter 8: Real Time

1. 'Self-Study Report and Self-Appraisal for the National Assessment and Accreditation Council', University of Allahabad, 2003, p. 9.
2. Amaranatha Jha, *A History of the Muir Central College*, The Indian Press, 1938, p. 133.
3. Ibid., p. 127.
4. Edward J. Di Bona, 'Change in A.U.', *The Allahabad University Magazine*, Vo. LI, II–III, p. 38.
5. Ibid.
6. Ibid., p. 36.
7. 'Please don't be offended. This is done in the friendly spirit of Holi.'
8. Alexander Aciman and Emmett Rensin, *Twitterature: The World's Greatest Books Retold Through Twitter*, Penguin, 2009, p. 12.
9. Di Bona, op. cit., p. 34.
10. Extracts taken from reports published in the *Hindustan Times*, Lucknow edition, on the given dates.
11. 'Effective Use of NKN', *Hindustan Times*, 11 March 2013.
12. *Hindustan Times*, 11 March 2013.
13. Extracts taken from reports in the *Hindustan Times*, Lucknow edition, on the given dates.
14. Extracts from reports in the *Hindustan Times*, Lucknow edition.
15. 'Project to Restore Heritage Structures of Allahabad University', *The Hindu*, 25 March 2013.

www.ingramcontent.com/pod-product-compliance
Lightning Source LLC
Chambersburg PA
CBHW020634230426
43665CB00008B/172